ORAL
INTERPRETING

Oral Interpreting: Principles and Practices is a volume in the PERSPECTIVES IN AUDIOLOGY SERIES—Lyle L. Lloyd, series editor. Other volumes in the series include:

Publisher's Note

Perspectives in Audiology is a carefully planned series of clinically oriented and basic science textbooks. The series is enriched by contributions from leading specialists in audiology and allied disciplines. Because technical language and terminology in these disciplines are constantly being refined and sometimes vary, this series has been edited as far as possible for consistency of style in conformity with current majority usage as set forth by the American Speech-Language-Hearing Association, the *Publication Manual of the American Psychological Association,* and The University of Chicago's *A Manual of Style.* University Park Press and the series editors and authors welcome readers' comments about individual volumes in the series or the series concept as a whole in the interest of making **Perspectives in Audiology** as useful as possible to students, teachers, clinicians, and scientists.

A Volume in the Perspectives in Audiology Series

ORAL INTERPRETING
Principles and Practices

edited by
Winifred H. Northcott, Ph.D.
Consultant and Lecturer in Private Practice
Educational Programming for the Hearing Impaired
Formerly President, Alexander Graham Bell
 Association for the Deaf, Inc.

University Park Press
Baltimore

UNIVERSITY PARK PRESS
International Publishers in Medicine and Allied Health
300 North Charles Street
Baltimore, Maryland 21201

Sponsoring editor: Janet S. Hankin
Production editor: Shelly Hyatt-Blankman
Text design by: S. Stoneham, Studio 1812, Baltimore
Typeset by: Maryland Composition Company, Inc.
Manufactured in the United States of America by:
Halliday Lithograph

Library of Congress Cataloging in Publication Data
Main entry under title:

Oral interpreting.

(Perspectives in audiology series)
Includes index.
1. Interpreters for the deaf—United States—Addresses,
essays, lectures. 2. Interpreters for the deaf—Study
and teaching—United States—Addresses, essays, lectures.
3. Deaf—United States—Means of communication—Addresses,
essays, lectures. I. Northcott, Winifred H. II. Series
[DNLM: 1. Lipreading. 2. Deafness. HV2487 063]
HV2402.72 1984 362.4′283 84-2314
ISBN 0-8391-1840-6

CONTENTS

CONTRIBUTORS

Barbara G. Biddle, B.S.
4001 Nassau Circle
Englewood, Colorado 80110

Rebecca H. Carlson, B.A.
109 North Dabney Drive
Slidell, Louisiana 70458

Barbara Chertok
5309 Mohican Road
Bethesda, Maryland 20816

William E. Castle, Ph.D.
Vice-President, Rochester
Institute of Technology
Director, National Technical
Institute for the Deaf
1 Lomb Memorial Drive
Rochester, New York 14623

Diane L. Castle, Ph.D.
National Technical Institute for
the Deaf
Rochester Institute of Technology
1 Lomb Memorial Drive
Rochester, New York 14623

Marilyn French-St. George, Ph.D.
Decibel Communications
605 East Fairmount Avenue
State College, Pennsylvania 16801

Kirsten Aase Gonzalez, M.S.
Specialist for the Hearing
Impaired
Mt. San Antonio College
Walnut, California 91789

Walter B. Green, Ph.D.
Department of Speech Pathology
and Audiology
Ithaca College
Ithaca, New York 14850

Kathleen W. Green, Ph.D.
Department of Speech Pathology
and Audiology
State University College at
Cortland
Cortland, New York 13045

Michael A. Karchmer, Ph.D.
Gallaudet Research Institute
Center for Assessment and
Demographic Studies
Gallaudet College
Washington, D.C. 20002

Ken H. Levinson, C.P.A.
11683 Goshen Avenue #407
Los Angeles, California 90049

Lyle L. Lloyd, Ph.D.
Department of Special Education
Purdue University
Lafayette, Indiana 47907

Sandra G. Maronde, B.A.
Chairman, National Certification
Board, RID
Southwest State University
Marshall, Minnesota 56258

James C. Marsters, M.S., D.D.S.,
F.I.C.D.
175 South El Molino
Pasadena, California 91108

Winifred H. Northcott, Ph.D.
Consultant and Lecturer, Private
Practice
Educational Programming for the
Hearing Impaired
4510 Cedarwood Road
Minneapolis, Minnesota 55416

Barbara Johnson Pulscher
Chairman, Minnesota Evaluation
Team, RID
People, Inc.
1885 University Avenue
St. Paul, Minnesota 55104

Mark Ross, Ph.D.
Department of Communication
Sciences
The University of Connecticut
Storrs, Connecticut 06268

Nansie S. Sharpless, Ph.D.
Departments of Psychiatry and
Neurology
Albert Einstein College of
Medicine
1300 Morris Park Avenue
Bronx, New York 10461

Linda A. Siple, M.S.
National Technical Institute for
the Deaf
Rochester Institute of Technology
1 Lomb Memorial Drive
Rochester, New York 14623

Mark L. Stern
Stanford University
Stanford, California 94305

Richard G. Stoker, Ph.D.
The Pennsylvania State
University
110 Moore Building
University Park, Pennsylvania
16802

Bonnie Poitras Tucker
Attorney-at-Law
Brown and Bain, P.A.
222 North Central Avenue
Phoenix, Arizona 85001

PREFACE TO
PERSPECTIVES IN AUDIOLOGY

Oral Interpreting: Principles and Practices edited by Winifred Northcott exemplifies many features of the *Perspectives in Audiology* series. First, and most importantly, it focuses upon an exciting, emerging area of concern for audiologists, educators of the hearing impaired (deaf and hard of hearing), and others involved in improving the communication of individuals with a significant hearing loss. Although the hearing impaired have used interpreters for many years, it has only been recently that the profession of interpreting has emerged. Initially, this profession was concerned primarily with translating speech into manual signs for hearing-impaired consumers or the manual signs of the hearing impaired into speech. For hearing-impaired individuals who do not know or may not use manual signs, oral interpreting offers a way of facilitating communication when conditions relating to the speaker or to the environment are highly unfavorable for speechreading.

Oral Interpreting reflects the ecumenical movement that exists in the interpreting field. It is a transdisciplinary approach to interpreting that enhances the interpreting profession's ability to help a hearing-impaired speechreader, upon request. Dr. Northcott has wisely selected a number of seasoned professionals from a variety of disciplines, as well as a number of persons with hearing impairment who use an oral interpreter routinely or selectively, to develop this basic source. The breadth and depth of the content of this book make it a basic reference for practicing professionals as well as a text for professional preservice and in-service instruction.

Lyle L. Lloyd, Ph.D.
Chairman and Professor of Special Education
Professor of Audiology and Speech Sciences
Purdue University

PREFACE

Oral interpreting is becoming more visible as a support service for speechreaders, upon request, as a result of contemporary respect for individual differences among the hearing impaired (deaf and hard of hearing) in preferred mode of interpersonal communication.

Since 1979, when the first oral interpreters in the United States were certified by the Registry of Interpreters for the Deaf, Inc. (RID), following formal evaluation, there has been an ever-increasing interest in setting up formal and more specialized educational programs for the preservice and in-service preparation of oral interpreters, beyond the established programs for sign language interpreters.

Participants at the Atlanta Conference on Interpreter Training (Yoken, 1979) and the 1980 Tucson Conference on Interpreter Research: Targets for the Eighties (Per-Lee, 1980) identified critical gaps in quality control of interpreter training programs—the paucity of qualified staff to teach oral or voice interpreting; basic textbooks; supplemental readings; instructional materials; audiotapes and videotapes for practice; and guides for practicum in formal and social situations, including both oral and manual hearing-impaired individuals. The lack of identified coursework in a core curriculum for all interpreter preparation programs was also cited.

THE SCOPE OF THIS TEXT

This is a textbook and primary reference book on the principles and practice of oral interpreting for speechreaders (lipreaders). It is designed as a practical book, with three major intended functions: 1) a consumer guide for speechreaders; 2) a basic text for instructors (hearing and hearing impaired) and students in interpreter preparation programs (sign language and oral specialization); and 3) a reference book for specialized libraries and advocacy agencies, institutions, or individuals involved in assuring the statutory rights of the hearing impaired to interpreter services under current federal and state laws protecting the handicapped. It is also written for teachers of the hearing impaired, instructors of speechreading classes, parents and specialists in the allied fields of speech pathology and audiology; medical and related health, legal, or social services; and senior citizen organizations, who relate to hearing-impaired persons in a direct service or advocacy role. To date, there is no comprehensive, single source textbook in print on the subject of oral interpreting.

BASIC DIMENSIONS OF THE TEXT

The purpose of this book is basically twofold. First, *it exposes the concept of oral interpreting and the heterogeneity of the speechreading population.* There are wide variations in linguistic abilities among speechreaders, which in turn can affect their desire and/or ability to make efficient use of an oral interpreter. Certain chapter authors explore the characteristics of speechreaders with varying etiological and educational backgrounds and work environments. It is an inductive approach to awareness of how hearing-impaired speechreaders function, given the range from congenital or prelingual hearing loss to the condition of postlingual deafness or the label, "hard of hearing," as an adult. The latter classification numbers more than 16 million persons in the United States in the 1980s, many of whom may be unaware of the role and function of an oral interpreter but would probably become interested if such services were available. Chapter 12 in this volume highlights the danger of generalizing about the impact of etiology or age of onset of hearing loss on speechreading performance or career expectations.

Second, the book delineates *a curriculum analysis and content—an inductive approach to the process of acquiring the competencies (knowledge or understanding, skills, and attitudes) presented in a comprehensive, professional preparation program for oral interpreters: a one-semester single course or a 1-week intensive training workshop.*

The book is divided into three sections: 1) Historical and Organizational Perspectives; 2) Educational Considerations and Curriculum Content; and 3) Role Models and Resource Networks.

The formal preparation of an oral interpreter does not begin with a description of adaptive techniques used in interpreting situations; hence, early chapters describe current educational practices (Chapter 2), psychoeducational aspects of deafness (Chapter 3), and legal rights to interpreter services, based on federal and state statutes and case law (Chapter 4). They also describe the system of evaluation and certification of oral interpreters and the major performance characteristics on which candidates are formally rated by an RID Evaluation Team (Chapter 5).

They prepare the reader to turn next to an intensive analysis of research studies identifying major factors (organic, phonetic, linguistic and environmental) that influence speechreading performance (Chapter 6). This chapter precedes a delineation of the process of speechreading (Chapter 7) because outmoded generalizations about "lipreading" can influence a reader's analysis of the oral interpreter requirements to meet the needs of the different types and styles of speechreaders. In any discipline, new information can be toxic to some.

In the description of a comprehensive curriculum, the author of Chapter 8 identifies eight major content areas in which competencies (knowledge, skills, and attitudes) must be demonstrated in order to function effectively as an oral interpreter. Through this process of task analysis, instructional goals and objectives have been written for each subject area to describe specifically what the student is expected to accomplish as a result of the instruction provided.

Chapter 9 presents a detailed analysis of the variety of skills and techniques used by an oral interpreter (the facilitator) to convey the message of an original speaker (the sender) to a hearing-impaired speechreader (the receiver). The importance of the prosodic features of language, such as stress, duration, and intonation, is emphasized because they are the means by which an oral interpreter conveys attitudes and feelings of the speaker. Nonverbal factors, such as posture, gesture, and facial expressions, are described as ways to enhance the speechreader's comprehension of words.

The content of practicum (Chapter 10) focuses on behavioral objectives related to observation and supervised interaction between oral interpreting students and speechreaders with hearing loss. Various activities within a group training session are identified along with a description of a variety of instructional strategies by which they can be individualized, in a range of format options combining both active and passive learning.

Hearing-impaired speechreaders are cast in such roles as professional staff member, curriculum consultant, supervisor of practicum, guest lecturer, or panelist in liaison with other speechreaders and resource networks in the community. The need for diversity in background, speech intelligibility, and speechreading capability is stressed.

Major tenets of the RID Code of Ethics and illustrations demonstrating "reasonable" interpretation of their application by oral interpreters are presented in Chapter 11.

Chapter 12 is a consumer effort, consisting of autobiographical sketches by six hearing-impaired adults on their experiences in educational, scientific, medical, and industrial settings, all of which involve the use of oral interpreters.

Certain terminology is used throughout this textbook. The terms have gained credibility and familiarity through formal definition and application in practice, although there is not precise uniformity of wording in every instance. For example, the generic term *hearing impaired*, which includes the subclassifications *deaf* and *hard of hearing*, is employed. It is an emotionally neutral concept and is used to refer to "any child with any type and degree of hearing loss" (Ross and Giolas, 1978, p. 2), whether qualified as mild, moderate, severe, or profound in terms of physiological impairment (Ling, 1981) (see Introduction for additional definitions of terms).

THE CHAPTER AUTHORS

A number of well-known specialists within the disciplines of special education and communication disorders, educational psychology and consumers of oral interpreting services, have responded to an invitation to develop an assigned chapter dealing with background information on deafness and its amelioration, or a critical dimension of the competencies required of oral interpreters and/or speechreaders. There has been no attempt to interfere with an author's distinctive literary style. The result is a meshing of philosophy, attitudes, strategies and data indispensable to the process of formal preparation of oral interpreters to assume a professional, direct service role following RID evaluation and certification.

Winifred H. Northcott, Ph.D.

REFERENCES

Ling, D. 1981. A survey of the present status of methods in English-speaking countries. In: A. M. Mulholland (ed.), Oral Education Today and Tomorrow, pp. 81–99. A. G. Bell Assoc. for the Deaf, Washington, DC.

Per-Lee, M. S. 1980. Interpreter research: Target for the eighties. Conf. Rep. October 6–10, Tuscon, AZ.

Ross, M., and T. G. Giolas (eds.). 1978. Auditory Management of Hearing-Impaired Children. University Park Press, Baltimore.

Yoken, C. (ed.). 1979. Interpreter Training: The State of the Art. The National Academy of Gallaudet College, Washington, DC.

FOREWORD

It is with particular pleasure that I write a brief foreword to this first extensive treatise on oral interpreting for the hearing impaired (deaf and hard of hearing) at a time when I am both president of the Alexander Graham Bell Association for the Deaf and director of the National Technical Institute for the Deaf (NTID). Both the A.G. Bell Association and the NTID have played significant roles in giving oral interpreting its place in the sun among other forms of interpreting for the deaf. The A.G. Bell Association champions the development of good oral, auditory, and speechreading skills among deaf people and the interests of oral deaf individuals who have a preference for oral interpreting. NTID has incorporated the training of oral interpreters into its interpreter preparation program because it knows that many speechreaders, including some of its own students, prefer oral interpreting and because it supports an eclectic position regarding the communication needs of hearing-impaired persons.

It is both the purpose and the accomplishment of this publication to answer with substance the following set of questions, among others: What is oral interpreting? Why is it needed? Why are many members of the A.G. Bell Association, the National Association of the Deaf (NAD), and the Registry of Interpreters for the Deaf, Inc. (RID) strong advocates of it and of certification standards for it? How did certification standards for oral interpreting come about? What are those certification standards? How do we best prepare people to meet those standards?

I first witnessed oral interpreting taking place when my wife was sitting before a group of the Oral Deaf Adults Section (ODAS) of the A.G. Bell Association at its 1968 meeting in San Francisco. The speechreaders focused their attention on her as she repeated everything being said by the speaker, occasionally paraphrasing for added comprehension. She did not use voice; rather, as I observed, she repeated each speaker's remarks by using her natural lip movements, facial expressions, and other gestures.

At the time of that first experience of mine, there were not more than a handful of persons who would have been called oral interpreters, and all of them were what one would call "naturals" because they achieved their status without any formal training. Since that time, it has been interesting for me to witness and participate in the development of general awareness of the need for more oral interpreters, for formal training programs to create more oral interpreters, for professional certification of such interpreters, and the possibility for accreditation of interpreter training programs.

The need for more oral interpreters and for formal preparation to create them rests primarily on the following facts: many hearing-impaired people do not know sign language; many do not care to or are unable to learn it; and some who have high-level speechreading skills find that the sign language used by simultaneous or manual interpreters is distractive rather than useful. In addition, because of Section 504 of the Rehabilitation Act of 1973, it is virtually a civil right of the hearing-impaired person to have an oral interpreter if that is his/her individual preference.

It is with some pride that I point out that the first formal interpreter training program was implemented at the NTID in the summer of 1970 and that the first formal training in oral interpreting took place in NTID's program but a few years later.

It is with similar pride that I point out that NTID was instrumental in bringing together representatives from the ODAS of the A.G. Bell Association for the Deaf, the International Organization for Education of the Hearing Impaired (IOEHI) of the A.G. Bell Association, the National Association of the Deaf (NAD), and the Registry of Interpreters for the Deaf, Inc. (RID) to draft a set of guidelines for the certification of oral interpreters which, with minimal revision, was adopted as Standards by the RID on May 3, 1979. In October of that year, A.G. Bell and NTID co-sponsored the First National Oral Interpreting Workshop, at which oral interpreter candidates were, for the first time, evaluated for RID certification. This workshop was funded by the Bureau of Education for the Handicapped, U.S. Office of Education, and was hosted by the St. Paul Technical/Vocational Institute in Minnesota. Dr. Winifred H. Northcott, then President of A.G. Bell, and Rebecca Carlson of St. Paul TVI were its co-directors.

Since 1979, there has been a strong drive, particularly on the part of A.G. Bell, to foster more formal programs for the professional training of oral interpreters, to increase the number of certified oral interpreters, and to strengthen the RID certification requirements for such specialists.

The design of the comprehensive curriculum suggestions presented herein is competency-based. Readers of this carefully documented volume, skillfully edited by Dr. Winifred H. Northcott, can acquire a solid foundation of knowledge, skills, and attitudes that are central to the professional role and function of an oral interpreter duly certified by the RID.

William E. Castle, Ph.D.
President, Alexander Graham Bell
Association for the Deaf
Director, National Technical
Institute for the Deaf
Vice-President, Rochester Institute
of Technology

*To the memory of
my father and mother
Edwin Winfred Nies, D.D.S. and Maud Peet Nies,
the first speechreaders I knew*

HISTORICAL AND ORGANIZATIONAL PERSPECTIVES

CHAPTER 1

INTRODUCTION

Winifred H. Northcott

CONTENTS

In 1894, when the Horace Mann School for the Deaf in Boston celebrated its 25th anniversary, Alexander Graham Bell, a teacher of the deaf, was its distinguished speaker at the ceremonies marking the event. Dr. Bell told how his original skepticism of the value of *speech reading* for a deaf child had led him to attempt to develop a machine that would "render visible to the eyes of the deaf the vibrations of the air that affect our ears as sound."

Dr. Bell concluded by saying that although he did not produce a visible speech apparatus:

> It is only right that it should be known that the telephone is one of the products of the work of the Horace Mann School for the Deaf, and re-

sulted from my attempts to benefit the children of this school. (Mackenzie, 1928, 56–57)

The term *speechreading* has returned to vogue in the 1980s in recognition of the fact that connected *speech* is read from the lips as a means of conveying thought, ideas, and attitudes. It is supplemented via the natural gestures and body language used by an average hearing person. "Speechreading" is defined in Webster's 3rd New International Dictionary (Gove, 1980) simply as "lipreading."

ORAL TRANSLITERATION AND ORAL INTERPRETING

The term *interpreting* is defined in Webster's Dictionary (Gove, 1980) as "to explain or tell the meaning of; to translate into intelligible or familiar language or terms."

> An oral interpreter is usually a hearing person. He or she will proceed at a normal rate of speed and enunciation and will generally be a few words behind a speaker in the smooth repetition of statements. A skilled oral interpreter will sometimes rephrase or add a word or phrase to give higher visibility on the lips for added comprehension. Natural body language and gestures give added flavor. (Northcott, 1979a, pp. 135–136)

Definitions of Terms (Guidelines, 1979; RID, 1982)

Oral Translating/Transliteration: Spoken to Visible (S/V)   Verbatim presentation of the speaker's remarks by means of natural lip movements, with or without voice, for the benefit of hearing-impaired individuals

Oral Interpretation: Spoken to Visible (S/V)   The occasional or substantial rewording of the speaker's remarks, preserving the essence, presented with or without voice and always with natural lip movements

Oral Translating/Transliteration: Visible to Spoken (V/S)   Vocal expression of the exact words of a hearing-impaired (deaf or hard-of-hearing) speaker who may or may not use understandable speech, standard inflectional patterns, and grammatical construction

Oral Interpretation: Visible to Spoken (V/S)   Verbal rephrasing of the message of a hearing-impaired (deaf or hard-of-hearing) speaker who may or may not use understandable voiced speech, standard inflectional patterns, and grammatical construction

Auditory memory skills, concentration, techniques of analysis, and presentation of appropriate wording to match the consumer's capacity to comprehend (Seleskovitch, 1978) clearly are significant factors in the development of a person's competence as an interpreter. Such skills must be demonstrated while the style and substance of an original speaker's statements are accurately mirrored. In order to present the knowledge, skills, and attitudes involved in exercising the role of oral interpreter, a sophisticated staff (hearing and hearing impaired) and multidisciplinary planning are required. Only then can a comprehensive preservice program of professional preparation be implemented (see Chapters 8 and 10, in this volume).

ORAL INTERPRETER/TRANSLITERATOR CERTIFICATES

Three oral interpreter certificates are presently issued by the Registry of Interpreters for the Deaf, Inc. (RID) after a person successfully completes the process established under RID's National Evaluation System (see Chapter 5 of this volume for definitions and a detailed description of the RID components of formal evaluation). These certificates are as follows:

1. Oral Interpreter Certificate: Comprehensive (OIC:C)
2. Oral Interpreter Certificate: Spoken to Visible (OIC:S/V)
3. Oral Interpreter Certificate: Visible to Spoken (OIC:V/S)

HETEROGENEITY AMONG SPEECHREADERS

In terms of the age of onset of hearing loss, hearing-impaired persons fall into three basic categories: 1) congenital or prelingual hearing loss; 2) adventitious hearing loss in early childhood (3–8 years of age); and 3) hearing impairment acquired in adulthood. This factor affects each individual's experience in different educational environments during the formal school years. *Some* members of each category are reasonable candidates as consumers of oral interpreting services during their secondary and/or adult years. Others can depend on listening, with or without a hearing aid, and the supplement of speechreading and will not need interpreting services.

Congenital or Prelingual Hearing Loss—Early Identification

Infants and toddlers with hearing loss are not automatically considered as candidates for oral or sign language interpreter services in later years because of four factors: 1) early differential diagnosis and educational intervention; 2) recent widespread availability of miniaturized individual binaural hearing aids; 3) the availability of carefully sequenced auditory skills curricula (Ling and Ling, 1978; Northcott, 1977a; Pollack, 1970; Vaughan, 1976) and 4) immediate focus on training to develop the dynamic use of residual hearing (detection, discrimination, identification, and comprehension) through oral exchange related to adult-child activities within the home and immediate environment, with or without speechreading as a supplement (Ling, 1981) (see Chapter 2 of this volume).

Pragmatic assessment is conducted primarily by a classroom teacher, who functions as a diagnostic-prescriptive teacher. Ling (1981) identified the major areas as: 1) speech reception (auditory, visual, or auditory/visual); 2) language growth (receptive and expressive/production); and 3) speech production (phonetic and phonological skills, including intelligibility when appropriate). PL 94-142 ensures periodic assessment as well as any appropriate changes in the educational environment regarding, for example, whether the method of instruction should be *oral* (auditory/verbal or visual/oral) or *simultaneous* or *combined* (adding a form of sign language and fingerspelling to the oral component).

Adventitious Hearing Loss in Early Childhood (Ages 3–8)

Hearing loss that occurs after the acquisition of expressive language is often the result of childhood illness or accident. The subsequent language curriculum for such children should encourage creative thinking and verbal expression as well as vocabulary enrichment, aural rehabilitation, and the opportunity for speech refinement and maintenance. As in the instance of the congenitally deaf child, speechreading is "caught" and not "taught" as a formal set of skills.

Hea.ing Impairment Acquired in Adulthood

The etiology of hearing loss may be familial; noise-induced; by accident; the result of old age (presbycusis); or occasioned by unsuccessful surgery to correct a minor otological defect. Formal speechreading lessons are required in most instances, following medical and audiological determination of the value of an individual hearing aid/s as a supplement or primary channel for oral communication. Enrollment does not assure future competency as a sophisticated speechreader, however.

Hearing impairment affects approximately 16.2 million Americans in one or both ears and approximately 1 in every 3 persons by 65 years of age or older (ASHA, 1982).

THE CASE FOR ORAL INTERPRETING

Why Oral Interpreting?

Kirsten Gonzalez, a postlingually deafened specialist for the hearing impaired at the largest community college in California, argued in favor of the availability of professionally trained oral interpreters upon a speechreader's request. Although her primary language is English, as spoken and speechread, she is proficient in signed English and reads American Sign Language (ASL). She outlined several situations in which a speechreader may be prevented from using his or her skills (Gonzalez, 1981):

1. When the speaker is not present (in telephone situations, public address system announcements; voice-overs; and narration accompanying audiovisual presentations)
2. When the speaker is present, but a moustache, beard or unclear speech (including gumchewing) makes him or her nearly impossible to speechread
3. When environmental factors cloud the effectiveness of a speaker who would otherwise be speechreadable (distance from the speaker; poor lighting; an obtuse angle from which to view the speaker; or visual or auditory background distraction, each contributing to the reduction of a speechreader's efficiency)
4. In group situations among hearing people, where it is difficult to find out "and find out fast" who is speaking (including courtroom proceedings, classroom seminars, consultations, and committee meetings)

Oral Interpreters and Sign Language Interpreters—Ambiguities They Face

Ambiguities in the English language and in ASL can become barriers to conveying the precise meaning of the speaker's remarks to either a speechreader or a sign language consumer.

In English, certain elements of speech are identical on the lips, e.g., the sounds of *t,d,* and *n,* where the flat tongue touches the upper gum. When combined into words that look just like other words, they are labeled *homophenes* (e.g., "rude" and "root") and can cause a speechreader to depend on the context in which each is presented for precise meaning. *Homophones*, which sound alike (e.g., *write* or *rite*), may also cause confusion upon occasion.

In ASL, many single signs have multiple meanings, e.g., "beautiful," "pretty," and "lovely"; or "pardon," "excuse," and "forgive." In turn, the concept of "run," for example, is expressed by different signs according to each of its multiple meanings—*run* for president (volunteer; compete); *run* an ad in the newspaper (file); *run* into a friend at the store (meet); or *run* a turret lathe (work on).

Why Not a Simultaneous Interpreter (Spoken and Sign Mode)?

Specific limitations can interfere with comfortable speechreading when a sign language interpreter using signs and voiceless speech (a *simul-*

taneous interpreter) is the only available option (Northcott, 1982). These limitations include instances when:

"I don't know sign language and it is distracting"

The rate of articulation for speaking is considerably higher than the rate of articulation for signing, with an increase in the percentage of time spent pausing, compared to the presentation of either modality separately (Bellugi and Fischer, 1972)

Occasional errors from spoken English appear in the signed version of the material being presented, or vice versa

Simultaneous presentation of signs and speech result in the deletion of significant portions of the spoken message, particularly under the Manual English condition (Cokely and Baker, 1980)

Words for which there are no formal signs must be fingerspelled frequently so that the normal rate and rhythm of speech are altered

A great many common signs obscure the mouth or the entire face momentarily, interrupting the speechreader's view and source of information (Gonzalez, 1981)

The rhythm of "silent speech" tends to follow the rhythm of signs being produced rather than that of natural spoken English

There is a sharp reduction in natural gestures and facial expression (nonverbal or body language), so valuable to a speechreader

There is a minimum of rephrasing of sentences for higher visibility on the lips because of the complex process of translating spoken language into precise, formal sign language

The fatigue factor sets in so that there may be a jerky unevenness of speech on the part of the simultaneous interpreter (the tendency to drop off word endings and to enunciate less clearly at times); "lip fatigue" may cause the oral interpreter to exaggerate mouth movements, which reduces his or her effectiveness to a consumer, and to add fewer natural gestures to convey the tone and mood of the speaker.

Informal Oral Interpreters: Unsung Pioneers

N. B. Lutes   The documented use of informal oral interpreters highlights the contribution of teachers of the deaf, friends, parents, spouses, siblings, and children of speechreaders in this helping role. An undated newspaper account (cited in *Deaf Heritage*) of N. B. Lutes, a deaf lawyer, tells of his appearance before the Ohio Supreme Court to argue a cause against the Tiffin National Bank: "He is said to have lipread his wife during the proceedings" (Gannon, 1981, p. 402).

Edwin W. Nies, D.D.S.   The author's father, Dr. Edwin W. Nies, was the second deaf person on record and the first Gallaudet graduate (after education at Lexington School for the Deaf in New York City) to earn a doctorate. Deafened in early childhood from meningitis, he received his Doctor of Dental Surgery degree from the University of Pennsylvania Dental School in 1914 (Gannon, 1981, p. 399). He relied primarily on classmates as note-takers and occasional informal oral interpreters and on a roommate, whom he taught to fingerspell, to supplement his speechreading skills.

Mabel Hubbard Bell   Mabel Hubbard suffered a total loss of hearing from scarlet fever at the age of 5. As the wife of Alexander Graham Bell and an excellent lipreader, she enjoyed attending the theater with her husband; there, Dr. Bell would turn his face toward his wife and repeat the dialogue silently so that she could follow it. Later, with captioned films, Dr. and Mrs. Bell attended the silent movies regularly. "Mabel . . . could read the lips at startling variance, especially during love scenes, with what captions purported was being said" (Bruce, 1973, p. 391).

When the telephone rang in the Bell home, Mrs. Bell used an intermediary to talk to those who were used to her speech. "One of the children or grandchildren . . . would listen at the receiver and repeat the other party's words for her to read from their lips while she spoke into the transmitter" (Bruce, 1973, p. 327-328).

Earnest Elmo Calkins   Deafened gradually during his elementary school years, this philosopher, author, and statesman in the setting of standards in planning and execution in advertising recognized the value of lipreading, "which all of us utilize to some extent. But it must be admitted that the good Lord has created few people with legible countenances" (Calkins, 1924, p. 253). One of the solutions was to "depend on an interpreter, one of those clear-speaking persons who will give him the leads" (p. 253). Calkins' efficient oral interpreter was his wife: ". . . a name or word, spoken without a sound, gives me the clue. . . . After each excursion into the hearing world, I receive a syllabus of what was said and find that my own impression was quite frequently wrong . . ." (p. 236).

Jack Ashley, Member of Parliament   In an autobiography bearing the poignant title, *Journey into Silence* (1973), this distinguished man reported about his return to a "completely silent House of Commons" in 1968 following a total loss of hearing and his subsequent triumph in reelection. He wrote of taking formal speechreading lessons, of "subtly changed relationships" with colleagues and friends, and of the clarity of speech of his wife and family: "If I encountered a difficult sentence, they would find an alternate form of words I could easily understand. Through their patience, I could converse as naturally, and almost as easily, as a man who could hear" (p. 160). The Honorable Ashley's wife, Pauline, a superb informal interpreter, also uses a shorthand-type of written cues at times; their teamwork was noted when the distinguished Member of Parliament was keynote speaker at the International Biennial Convention of the Alexander Graham Bell Association, held in Toronto in June, 1982. In telephone conversations, Ashley is able to have "almost normal conversations," using the ordinary handset, while his wife listens on an additional earpiece and "simultaneously and silently repeats the caller's words while I lipread her" (p. 171).

The unevenness of opportunity for supplementary casual interpreter assistance to the indomitable individuals described above is in sharp contrast to the testimony of speechreaders who function in the 1980s with certainty in lead roles in their professional work with the assistance of a professionally trained and certified oral interpreter (see Chapter 12 in this volume).

LEGAL GUARANTEES FOR THE HEARING IMPAIRED

In the mid-1960s, Congress legislated in rapid succession legal assurances and guarantees of protection of the rights of the handicapped and access to full participation in an integrated society. In addition, Congress legislated a philosophy as well as procedures for implementation of its new laws.

PL 94-142 (Education for All Handicapped Children Act, 1975)

Its assurances include a free appropriate education suited to each child's individual needs. The law refers to the "least restrictive alternative," giving surety that, to the extent appropriate, children and youth who are handicapped will receive their education in regular classes with children who do not have handicaps. The burden of proof is on the local education agency (school district of the child's residence) that it cannot provide appropriate service including an oral or sign language interpreter, when specified, before removing the handicapped child (hearing impaired, in the framework of this book) from the regular educational environment.

Certain procedural safeguards involving active participation of parents in major educational decisions that affect their child and the steps in due process that must be afforded in developing an individualized education plan (IEP) are now being analyzed in public hearings on proposed changes to the law itself, including the frequency and duration of supplemental support services during the school day.

Section 504 (Regulations) of the Rehabilitation Act of 1973

These regulations forbid discrimination against the handicapped by recipients of federal Health, Education, and Welfare (HEW) funds:

No otherwise qualified handicapped individual in the United States shall, solely by the reason of handicap, be excluded in the participation in, be denied the benefit of, or be subjected to discrimination under any program or activity receiving federal financial assistance.

Part of the regulations exclusively deal with preschool through postsecondary school years. They carry the threat of sanctions, permit witholding of funds for demonstrated discrimination, and are administered by the Office of Civil Rights.

Section 304d of PL 95-602 (Interpreter Training Programs)

The first stated objective of the Training Program for Interpreters for Deaf Individuals, which permitted a maximum of 12 grants to establish a training program or provide financial assistance for ongoing interpreter training programs, read:

To increase the supply of skilled manual and oral interpreters available throughout the country for employment in public and private agencies, schools and other institutions . . . and those other areas of service in which deaf persons can share equally with non-deafened citizens through the use of interpreter assistance. (Office of Human Development Services, 1980, p. 1)

The training grant application review rating form required a rating of the extent to which:

. . . the curriculum and teaching methods provide for both manual and oral interpreting and provide a balance between and integration of theory and practice relevant to the educational objectives of the program. (p. 3)

(The impact on the right of hearing-impaired individuals to receive interpreting services and the question of responsibility for payment for such services are discussed in Chapter 4 of this volume.)

DEVELOPMENT OF STANDARDS
FOR ORAL INTERPRETER CERTIFICATION

Historical Perspective

A Speechreader Speaks   Two decades ago, Simon (1964) stated forthrightly in a letter to the editor of the Volta Review that: ". . . It is difficult to lipread lectures and speeches. However, it is not necessary to have manual interpretation." He explained that a group of lipreaders at a convention of the Alexander Graham Bell Association for the Deaf "listened" to one of the speeches ". . . through reading the lips of a hearing person next to us, who was able to repeat what was being said, sotto voce. . . ." He clarified his position by stating that through this exact translation, they were able to appreciate all the "nuances and the flavor," which not only expressed the style, tone, and mood of the original speaker but were "so important in conveying the exact meaning of whatever is spoken or written" (p. 52).

A Professional Organization for Interpreters (Sign Language and Oral) In that same year, 1964, the National Registry of Professional Interpreters and Translators for the Deaf, later known as the Registry of Interpreters for the deaf, Inc. (RID) was established at a Workshop on Interpreting for the Deaf at Ball State Teachers' College in Muncie, Indiana. Its stated purpose was: ". . . to promote recruiting and training of more interpreters for the deaf, both manual and oral, and to maintain a list of qualified persons" (Smith, 1964).

In the spirit of harmony that generally prevailed at the workshop, the past president of the Utah Association of the Deaf, Robert Sanderson, stated:

> For those oral deaf who are highly educated and successful in life by any standard, I have only respect. Undoubtedly they need only a minimum of interpreting in close situations. . . . I am led to wonder how the oral deaf person . . . will fare in a large meeting where the speaker is some distance away. I hope this workshop will provide some answers and that the oral deaf who are with us will help us develop them. (Smith, p. 33)

Interagency Action: 1976–1979   The time line of major events that led to RID evaluation and certification of the first 51 oral interpreters in the United States in 1979 is as follows (Dirst, 1980; Northcott, 1979a; Northcott et al., 1980):

1976
    June
        Carl Kirchner, President, RID, stated the formal readiness of the RID to "work with the A. G. Bell Association for the Deaf and its hearing-impaired members to establish a certificate for oral interpreting" (A. G. Bell Association Biennial Convention, Boston. Section: Oral Interpreters: A Missing Link).

1977
    April
        Publication: W. H. Northcott published "The oral interpreter: a necessary support specialist for the hearing impaired" (Volta Rev. 1977. 79:136–144).
    November
        Dr. William Castle, Director of the National Technical Institute for the Deaf (NTID), served as chairperson of a committee representing the six federally sponsored postsecondary programs.

Dr. Castle directed the drafting of Regulations for Implementation of the National Interpreter Training Act, inviting A. G. Bell members, including the A. G. Bell Association Oral Deaf Adults Section (ODAS), to participate.

1978

June

A Council on Education of the Deaf (CED) resolution recommended that: ". . . agencies involved with the provision of training or certification of Simultaneous or Manual Interpreters consider the establishment of guidelines, competencies, and criteria for certification of oral interpreters as soon as practicable."

October

A. G. Bell Association hosted a workshop, "Focus on the Oral Interpreter," to revise a first draft of the *Guidelines for the Preparation of Oral Interpreters* (see Appendix I on p. 258) written by W. H. Northcott. Participants included representatives of NTID, RID, NAD, the International Parents Organization (IPO) of the A. G. Bell Association, and the International Association of Parents of the Deaf (IAPD) (Guidelines, 1979).

November

Ray Fuller, Program Evaluation Specialist, Arkansas Division of Rehabilitation Services and member of ODAS, conceptualized and hosted the first Oral Interpreter Training Workshop in the United States, Little Rock, Arkansas. Co-sponsors were the University of Arkansas (Medical Sciences and Communicative Disorders Program); Arkansas Division of Rehabilitation Services; A. G. Bell Association; and Arkansas Association for Hearing-Impaired Children.

December

American Association for the Advancement of Science (AAAS) (via Virginia Stern, Senior Program Associate, Project on the Handicapped in Science), A. G. Bell Association, and NTID co-hosted an Oral Interpreter Training Workshop in Houston, Texas to prepare for the AAAS Convention, held in that city the following month.

1979

January

James Stangarone, President, RID, designated that A. G. Bell Association and NTID would work with the RID in the "joint leadership role of developing standards and implementing training for oral interpreters."

April
RID Board of Directors approved the inclusion of the oral interpreter certification process within the existing RID evaluation system.

May
A.G. Bell Board of Directors passed a resolution: "WHEREAS the United States Congress has recognized the need for handicapped persons to have full access to public facilities and meetings and WHEREAS Secretary Califano has issued a directive that manual interpreters will be provided at all HEW meetings. . . . THEREFORE BE IT RESOLVED that the Board of Directors of the Alexander Graham Bell Association for the Deaf respectfully request that HEW provide oral interpreters in order to ensure full compliance with federal law and full participation by the hearing-impaired citizenry."

May
A conference on Oral Interpreter Certification was sponsored by NTID, Rochester, New York. Chairperson was Dr. William E. Castle, Director, NTID. Purpose: To revise the first draft of proposed certification standards, written by Dr. Diane Castle, Marjorie Jacobs, James Stangarone, and Anna Witter of NTID. Representatives included six from A.G. Bell Association (four from ODAS); six from NTID; two from RID; and two from the National Association of the Deaf (NAD).

Summer
RID Board of Directors approved oral interpreter standards.

October
The first National Oral Interpreter Evaluation/Certification Workshop was hosted by the St. Paul, Minnesota Technical Vocational Institute, Regional Programs for Deaf Students (Robert Lauritsen, Director). Co-sponsors were A.G. Bell Association, NTID, and RID (through federal grant from the Bureau of Education for the Handicapped, U.S. Office of Education). There were 69 invited registrants. The first 51 oral interpreters in the United States received RID certification.

1980

NAD at its 35th Biennial Convention resolved to: ". . . actively work to eliminate discrimination against any deaf person because of his/her chosen method of communication." This furthered the cooperative interagency and organizational efforts to ensure the preservation of equal access to professional interpreter services in the individual consumer's choice of specialist—the oral interpreter or the sign language interpreter.

THE VOLTA SERIES: PROFESSIONAL GROWTH WORKSHOPS

During the summer and fall of 1983, the A.G. Bell Association hosted the Volta Series, a group of four intensive 1-week (40 to 50 hour) regional courses, which were conducted throughout the United States for the instruction and preparation of oral interpreters. Various members of a national team of guest faculty supplemented the site specialists as instructors in each course. The final course was reserved for instructors of oral interpreters in formal programs of preparation.

At the request of the donor whose financial gift made the series possible, the target population for registration was the seasoned *informal* oral interpreter (e.g., teacher, parent, or sibling of a hearing-impaired individual or the hearing-impaired speechreader). The course addressed curriculum development, updating of interpreting skills, including critique as well as orientation to the Code of Ethics (see Appendix II on p. 266) and current information on available resource networks and materials.

During the preceding year, as part of preplanning for the Volta Series, a consortium of members of the A.G. Bell Association Committee on Oral Interpreting, including representatives of NTID, the RID, and the Conference of Interpreter Trainers (CIT), gathered at NTID to set entry criteria for participant eligibility in the Volta Series courses. They reviewed the curriculum for the Volta Series and also established pre-evaluation criteria associated with the Oral Interpreter Certification System, which had been lacking.

THE REGISTRY OF INTERPRETERS FOR THE DEAF, INC. (RID): A SINGLE PROFESSION EMBRACING ROLE SPECIALIZATION

The human communication process is central to the interaction between any hearing and hearing-impaired individual. The interpreter (oral or sign language) is the primary facilitator in situations requiring such support.

The RID is currently recognized as the national organization that coordinates the process of evaluation and certification of *oral* interpreters and *sign language* interpreters through its National Evaluation System, established in 1972. After standards for the oral interpreter certifications were approved in 1979 by its Board of Directors, the RID ". . . formally recognized oral interpreters through the development of an evaluation process as part of the National Evaluation System" (Dirst, 1980, pp. 1–2). The certification system for oral interpreters is separate from the certification system for sign language interpreters but parallel to it. Currently, most states have RID chapters or affiliates working on the local level through a local evaluation team, which formally evaluates candidates for either specialization.

In 1972, the first sign language interpreters were evaluated and recommended for certification by the RID at the National Evaluation Workshop (NEW), held in Memphis, Tennessee October 20–23 (Kirchner, 1976; RID, Inc., 1976). Seven years later, the first 51 oral interpreters were evaluated and certified in St. Paul, Minnesota at the First National Oral Interpreter Training and Evaluation Workshop, October 25–27 (Castle, 1982; Dirst, 1980; Northcott et al., 1980). The current ratio of oral interpreters to sign language interpreters is roughly 1:10.

Not all public expression was supportive of including oral interpreters in the RID National Evaluation System. Caccamise (1978), for example, urged that RID members "decide for themselves how their organization can best continue to service the communication need of deaf people" on the basis of research that: ". . . compares the effectiveness of 'strict' oral interpreting (mouthing what the speaker says) and simultaneous interpreting (mouthing and manually communicating what the speaker says)." Northcott's (1979b) response attempted to bring the focus back to the rights of every hearing-impaired individual to equal access to quality interpreter services, in their preferred mode of communication.

RID: Model for the Eighties

The RID business meeting held during the National Convention of RID in Hartford, Connecticut in July, 1982 was the scene of further discussion related to oral interpreters. With no debate, the membership approved a resolution affirming that ". . . the stated purpose of the RID is to serve all deaf persons as communication facilitators" and its purpose is "service to all deaf persons, regardless of their communication preference."

SUMMARY

Modes of Communication: A Humanistic Approach

As a result of certain legal guarantees of the past decade, hearing-impaired individuals in the 1980s are increasingly inner-directed as they search for purpose, direction, and control in their daily lives. The concept of homogeneity of "the deaf" is being replaced through public awareness of the heterogeneity of individuals who are hearing impaired. Personal values, priorities, and preferred social and economic environments are a matter of self-determination; central to personal fulfillment is freedom of choice in preferred mode of communication and assistance through support services, if requested.

The certification of *oral* interpreters and *sign language* interpreters by the RID permits a hearing-impaired consumer to use the support specialist of his or her choice. The concept is one of matched characteristics of the consumer and interpreter. This has enabled professionally competent, certified interpreters (*oral* or *sign language*) to drop their advocacy for a particular mode of communication and their concern that a hearing-impaired consumer will not choose "correctly" to focus on role specialization—in this instance, the competencies demanded of an oral interpreter in order to serve efficiently as a communication facilitator for speechreaders.

Critical Needs   Oral interpreters can be found in specialized settings where speechreaders function. This may be in an academic/vocational; professional (including legal or medical); media (telephone, TV, radio, or performing arts); or social environment. The variety of direct service surroundings ensures the existence of specialists on oral interpreting who are logical candidates for appointment as instructors, practicum supervisors, guest lecturers, and community consultants in preservice or professional growth programs and coursework for the preparation of oral interpreters. The personal background, preparation, and milieus in which an interpreter functions combine to identify an instructor's specialization area of competence—as an instructor in the preparation of oral interpreters or as an instructor in the preparation of sign language interpreters. Role specialization is the cornerstone in careful preparation of each classification of specialist.

Participants at the Conference on Interpreter Training, convened in June of 1979 by the National Academy of Gallaudet College in Atlanta, concluded that: "Few of the current generation of traditional interpreter trainers are comfortable teaching oral or voice interpreting; scientifically developed training procedures are needed" (Yoken, 1979, p. 20). Attitudes of hearing-impaired persons toward interpreting procedures and interpreters and interpreters' attitudes about hearing-impaired people in general, and special groups in particular, were identified as related topics for future inquiry (pp. 19–21).

Oral Interpreting: Principles and Practices   This book offers a structural frame of reference for students, instructors, and administrators who are or will become actively involved in the design and implementation of a comprehensive educational program of professional preparation of oral interpreters. It is designed as both a state-of-the-art presentation of functional practices and procedures in coursework and practicum and as a reference book that links current trends and issues related to deafness and its amelioration with events, past and present, that can redirect the focus of interpreter preparation in the future.

As a working tool in the hands of those who pursue quality control of oral interpreter preparation and service . . . a springboard for creative discussion at workshops and conferences on "How can we do it differently or better?". . . . a reference book in the development of a public awareness program. . . . an outstretched hand to speechreaders in states where only a handful of oral interpreters now exist . . . this book is offered with an invitation to open-ended adaptation of its contents by thoughtful readers.

REFERENCES

ASHA. 1982. Hearing impairment and the audiologist. ASHA, Rockville, MD.

Ashley, J. 1973. Journey into Silence. The Bodley Head, London.

Bellugi, U., and S. Fischer. 1972. A comparison of sign language and spoken language rate and grammatical mechanisms. Cognition 1:178–200.

Bruce, R. V. 1973. BELL: Alexander Graham Bell and the conquest of solitude. Little, Brown and Co., Boston.

Caccamise, F. 1978. New myths to replace old myths? Am. Ann. Deaf. 123:513–515.

Calkins, E. E. 1924. "Louder, Please!": The Autobiography of a Deaf Man. The Atlantic Monthly Press, Boston.

Castle, W. E. 1982. Oral interpreting. RID Views VII:8.

Cokely, D., and C. Baker. 1980. Problems with rate and deletions in simultaneous communication. Directions 1:22.

Dailey, S., and E. N. McMillan (eds.). 1978. Interpreting for International Conferences; Problems of Language and Communication. Translation of the original author's work: D. Seleskovitch. Pen and Booth, Washington, DC.

Dirst, R. D. (ed.). 1980. Oral Interpreter Evaluation Manual for Evaluators. RID, Inc. National Evaluation System, Silver Spring, MD.

Gannon, J. R. 1981. Deaf Heritage: A Narrative History of Deaf America. NAD, Silver Spring, MD.

Gonzalez, K. A. 1981. Why oral interpreting? RID Views VII:6.

Gove, P. B. (ed.). 1980. Webster's 3rd New International Dictionary. G. and C. Merriam Co., Springfield, IL.

Guidelines for the preparation of oral interpreters. 1979. Volta Rev. 81:135–145.

Kirchner, C. 1976. Preface. Registry of Interpreters for the Deaf, Inc. Directory of Membership. The Center for Continuing Education. Gallaudet College, Washington, DC.

Ling, D. 1981. A survey of the present status of methods in English-speaking countries. In: A. M. Mulholland (ed.), Oral Education Today and Tomorrow, pp. 81–94. Alexander Graham Bell Association for the Deaf, Washington, DC.

Ling, D., and A. H. Ling. 1978. Aural Habilitation. Alexander Graham Bell Association for the Deaf, Washington, DC.

Mackenzie, C. 1928. Alexander Graham Bell. Houghton Mifflin, Boston.

Northcott, W. H. 1977a. The oral interpreter: a necessary support specialist for the hearing impaired. Volta Rev. 79:136–144.

Northcott, W. H. (ed.). 1977b. Curriculum Guide: Hearing-Impaired Children (0–3 Years) and Their Parents. Alexander Graham Bell Association for the Deaf, Washington, DC.

Northcott, W. H. 1979a. Introduction. In: Guidelines for the preparation of oral interpreters. Volta Rev. 81:135–145.

Northcott, W. H. 1979b. Letter to the editor: Oral interpreting. Am. Ann. Deaf 124:4.

Northcott, W. H. 1979c. Oral interpreting—into the major leagues. A paper presented at the First National Oral Interpreter Evaluation/Certification Workshop, October 25–27, St. Paul, MN.

Northcott, W. H. 1982. The professional oral interpreter. A. G. Bell Association for the Deaf, Washington, DC.

Northcott, W. H., R. H. Carlson, J. D. Flack, H. Draving, and M. Schommer. 1980. Oral interpreting. In: F. Caccamise, R. Dirst, R. D. DeVries et al. (eds.), Introduction to Interpreting. RID, Inc., Silver Spring, MD.

Office of Human Development Services. 1980. Program information for training programs for interpreters for deaf individuals. Division of Manpower Development, Rehabilitation Services Administration, Department of Health, Education and Welfare, Washington, DC.

Per-Lee, M. S. 1980. Interpreter research: Targets for the eighties. Conference Report: October 6–10, Tucson, AZ.

Pollack, D. 1970. Educational Audiology for the Limited Hearing Infant. Charles C Thomas, Springfield, IL.

Research: Topics for future investigation. 1979. In: C. Yoken (ed.), Interpreter Training: The State of the Art. The National Academy of Gallaudet College, Washington, DC.

RID, Inc. 1973. Directory of Members. P.O. Box 1339, Washington, DC.

RID, Inc. 1982. Oral interpreters: A communication dimension. RID, Inc., Silver Spring, MD.

Ross, M., and T. G. Giolas (eds.). 1978. Auditory Management of Hearing Impaired Children. University Park Press, Baltimore.

Seleskovitch, D. 1978. Interpreting for International Conferences. Translated by S. Dailey and E. N. McMillan. Pen and Booth, Washington, DC.

Simon, A. B. 1964. Letter to the editor: Oral interpreting. Volta Rev. 66:52.

Smith, J. (ed.). 1964. Interpreting for Deaf People. U.S. Department of Health Education and Welfare, Washington, DC.

Vaughan, P. 1976. Learning to Listen. New Press, Don Mills, Ontario.

Waite, H. E. 1961. Make a Joyful Sound: the Romance of Mabel Hubbard and Alexander Graham Bell. Macrae Smith Co., Philadelphia.

Woolf, H. B. (ed.). 1977. Webster's New Collegiate Dictionary. G. and C. Merriam Co., Springfield, IL.

Yoken, C. (ed.). 1979. Interpreter Training: The State of the Art. The National Academy of Gallaudet College, Washington, DC.

CHAPTER 2

CURRENT EDUCATIONAL PRACTICES

Mark Ross

CONTENTS

CLASSIFICATION OF HEARING LOSS

The isolated fact that a child has a hearing loss provides virtually no useful information concerning educational programming. There are different types of hearing losses and they come in differing degrees and shapes, many of which may have profound educational significance. Therefore, the first step in developing an educational plan for a particular child involves ensuring that current and comprehensive audiological information is available and the communication and educational implications of the loss are fully explored and understood.

There are two basic kinds of hearing loss: *conductive* and *sensorineural*; a third type is a combination of the two (Martin, 1980). In a conductive hearing loss, the sensory organ (the cochlea) and the neural structures (nerve VIII and higher auditory pathways) are intact; the problem lies in some obstruction in either or both the outer and middle ears, which reduces the sound energy reaching the cochlea. Such conditions may be temporary, recurring, or permanent; they are frequently amenable to successful medical and/or surgical treatment. However, a longstanding or chronically intermittent problem that occurs in infancy may affect auditory processing and educational achievements. These potential problems should be considered in any such instance (Gottlieb et al., 1979; Kessler and Randolph, 1979; Masters and Marsh, 1978; Sarff et al., 1981; Zinkus and Gottlieb, 1980).

A sensorineural hearing loss is of primary concern in educational settings. The sound reaches the cochlea with no obstruction, but damage to the cochlea and/or the neural structures either prevents sounds from being detected or requires more sound before detection can take place. Because portions of the cochlea and the neural structures are "tuned" to respond best to certain sound frequencies, a sensorineural hearing loss may affect some sound frequencies more than others, depending upon the locus and severity of the damage. This differential responsivity of the sensorineural structures gives rise to the audiogram, which is simply a graph of the degree of loss across frequency.

There are two important concepts of consider regarding a sensorineural hearing loss:

1. *The shape of the audiogram*   The degree of loss across frequency has important educational and communicative implications. The normal auditory channel has evolved to maximally detect the sounds of speech, which spread across frequency from a low of about 80 or 100 Hz to above 8000 kHz (Levitt, 1978). A greater degree of loss at the higher frequencies, which is common, means that the higher frequency components of speech, such as all the voiceless consonants, will be perceived poorly, if at all, if no amplification is employed.

2. *Hearing loss is rarely total*   Only about 5% of children with the most severe hearing losses are unable to hear any sounds, regardless of frequency or intensity. The term "deaf" is reserved for those children with the most profound losses—those whose residual hearing is insufficient to serve as a primary communication modality, even after optimal auditory management procedures. The residual hearing of the majority of hearing-impaired[1] children, therefore, can still be viewed as the therapeutic "frontline" in planning an educational program.

PRIMACY OF THE AUDITORY CHANNEL

The emphasis on the auditory channel is based on the fact that audition normally serves as the primary means by which children develop

---

[1] The term *hearing impaired* is used generically to refer to any child with hearing loss, regardless of severity or type. It is not a synonym for *hard of hearing* or *deaf*, but includes both classifications.

speech and language. Educators of hearing-impaired children too often emphasize the *teaching* of language when, by its nature, language is most effectively *learned* rather than taught. Children with normal hearing have an innate capacity for organizing their experiences and attaching verbal symbols (words) to these experiences. Given relevant auditory linguistic inputs associated with ongoing activities, in step with a child's evolving maturational and cognitive development, hearing children will rather easily and effortlessly make the necessary linguistic-experiential associations (Fry, 1978). In a brief period of time, they will not only learn the linguistic labels for objects and events in their environment, but will also induce the grammatical rules for combining linguistic elements and very shortly thereafter become very effective oral verbal communicators.

Hearing-impaired children have the same capacity for creating language symbols as do normally hearing children. However, they lack a sufficient quantity and quality of auditory linguistic inputs to stimulate their biological potential for learning the language of their surroundings. With modern sound amplification technology, relatively few hearing-impaired children are unable to employ their natural predisposition for evolving a primarily auditory-based linguistic system. In many places, the profession of education of the hearing impaired functions as if these technological developments have never taken place. Many educators still consider children with 60 to 90 dB losses to be educationally deaf and expose them to educational practices that virtually ignore the presence of residual hearing. These practices constitute in reality a self-fulfilling prophecy, the outcome of which is a functionally "deaf" as opposed to a functionally "hard-of-hearing" person (Northcott, 1973, 1975; Ross and Calvert, 1967; Wilson et al., 1974).

We do not know the precise limits of hearing loss beyond which audition cannot serve as the primary channel for developing a verbal communication system. The evidence from a number of research projects (reviewed in Stark, 1974) suggests that there is a discontinuity in the ability to comprehend and produce intelligible speech in the 90–95 dB range. This may be slightly on the conservative side. The children who were the subjects of these studies did not necessarily receive amplification at a sufficiently early age to prevent the occurrence of auditory sensory deprivation, which would impose limits on the potential capabilities of the auditory system. These children did not necessarily receive early binaural amplification, or individually selected electro-acoustic responses to produce an optimal pattern of aided sensation levels across frequency. In using amplification devices in a classroom, these children did not necessarily receive the teacher's voice at a 25–30 dB level above the noise and sound reflections existing in the classroom (all of these variables are discussed fully in Ross et al., 1982). Had these and other factors affecting the maximum use of amplified sound been considered, children with greater degrees of hearing loss could also possibly have functioned primarily as hard-of-hearing individuals. There are many such children; usually, their accomplishments are dismissed as "exceptions," with little thought given to what factors make these children "exceptions" and why other children with similar capabilities do not reach the same level of accomplishment. Two essential factors are 1) appropriate amplification; and 2) teamwork involving dedicated and knowledgeable parents and teachers.

Emphasis on the primacy of the auditory channel for most hearing-impaired children reflects, of course, personal values; but, it goes beyond this. Hearing is a human birthright, and even when it is impaired, it is the obligation of professionals to develop and stimulate it to the maximum extent feasible. If this is done, many children with severe and profound losses will be able to function as hard-of-hearing rather than deaf persons while others, who are functionally deaf, will be able to employ their limited residual hearing as an important supplement to their overall communication capacities. Audition is a time-locked sensory avenue; unstimulated and unused early in life, its potential contribution is markedly reduced. Although the theme of this book is *oral interpreting*, which primarily implies dependency upon a visual means of communication, such an eventuality should be preceded by extensive and continuing efforts to initially exploit the auditory channel.

CURRENT EDUCATIONAL PRACTICES

Family-Oriented Preprimary Programs

It is a truism in the 1980s that the education of a hearing-impaired child should begin as early as possible (Simmons-Martin and Calvert, 1979). Few professional personnel involved in early educational intervention would disagree with this statement. Young children have a phenomenal natural capacity to learn language, and management efforts must begin in early childhood before this natural ability is lost. When management procedures are instituted at the time the hearing loss is first detected, there is an opportunity to assist parents while they are first trying to come to terms with the shock, anxieties, and guilt of learning that their child has an irreversible hearing loss. Luterman (1979) expressed it very aptly: Our first clients are the parents and not the child. They are, and remain for many years, the most important influences in a child's life. If parents are confused and despondent, unable to progress beyond the stages of shock and denial, if the defense mechanisms they establish to ease the pain are self-defeating, then any direct efforts with the child will, at best, not be reinforced by them, and at worst, be unknowingly sabotaged by parents who follow their own agenda. Parents are not an intrusion in our therapeutic efforts nor adversaries we have to overcome in order to reach the child. At first, they *are* our therapeutic focus.

Parent-Home Programs (0–3 Years of Age)

The first teachers of any child are the parents and the first school is the home. This obvious basic premise has often been ignored in practice. The child's mother is generally considered the primary caretaker for the first 2 or 3 years of a toddler's life. This departs from previous educational practices, which emphasized the periodic visits of a mother and child to the clinic or school, where a teacher, audiologist, or speech-language pathologist would "work" with the child and then "counsel" the parent. The results were usually only marginally beneficial and frequently detrimental to the parent's relationship with the child. The parent's role in these instances was secondary and supportive of the professional.

Current procedures emphasize and capitalize on reinforcing or building a helpful relationship between the parents and child; through parents, the child is reached. Once they accept the reality of their child's condition, parents will have the greatest initial impact upon a child's development. The limited professional time available is most effectively spent in assisting parents in: 1) providing an enriched communicative atmosphere for the child; 2) helping them understand the incremental advances in receptive and expressive communicative development; and 3) differentiating behavior attributable to the hearing loss in contrast to that occurring normally among most young children. Young parents, in particular, often implicate the hearing loss in difficulties that have nothing to do with audition.

Visits to the child's first school, the home, are a frequent necessity because that is where the raw material of the child's nonlinguistic world is primarily found. In the home, the child is surrounded daily by familiar objects, people, and events; they act upon the child and, in turn, the child interacts with them. The child has a need to develop symbols to comprehend and communicate experiences that occur most frequently and naturally in the home. The naming of familiar objects, such as the family pet, favorite toys, or people, and familiar routines, such as eating, bathing, bedtime, or household chores, serve as the experiential basis for linguistic growth. In the home, too, parents are in charge; they are consequently relaxed and more receptive to the information presented by the professional. The professional can observe the usual interactions between parent and child and make suggestions of immediate relevancy. In respect to auditory development, the most salient stimuli for beginning auditory training occur naturally in the home. One early objective of home visits is to conduct an auditory inventory; that is, to point out to the parents all of the naturally occurring, sound-producing events that can be brought to the child's attention for detection, discrimination, and verbal labeling in a natural manner.

A parent support group is essential. No professional can offer the same insights and shared experiences or has the same credibility as other parents of hearing-impaired children. Such groups are usually organized under the aegis of a center or school and coordinated by a professional, who should be knowledgeable about child development, psycholinguistics, audiology, and the dynamics of group therapy. One person usually cannot fill this role; thus, responsibility for the group may be shared by several persons, or consultants may be sought on frequent occasions (Northcott, 1975; Simmons-Martin, 1979).

Luterman (1979) outlined the general and specific format of such a group. The goal is to assist parents in working through the intense emotional impact of having a hearing-handicapped child and, with the information presented in the group supplemented by several site visits, to make their choices among the educational alternatives available to their child. No other therapeutic procedure designed for young hearing-impaired children is more important (save, perhaps, amplification) than the focus on parents as the prime deliverer of services to their child.

Concurrent with or preceding the parent-infant program, the child must be provided with effective, wearable amplification. Because the primary source of the child's difficulties is the hearing loss (except for children with multiple handicaps), some problems can be prevented or minimized by giving the child more "hearing" through amplified sound. The provision of optimal amplification is more complex than simply "sticking" a hearing aid in a child's ear. Amplification as a therapeutic procedure generally receives inadequate emphasis at all levels in educational programming (Ling and Ling, 1978; Ross and Tommassetti, 1978; Ross, 1981a, 1981b), possibly because of the limited exposure offered in teacher-training programs.

The process is, unfortunately, circular. If amplification is not employed in a sophisticated manner, the potential for auditory verbal communication will not be realized; if there are few "success" stories to examine, then there is little pressure to modify curricula to incorporate an auditory management model. Simple inertia further complicates the situation. The antidote is the continuing dissemination of the positive results achieved by many children and some exemplary programs, by means of books, articles, videotapes, and personal examples; attitudes must change before the widespread application of appropriate amplification can be realized.

Amplification is not a weak reed or a cruel hoax to play on children and their parents; if properly utilized, it can serve as an entrée to much our culture has to offer. Unfortunately, we live at a time when the imperatives of gaining acceptance as a deaf person that equals the value of any hearing person has led some leaders of the deaf community to reject efforts to improve the integration of hearing-impaired people into society. This is precisely what the development of functional auditory-oral communication skills will do. The attitude of some people seems to be that by fostering auditory-oral communication, hearing-impaired people must thereby be rejecting to themselves or the deaf community. This is a false issue. A person can develop the residual hearing with which he or she was born without placing negative values on those with less auditory-oral potential. The actualization of potential is a human imperative; being content with less is diminishing.

Optimally, the hearing aid should deliver an amplified speech signal at approximately 30 dB above the child's impaired thresholds across all the frequencies important for speech reception and, thus, for speech and language development (Ross et al., 1982). It should not be so intense as to exceed loudness discomfort levels or possibly produce further damage (see Ross and Giolas, 1978, Chapter 9). Distortion levels should not exceed 10% and preferably should be much less. Earmolds should fit comfortably and include the kinds of modifications necessary to alter the amplified signal in a positive manner (Killion, 1980). Binaural aids should be the normal recommendation (Libby, 1980; Ross, 1980).

Because we are dealing with preverbal children, it is not possible to make the kinds of precise behavioral measurements necessary to ensure that an optimal amplified signal is being received. It is often necessary to readjust the amplified signal as more data regarding the child's hearing status are collected. For these young children, our criterion for a successful "fit" is not superior word discrimination scores but, instead, progress in auditory linguistic development consistent with professional expectations. Admittedly, this is a very subjective judgment; our standards must be high enough to be challenging without being impossible or too frustrating. The use of aided audiograms (Ross et al., 1982, Chapter 4), which is feasible even with the very young child, can provide some assurance regarding the maximum detectability of a speech signal. Given the maximum amount of acoustic raw material, as judged by the aided thresholds, auditory linguistic development should then respond to the quality and quantity of linguistic input to which the child is exposed.

Nursery and Kindergarten Programs

Around 3 years of age, group educational experience via enrollment in a formal nursery program is highly desirable. The specific age of a child is less important than his or her ability to benefit socially and linguistically from a group situation. This decision is best made as the result of the informed involvement of a number of specialists, including the parent, teacher, social worker, speech-language pathologist, and audiologist. No written "guide" can be a substitute for active team deliberation.

The Neighborhood Nursery School

The child can be recommended for a regular nursery school if he or she:

1. Demonstrates acceptable social behavior according to chronological age
2. Is able to learn language by an auditory-oral and/or visual oral mode of communication
3. Functions on standardized tests of auditory-oral comprehension at the 2–6 age level or beyond
4. Is able to follow simple directions and questions
5. Uses two or more words spontaneously in self-expression
6. Is assured of supportive help (special teacher, educational audiologist, and the speech-language pathologist)
7. Is assured of parental willingness to be heavily involved in child's education

The Special Nursery

Special nursery programs come in a variety of models. For the child with a significant hearing loss, a preferred situation may be one in which there are about twice as many normally hearing children as hearing-impaired children (Jury, 1981). In these instances, the normally hearing children can serve as role models in such activities as cooperative play, taking turns, school routines (e.g., juice and cookie time), and the moves and rules in children's games. Through observation, a hearing-impaired child can learn what behaviors are acceptable and what are not. The special nursery is operated as a *nursery*, in which child development specialists play a dominant role. Superimposed on the normal routines is the special assistance that the hearing-impaired child requires. Each day, the child can receive daily individual tutoring in language and speech; it is expected one or both parents will observe, and occasionally assist, in the nursery several times a week. Ideally, parental involvement is scheduled in conjunction with an ongoing parent group. Hearing aids are checked daily, the acoustical conditions made as optimum as possible, and the use of FM auditory trainers (see below) considered.

The average special nursery extends for 2 years. At the end of the first year, the child should be reevaluated.

If the child now meets the criteria for a neighborhood nursery school (as above), then his or her placement can be considered. If the child's progress is acceptable in terms of auditory-oral or visual-oral skills and/or there is a need for further diagnostic appraisals, then the second year in the same nursery program can be recommended. If neither of these conditions occurs, then the child may be considered a candidate for a total communication[2] nursery. It should be explicitly noted that any decision to place or modify a child's educational setting requires a full team meeting.

Total Communication Nursery

The decision to recommend a total communication nursery should be made following the first year in the auditory-oral special nursery. The basis for this judgment would be 1) the child's clearly apparent inability to make acceptable auditory-oral progress; 2) extreme frustration exhibited regarding communication limitations; and 3) social isolation from the other children directly or indirectly attributable to communication problems. An informed parental preference must also be given great weight. However, a change in the communication method in itself, gives no assurance of any significant increase in communication skills.

Kindergarten Programs

The choices for a child after completion of nursery school are: 1) a regular kindergarten in a neighborhood school; 2) continuation in the auditory-oral special program; or 3) enrollment in a total communication program in a class taught by the *simultaneous method* of instruction. The neighborhood school would be recommended when the child has the capability to *directly* gain information from hearing classmates and teachers without an oral interpreter (Resolution, 1980), has the personality to cope with the demands of a regular school environment, and where the appropriate supportive help is available for both the regular teachers and the child. Continuation of a child in the

---

[2] The following definition of "total communication" was adopted by the 48th meeting of the Council of Executives of American Schools for the Deaf: "Total communication is a philosophy requiring the incorporation of appropriate aural, manual, and oral modes of communication in order to ensure effective communication with and among hearing-impaired persons."

auditory-oral special program is warranted when the above conditions are *not* met, but when regular progress in communication and social skills suggest that regular kindergarten placement is a reasonable future goal. Recommendations to a total communication nursery would be where neither of the above conditions apply, or where there is a cogent reason (such as manually deaf parents who express a strong preference) for giving such a placement priority. Our transcendent concern is always the welfare of the child and not a particular communication mode or educational placement.

Multidisciplinary Team Members

Decisions regarding educational options require an ongoing assessment of the child's progress. No specific test or criteria can take the place of the day-to-day observations of the child made by individuals who are in frequent contact with him or her. Each professional who sees a child, as well as the parents, makes observations consistent with his or her own orientation. Such observations, when reported, are valuable to the team's ultimate decision.

The permanent core members of a team include the parents, the child's teacher, and a school administrator (Nober, 1978). A number of other individuals may join in the team's deliberations, particularly if alternative educational programming is contemplated. The educational audiologist, speech and language pathologist, social worker, psychologist, special teacher, and personnel from a receiving facility are possible members of the team. Attendance at team meetings is restricted to the minimum number consistent with the detailed information necessary in any particular case. A team member should not leave a child or the classroom to join a meeting unless the information and input provided is considered central to planning a continuing program or determining alternative placements.

A case coordinator is designated for each team; the term *coordinator* rather than "manager," conveys the attitude that this individual relates to professional colleagues and not to subordinates (Dublinske, 1978). It can be anyone who knows the child fairly well, is familiar with the effects of a hearing loss upon all dimensions of performance, and has the flexible schedule necessary to accomplish the many organizational and clerical chores involved. Often, the special education administrator assumes this role. When, however, a school system employs the services of an educational audiologist, the case coordinator's role can be viewed as a logical extension of his or her clinical and educational responsibilities. The speech-language pathologist may be an appropriate coordinator for a hard-of-hearing child, while a teacher of the hearing impaired could serve the same function with the deaf child. Although classroom teachers usually can provide the most relevant insights, their schedules ordinarily lack the necessary flexibility to assume the role of coordinator.

The case coordinator has the following responsibilities:

1. *To inform parents of an impending meeting and advise them of their rights under PL 94-142*   These rights include being accompanied by a knowledgeable advocate, being entitled to an independent assessment, and being informed of the steps in the appeals process (Nober, 1978). To be truly effective, the case coordinator (as well as the rest of the multidisciplinary team) must be sensitive and empathetic to the parents' anxieties and concerns (Northcott, 1975, 1980b).

2. *To communicate the purpose of each meeting and the background of each agenda item to the selected participants*   The writing of a routine individual educational program (IEP) may require different specialists (depending on the purpose of the meeting), such as an oral interpreter to fulfill the immediate need for support services.

3. *To ensure that all necessary evaluations are completed prior to the meeting*   An open-ended list includes: comprehensive audiological tests, electroacoustic and behavioral analysis of hearing aids and auditory training systems, the need for an FM auditory training system to overcome poor classroom acoustics, oral communication skills (speech and language), academic achievement tests including standardized language measures, individually administered performance and verbal intelligence tests, organized classroom observations, and psychosocial status (Ross et al., 1982).

4. *To summarize the current status of the child after each of the attendees has reported his or her observations* (For example, have academic and communication goals been met?) This would serve as a basis for the group discussion regarding recommendations to rectify specific problems (i.e., increased tutoring, FM auditory trainer in classroom, oral interpreter) and/or the development of an upgraded IEP.

5. To translate the often unintelligible professional jargon into common American English for the parents. Parents may already by intimidated by the formal atmosphere of the meeting. The case coordinator (always with the assistance of colleagues) should endeavor to ensure a two-way communication with the parents—that parents are *listened* to, as well as *spoken* to, in any team meeting.

6. *To follow up on the recommendations of the team*   He or she should bring the team's recommendations for specific support ser-

vices to the attention of the appropriate department, facility, or administrator. Responsibilities must be explicitly delegated, with a specific time frame for each recommendation.

7. *To request during the course of the year a formal or informal status report on selected children*   Are short-term objectives being met? What is the status of some stipulated support service? If a problem is apparent and if informal contacts do not resolve the issue, then the case coordinator (with the authority of the appropriate administrator) may request an interim meeting.

In brief, the activities of the multidisciplinary team, coordinated by one of its members, are designed to blend the varied insights and information regarding a child into a comprehensive management program. The classroom teacher is the primary professional educator for hearing-impaired children who are mainstreamed for all or part of the school day. Other services are designed to reinforce his or her efforts in the classroom, where the most important educational action occurs. Furthermore, no educational plan is complete unless the parents' input and the parents' role are fully considered. One truism in the education of the hearing impaired is that the children who "make it," who somehow realize their educational and communicative potential, are those whose parents play an active and informed role as informal teachers and reinforcers of desirable behavior. A multidisciplinary educational team is no substitute for effective parenting.

PLACEMENT ALTERNATIVES IN ELEMENTARY AND HIGH SCHOOLS

Criteria

The decision to place a hearing-impaired child in a regular elementary school program requires a careful analysis of the child's educational, communicative, and psychosocial status, as well as evidence of parental understanding and cooperation (Nober, 1981; Northcott, 1973). Some general considerations regarding the decision to place *this* particular child in *that* specific setting, are:

1. *Does the candidate have sufficient communicative skills upon entrance to engage in meaningful verbal communication with peers and teachers?*   Normal speech and language skills are not expected, but it is assumed that classroom lessons and peer conversation can be comprehended with some effort on the part of all concerned and that intelligible messages can be exchanged. Under these conditions, the standards and expectations in a regular class-

room can stimulate further progress in verbal communication (Ross et al., 1982, pp. 41–45).

2. *Does a first-grade child, when first being mainstreamed, score no more than 2 or occasionally 3 years below his or her classroom peers in standardized language tests?* Normally hearing children exhibit a wide range of language ability; thus, fully age-appropriate language ability is not expected of a hearing-impaired child. Sufficient language knowledge is required, however, so that the child can benefit from the material presented and the verbal exchanges that occur (Northcott, 1978).

3. *Is a full and appropriate range of supportive help available to the child?* The overwhelming majority of hearing-impaired children require additional assistance in the regular school; however, not all children need all support services. Examples of supplemental support are:
   a. Ongoing audiological consultation and management
   b. Classroom "troubleshooting" of personal and classroom amplification systems
   c. The use of an FM auditory training system, which should be a routine provision in most educational settings for most hearing-impaired children
   d. Pre- and post-teaching of classroom material by a qualified general or special educator, after coordinating material with the classroom teacher (Birch, 1976; Northcott, 1973)
   e. Speech and language therapy provided by a speech-language pathologist, including coordination and consultation with the classroom teacher and frequent classroom observations
   f. Observation and consultation by the school psychologist and/ or social worker
   g. The services of an oral or sign language interpreter for certain teachers and subjects, when direct speechreading of a teacher and/or peers is not possible (this provision would be more relevant to the older child or youth)

4. *Does the child possess the requisite social skills to interact appropriately with his or her classmates?* This provision requires careful observation of the child in many unstructured situations, including recess and lunch (Davis, 1981). Placement in a regular school entails more than academic challenges; the child must also be able to join a social group. An isolated, unhappy child whose self-image is eroded or deformed by his or her contacts with classmates is poor testimony to our efforts, no matter how well other dimensions of school performance are advancing (Ross, 1978a).

5. *What is observed about the child's ability to deal with frustration?* Is the child able to initiate contacts and pursue them? Does he or she possess some special skills or capabilities that are admired by peers? Is the child able to make him- or herself understood in spite of the difficulties? In other words, does the child possess a tough, resilient personality? Often, a hearing-impaired child is "adopted" by well-meaning classmates, to the detriment of the child's ability to develop self-esteem and an independent personality. Obviously, this is not a desirable state of affairs.

6. *Is the receiving program fully prepared to enroll the hearing-impaired child?* Will there be specific support from the school administrators, and will an orientation and a continuing in-service program be provided (Teitelbaum, 1981)? The general effects of hearing impairment and the specific problems and remedies for a particular child must be described as well as the role and function of prescribed support specialists who assist the teacher and pupil. Teachers are often reluctant to have a hearing-impaired child in their classroom, although they may be conscientious individuals, because they feel inadequate to educate such a child. Information and continuing support can overcome this reluctance. Informed teachers can be very effective salespersons in convincing colleagues to willingly accept another hearing-impaired child.

7. *Are the parents willing to have their child placed in a regular school?* If so, their complete and informed cooperation is an absolute necessity (Meltzer, 1981; Northcott, 1980b).

Educational Placement Alternatives

Twenty-five years ago, there were just two educational options available to most hearing-impaired children: 1) enrollment in a neighborhood school with whatever supportive help and special arrangements that could be worked out locally (often paid by parents who secured private tutors or speech therapists after school hours), or 2) placement in the state public residential school.

Times have changed for the better; there are now available, as discussed earlier, many preprimary school programs for hearing-impaired children in both special and regular educational settings throughout the country.

Alternative educational programs must also be available for the older child and youth beyond the integrated classroom. Regular school placement is stressed here because the theme of this book is oral interpreting, which is only relevant in a regular school setting. It should not be forgotten, however, that a special day or residential school (public or private) may be the most appropriate educational placement for some hearing-impaired children. One such setting is not "better" than another, conceptually or absolutely; each is a viable alternative for some children (Deno, 1970; Northcott, 1980a; Ross, 1976). Preferably, any regional or large city program should be comprised of two tracks under a single coordinator. One track should employ the *simultaneous* method of instruction (the oral method plus sign language and finger-spelling), although mainly self-contained, and permit some social and limited classroom (art, physical education, shop, etc.) integration with normally hearing peers. The other track would employ the *auditory-oral* method, with specific alternatives as indicated below.

Special Classes in Regular Schools   Children who are enrolled in a segregated class in a regular school are primarily those who have the greatest hearing loss and the greatest academic and communicative needs. The curriculum is usually produced locally and taught by a teacher of the hearing impaired. Whatever special assistance is available to normally hearing children in the school system, such as speech therapy or individual tutoring, is also available to them. This setting is usually closer to the child's home than a special day school, thus requiring less travel time, and assures the stimulating daily presence of hearing children. A hearing-impaired child can receive valuable education via games, conversation, or other friendly social overtures with normally hearing peers at recess and lunchtime. Here, all children are equals. In special class placement, however, the primary social and academic group is composed of hearing-impaired children.

The special class in a regular school affords some children an opportunity to participate on a trial basis in certain nonacademic and academic activities in the regular program. Art, shop, physical education, and even music experiences are perfectly within the capability of most hearing-impaired children, and they deserve the same opportunity to benefit from the services of a skilled specialist as normally hearing children. Other subjects, such as science, lab exercises, computer courses, mathematics, and perhaps even language-related subjects, can be attempted by selected children, depending upon the child's motivation and ability as determined by his or her teacher (and if approved by the multidisciplinary team). The presence of an oral interpreter who holds teacher certification may make such placements feasible. In the special classroom in a regular school, the setting is considered to be a stepping stone to the next level of integration—the transitional class, or resource room.

The Transitional Class or Resource Room   In practice, the distinction between these two presumably different placement alternatives is very loosely defined; because they share the same conceptual basis, they are discussed together. In such classes, the commitment is to integrate as many hearing-impaired children into as many of the regular subjects as possible. A special curriculum may be followed for many language-related subjects, although more often, the regular school curriculum is modified. The "transition" takes place for each child individually, depending on the child's capabilities to comprehend the material and participate in different classrooms with different demands. The preference is for children to be able to gain direct information from a teacher or other children without the need for an interpreter. However, unique situations existing in particular cases (such as lectures taking place in a large auditorium or a teacher with immobile lips or a heavy beard) may necessitate the services of an interpreter. In transitional and resource room placements, it is expected that the children will be fully mainstreamed and, hopefully, assimilated in all nonacademic subjects.

These classes require continuing communication and cooperation between the regular and special teachers. Flexibility is the keynote. Often a lengthy trial period is required in order to determine the suitability of a particular regular classroom placement. Such trials are preceded by evaluations, intensive preparatory help, and ongoing assessment of performance. The regular classroom teacher needs assurance that the services of qualified support personnel are always available. If an auditory training device is necessary, they must be given instruction in its use and a place to go when there is a problem. The goal in transitional and resource room placements is as much full mainstreaming as is consistent with the ability of the child to cope and profit.

Educational Amplification

The average classroom is a noisy place (Ross, 1978b). The impact of noise and reverberation upon the ability to understand speech is greater for those with hearing losses than those with normal hearing, who may find a particular classroom only mildly interfering in terms of speech reception. The acoustical conditions in the same classroom may completely obliterate speech comprehension for a hearing-impaired child (Ross and Giolas, 1978). The best way to overcome this problem is to increase the intensity level of speech with reference to background noise. In most classrooms, the speech-to-noise ratio is in the order of 5 dB; that is, speech arrives at a child with only 5 dB greater sound level than does background noise. By locating a microphone close to the talker, the effective level of speech can be increased by 20 to 25 dB, compared to the speech level arriving at a child's hearing aid 4 or 5 feet from the talker. The major advantages of any classroom amplification system are a function of the distance between the microphone and the teacher. All studies that have investigated this phenomenon have shown that speech comprehension is increased as the distance between the microphone and the talker is reduced (Ross, 1978b).

In a regular school setting, the most feasible classroom amplification system is the frequency modulated (FM) auditory training system. The system functions as a personal radio link between the talker and the child. The teacher wears the microphone/transmitter, while the child uses the radio receiver/hearing aid. Such devices are easy to use, and their benefits are immediate and often profound (Ross et al., 1973). For the child who has the capacity to recognize language auditorially, there is no more effective therapeutic device than a classroom auditory training system. For the child who can or has the potential to employ audition as a valuable supplement to speechreading, an auditory training system in the classroom provides the maximum amount of acoustic information. In order for all hearing-impaired children to capitalize on the dynamic use of residual hearing to the maximum extent possible, the FM auditory training system is a necessity. It greatly aids the development of more intelligible speech and the mastery of academic subjects through audition.

CONCLUSION

In this brief chapter, several overriding themes are presented:
1. *The necessity of early detection and management of hearing* Here, parents play a key role from the very beginning.
2. *The need for availability of educational alternatives, including appropriate support services, for every hearing-impaired child* These alternatives are of limited value unless the child is comprehensively evaluated at stated intervals throughout his or her school career.
3. *The necessity of stimulating a child's residual hearing to the maximum extent feasible* As an educationally oriented audiologist who has visited many programs and is familiar with current professional literature on the subject, the author believes this crucial goal has been realized only on relatively rare occasions.
4. *The required availability of a sound educational system to give children genuine alternatives as they grow up, not only with respect to mode of communication but to the life-style they elect to choose for themselves* This theme relates to the observation that, when educational programming is involved, professional decisions are too often made on the basis of a personal set of values and not on the child's capabilities. Early and intensive auditory-oral management, with sensitivity to the availability of other options when

necessary, will permit the developing hearing-impaired person to make mature decisions regarding a personally satisfying future.

REFERENCES

Birch, J. W. 1976. Hearing Impaired Pupils in the Mainstream. Council for Exceptional Children, Reston, VA.

Brill, R. 1976. Total communication definition adopted. Am. Ann. Deaf 121:358.

Davis, J. 1981. Psychosocial considerations and evaluations. In: M. Ross and L. W. Nober (eds.), Educating Hard of Hearing Children, Special Education in Transition Series. A. G. Bell Assoc., Washington, DC.

Deno, E. L. 1970. Special education as developmental capital. Except. Child. 37:229–240.

Dublinske, S. P. 1978. PL 94-142: Developing the individualized educational program. ASHA 20:393–397.

Fry, D. B. 1978. The role and primacy of the auditory channel in speech and language development. In: M. Ross and T. G. Giolas (eds.), Auditory Management of Hearing-Impaired Children, pp. 15–44. University Park Press, Baltimore.

Gottlieb, M. E., P. W. Zinkus, and A. Thompson. 1979. Chronic middle ear disease and auditory perceptual deficits. Clin. Pediatr. 18:725–732.

Jury, V. L. 1981. Assessment and management of the preschool child. In: M. Ross and L. W. Nober (eds.), Educating Hard of Hearing Children, Special Education in Transition Series. A. G. Bell Assoc., Washington, DC.

Kessler, M., and K. Randolph. 1979. The effects of early middle ear disease on the auditory abilities of third grade children. JARA 12:6–20.

Killion, M. C. 1980. Problems in the application of broadband hearing aid microphones. In: G. A. Studebacker and I. R. Hochberg (eds.), Acoustical Factors Affecting Hearing Aid Performance. University Park Press, Baltimore.

Levitt, H. 1978. The acoustics of speech production. In: M. Ross and T. G. Giolas (eds.), Auditory Management of Hearing-Impaired Children, pp. 45–116. University Park Press, Baltimore.

Libby, E. E. (ed.). 1980. Binaural Hearing and Amplification. Zenetron, Inc., Chicago.

Ling, D., and A. H. Ling. 1978. Aural Habilitation: The Foundations of Verbal Learning in Hearing-Impaired Children. A. G. Bell Assoc., Washington, DC.

Luterman, D. 1979. Counseling Parents of Hearing-Impaired Children. Little, Brown, and Company, Boston.

Martin, F. M. 1980. Introduction to Audiology, 2nd Ed. Prentice-Hall, Englewood Cliffs, NJ.

Masters, L., and G. E. Marsh. 1978. Middle-ear pathology as a factor in learning disabilities. J. Learn. Disabil. 11:54–57.

Meltzer, D. R. 1981. Parents as consumers: A personal viewpoint. In: M. Ross and L. W. Nober (eds.), Educating Hard of Hearing Children, Special Education in Transition Series, pp. 77–81. A. G. Bell Assoc., Washington, DC.

Nober, L. W. 1978. Developing effective IEP's for the hearing-impaired: Considerations and issues. In: B. B. Weiner (ed.), Periscope: Views of the Individualized Education Program. Council for Exceptional Children, Reston, VA.

Nober, L. W. 1981. Developing IEP's for hard of hearing children. In: M. Ross and L. W. Nober (eds.), Educating Hard of Hearing Children, pp. 88–101, Special Education in Transition Series. A. G. Bell Assoc., Washington, DC.

Northcott, W. H. (ed.). 1973. The hearing-impaired child in a regular classroom: Preschool, elementary, and secondary years. A. G. Bell Assoc., Washington, DC.

Northcott, W. H. 1975. Normalization of the preschool child with hearing impairment. In: M. D. Glasscock (ed.), Symposium on sensorineural hearing loss in children: Early detection and intervention. Otolaryngol. Clin. North Am. 8:159–186.

Northcott, W. H. 1978. Integrating the preprimary hearing-impaired child: An examination of the process, product and rationale. In: M. J. Guralnick (ed.), Early Intervention and the Integration of Handicapped and Nonhandicapped Children, pp. 207–238. University Park Press, Baltimore.

Northcott, W. H. 1980a. Implications of mainstreaming for the education of hearing-impaired children in the 1980s. Colloquium address, presented at the National Technical Institute for the Deaf, May 2, Rochester, NY. A. G. Bell Assoc., Washington, DC.

Northcott, W. H. 1980b. On behalf of parents in the IEP process. Volta Rev. 82:7–15.

Resolution on interpreters in the classroom clarified. 1980. Newsounds 5(9):1. A. G. Bell Assoc., Washington, DC.

Ross, M. 1976. Model educational cascade for hearing impaired children. In: G. Nix (ed.), Mainstream Education of Hearing Impaired Children and Youth. Grune and Stratton, New York.

Ross, M. 1978a. Mainstreaming: Some social considerations. Volta Rev. 80:21–30.

Ross, M. 1978b. Classroom acoustics and speech intelligibility. In: J. Katz (ed.), Handbook of Clinical Audiology, 2nd Ed. Williams and Wilkins, Baltimore.

Ross, M. 1980. Binaural vs. monaural amplification. In: C. Libby (ed.), Binaural Hearing Aids, pp. 1–22. Zenetron, Inc., Chicago.

Ross, M. 1981a. Classroom amplification. In: W. R. Hodgson and P. H. Skinner (eds.), Hearing Aid Assessment and Use in Audiologic Habilitation, 2nd Ed., pp. 221–243. Williams and Wilkins, Baltimore.

Ross, M. 1981b. Personal versus group amplification: The consistency vs. inconsistency debate. In: F. H. Bess, J. S. Sinclair, and B. A. Freeman (eds.), Amplification for Education, pp. 139–150. A. G. Bell Assoc., Washington, DC.

Ross, M., D. Brackett, and A. Maxon. 1982. Hard of Hearing Children in Regular Schools. Prentice-Hall, Englewood Cliffs, NJ.

Ross, M., and D. R. Calvert. 1967. The semantics of deafness. Volta Rev. 69:644–649.

Ross, M., R. J. Duffy, H. S. Cooker et al. 1973. Contribution of the lower audible frequencies to the recognition of emotions. Am. Ann. Deaf 118:37–42.

Ross, M., and T. G. Giolas. 1972. Effect of classroom listening conditions upon speech intelligibility. Lang. Speech Hear. Serv. Schools 4:72–76.

Ross, M., and T. G. Giolas. 1978. Auditory Management of Hearing-Impaired Children. University Park Press, Baltimore.

Ross, M., and C. Tommassetti. 1978. Hearing aid selection for pre-verbal hearing-impaired children. In: M. Pollack (ed.), Amplification for the Hearing Impaired, 2nd Ed., pp. 213–250. Grune and Stratton, New York.

Sarff, L. S., H. R. Ray, and C. L. Bagwell. 1981. Why not amplification in every classroom? Hear. Aid J. 34:44–52.

Simmons-Martin, A., and D. R. Calvert (eds.). 1979. Parent-Infant Intervention: Communication Disorders. Grune and Stratton, New York.

Stark, R. E. (ed.). 1974. Sensory Capabilities of Hearing Impaired Children. University Park Press, Baltimore.

Teitelbaum, M. L. 1981. Teachers as consumers: What they should know about the hearing impaired child. In: M. Ross and L. W. Nober (eds.), Educating Hard of Hearing Children, Special Education in Transition Series, pp. 82–86. A. G. Bell Assoc., Washington, DC.

Wilson, G. W., M. Ross, and D. R. Calvert. 1974. Experimental study of the semantics of deafness. Volta Rev. 76:408–414.

Zinkus, P. W., and M. I. Gottlieb. 1980. Patterns of perceptual and academic deficits related to early chronic otitis media. Pediatrics 66:246–253.

CHAPTER 3

HEARING-IMPAIRED STUDENTS AND THEIR EDUCATION: POPULATION PERSPECTIVES

Michael A. Karchmer

CONTENTS

It is difficult to assess the educational needs of an individual child with hearing loss without first understanding the broader context of education for hearing-impaired (deaf and hard-of-hearing) children in the United States. In what educational settings are hearing-impaired students found, and what special services are they receiving in those settings? What is the nature and extent of their disabilities? What individual characteristics influence their educational placement? What communication modes are being used by and with hearing-impaired children at school and at home? Understanding these and other questions about this special population sets the stage for understanding the specific environments in which individual hearing-impaired children function.

The unifying theme of this chapter is *diversity*. The children and youth who share the common characteristic of hearing loss constitute a very heterogeneous population. There is no such thing as a single "deaf" group whose abilities, needs, and limitations can be characterized simply. Indeed, the existence of diversity poses the biggest challenge for people who work with hearing-impaired children and youth. The dissimilarities that exist must be understood in order to design effective strategies that will meet the full range of needs of students who may well have common degrees of hearing loss as shown on an audiogram.

This chapter deals primarily with three areas of interest: 1) the settings in which hearing-impaired children are receiving their education, in order to understand how specific characteristics of these children relate to program placement; 2) communication modes that are used by hearing-impaired children, their teachers, and their parents in interaction at home and school; and 3) issues that relate to the problems of assessing the academic achievement of hearing-impaired children. This chapter does not attempt to provide comprehensive coverage of these three areas. Instead, the issues are presented from a population perspective. In doing so, the intention is to underscore the theme of the diversity of student characteristics and needs.

SOURCES OF DATA

Much of the information presented in this chapter comes from a continuing national study of hearing-impaired students in the United States—the Annual Survey of Hearing Impaired Children and Youth. Each year since 1968, Gallaudet College's Center for Assessment and Demographic Studies (formerly the Office of Demographic Studies) has solicited participation in the Annual Survey from all special education programs in the United States known to be offering services to hearing-impaired students. Each program is asked to submit relevant information on the students it serves. The survey attempts to gather data that describe student characteristics in relation to the educational services being received. Specific items on the survey relate to the student's age, sex, ethnic background, audiological characteristics, etiology and age at onset of hearing loss, additional handicaps, and types of educational services. Additional issues are dealt with by the survey from time to time.

The data presented here are taken from the 1977–78 and 1981–82 school year projects. The 1977–78 survey solicited information on integration; the 1981–82 project is the most recent for which data are available. Both surveys contain information on almost 55,000 hearing-impaired students, about 75% of the number of hearing-impaired students in the United States estimated to be receiving some kind of special education.

The data in this chapter related to speech intelligibility and communication resulted from a 1974 survey conducted by the Center using a national sample of teachers and parents of hearing-impaired children (Jensema and Trybus, 1978; Jensema et al., 1978).

The data presented here pertain primarily to hearing-impaired students, ages 3 to 21, who are receiving some kind of special instructional or support service related to their hearing impairment. Regardless of their degree of hearing loss, students who were maintained in regular classes from the outset of their formal elementary school years are not commonly reported to the Annual Survey of Hearing Impaired Children and Youth. Additionally, there are hearing-impaired students who have multiple handicaps so severe that the types of service they receive are other than educational. These hearing-impaired individuals also tend to be underrepresented in the survey.

EDUCATIONAL SETTINGS AND SERVICES

Hearing-impaired children in the United States receive their education in a variety of regular and special education programs. The settings of these programs also vary, ranging from special facilities such as residential or day schools for the deaf (which are entirely devoted to the education of hearing-impaired students) to public schools that offer a range of full- or part-time special or regular education service options. These may be self-contained classrooms, resource rooms, and other part-time special education classes. The focus of this section is not on the type of facilities in which hearing-impaired students are educated, but rather on the nature of services hearing-impaired children are receiving.

"Integration" is a term that figures prominently in discussions about the education of hearing-impaired children but which tends to be used rather loosely. In fact, a distinction should be made between two types of integration: *academic* and *nonacademic*. Hearing-impaired students are integrated academically when they attend instructional classes with normally hearing students (e.g., in reading, science, and math classes). Nonacademic integration refers to school settings, such as physical education, art, lunch, recess, or homeroom. In an attempt to understand the patterns of integrating hearing-impaired students, the Annual Survey of Hearing Impaired Children and Youth for the 1977–78 school year solicited information on these two kinds of integration (Wolk et al., 1982). The findings were quite striking. As illustrated in Figure 3.1, of the students on whom data on integration were obtained, almost half were reported to be nonacademically integrated to some extent, compared to 32% for academic integration. Thus, hearing-impaired students were far more likely to be placed with their hearing peers in social, recreational, and other nonacademic situations than in academic settings. It is open to question whether for many children nonacademic integration constitutes "mainstreaming" at all. As Wolk et al. (1982) stated in commenting about a large number of children who received nonacademic, but no academic, integration:

> For these hearing-impaired students, integration may be more a by-product of physical proximity to hearing students, an "integration" in name only, rather than a planned activity in which normally hearing and

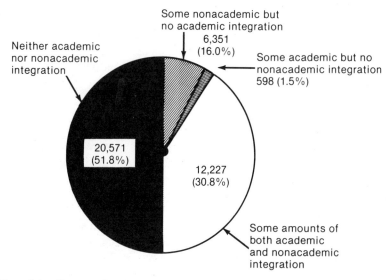

Figure 3.1.   Patterns of academic and nonacademic integration for hearing-impaired students, from the Annual Survey of Hearing Impaired Children and Youth (Reprinted by permission from Wolk et al., 1982, p. 3).

hearing-impaired children intermingle and interact and are able to share common non-academic experiences. (p. 3)

The Wolk et al. (1982) study also investigated the extent of integration in the various types of educational programs. They found that only 6% of the students at residential schools were integrated at all. The percentage at day schools was somewhat higher, with 15% receiving some academic integration and 38% integrated into nonacademic settings. The situation differed for students in full-time special education classes ("self-contained classes") located in schools that also served hearing students. Nearly 40% of the hearing-impaired students in this type of program were integrated in academic settings. However, the amount of such integration was small; the modal amount was an hour or less a day. On the other hand, more than 80% of the hearing-impaired students receiving their academic work in self-contained classes were integrated with normally hearing peers in nonacademic school settings. Finally, over 90% of the students reported to be receiving part-time special education services were integrated with normally hearing students to some degree in both academic and nonacademic settings. The amount of academic integration was likely to be substantial, with more than two-thirds of the group averaging over 3 hours a day in instructional settings with normally hearing students.

Table 3.1.   Type of classroom instruction received by hearing-impaired students in the United States (Annual Survey of Hearing Impaired Children and Youth, 1981–82)

	Number of students	Percentage of total
Special education instruction only	22,518	52.4
Both regular and special education instruction	16,713	38.9
Regular education instruction only	2,761	6.4
Neither regular nor special education instruction	954	2.2
Total	42,946[a]	100.0

[a] Information on either regular or special education service was not reported for 2,307 students (5.1% of the 45,253 total).

More recently, the Annual Survey attempted to focus on the nature of the regular and special education instructional settings and the types of services hearing-impaired students received in those instructional settings.

Table 3.1 shows the instructional services received by hearing-impaired students in the United States during the 1981–82 schools year.[1] The largest group, representing slightly more than half (52.4%) of the students, received instruction only in special education settings. However, a large minority, 38.9%, received both special education instruction and some regular classroom instruction with normally hearing students. The other groups were smaller: 6.4% of the total received regular education instruction only, and 2.2% were provided neither regular nor special education instruction. (A large proportion of the latter group were preschool children involved in parent/child programs.)

Perhaps the most noteworthy feature of Table 3.1 is the high percentage of hearing-impaired students who received classroom instruction with normally hearing students. Altogether, 45.3% of the students in 1981–82 received some regular education services, either alone or in combination with instruction in special education settings. For close to half of the hearing-impaired students reported in this survey, "mainstream" education was the norm.

The 1981–82 Annual Survey also sought information on settings of services for the students who were receiving special education, as shown in Table 3.2. Most of the students were in settings designed for: 1) hearing-impaired students (73.9% of the total); 2) multiply handicapped, hearing-impaired students (8.9%); or 3) a combination of these

---

[1] The author is indebted to Susan Jablonski at the Center for Assessment and Demographic studies for providing this analysis.

two settings (5.6%). There were 3,158 hearing-impaired students (8.5% of the total) who received their instruction with students with various handicaps, not all of whom were hearing-impaired. Grouping students with different handicaps together ("noncategorical" special education) is an approach to special education that seems likely to be increasingly utilized, considering the forecasts for dwindling resources. Certainly, it is a trend worth studying in the 1980s. However, students educated in this way truly represent a group of students who may be *integrated* with hearing students, but who are not *mainstreamed* in the usual sense.

If so many students are now receiving regular education instruction, what is being done to support them while they are integrated with normally hearing students? Table 3.3 shows the support services given to hearing-impaired students while in the regular classroom receiving instruction with normally hearing students. Although no support services were provided to one-third of the students, a majority did receive at least one support service. The most commonly reported services, either alone or in combination with other services, were interpreter (29% of the total in regular education) and tutor (26%). The nature of the interpreter services was not specified, so the services reported could refer to either sign language or oral interpreting. However, a 1980 resolution of the A. G. Bell Association recommended against the use of oral interpreters at the preschool and elementary school levels.[2] Other support services were reported for 22% of the the group. Under the last category, the "other" services specified were varied, but many involved the use of a teacher's aide or the equivalent.

Merely to list these support services leaves many questions unanswered. These data are very general and do not speak to important issues, such as the quality of services provided or their appropriateness for the individual student. For example, what were the levels of training of the providers of support services? What percentage of the interpreters were certified? Were note-takers and tutors formally trained to work with hearing-impaired students? What was the average time

---

[2] Resolution of the Board of Directors, A. G. Bell Assoc. for the Deaf, April 1980: "RESOLVED: That the Alexander Graham Bell Association for the Deaf endorses the concept that a hearing-impaired child placed in a regular classroom for a portion or all of the day, during the preschool or elementary years, be so placed on his/her ability to gain information *directly* from the teacher and hearing classmates, without the use of an interpreter, and to speak for him/herself and be understood.

FURTHER that the Association reaffirms the concept of a continuum/cascade of services for handicapped children and affirms that: working within the framework of Individual Educational Program Planning, each child should be placed in the communicative, academic, and social setting which best meets his or her particular needs." (Resolution, 1980, p.1)

Table 3.2.   Hearing-impaired students in special educational settings, 1981–82

Setting designed for:	Number of students	Percentage of total
Hearing-impaired students (who were not multiply handicapped)	27,444	73.9
Multiply handicapped, hearing-impaired students	3,317	8.9
Students with various handicaps (not all of whom were hearing impaired)	3,158	8.5
Home instruction students	305	0.8
Combination of first two categories	2,082	5.6
All other combinations of the above categories	838	2.3

Missing information: A specific setting was not reported for 1,600 students who were reported to be receiving special education services.

per day or week spent in speech therapy and auditory training? Were the service providers paid, or were they volunteers? How did programs determine the specific support services to be provided for each student? Were support services selected on the basis of the individual student's needs, or simply assigned according to school philosophy or determined by economic constraints or considerations?

Table 3.3.   Support services given to hearing-impaired students while receiving regular classroom instruction with hearing students (1981–82)

Number of support services	Total by number of services		Percentage of total
No support services	6,198		33.4
One support service	9,755		
Interpreter		3,247	17.5
Note-taker		153	0.8
Tutor		2,786	15.0
Other		3,569	19.2
Two support services	2,077		
Interpreter-Note-taker		264	1.4
Interpreter-Tutor		1,264	6.8
Interpreter-Other		163	0.9
Note-taker-Tutor		193	1.0
Note-taker-Other		32	0.2
Tutor-Other		161	0.9
Three or more support services	536		2.9
Total	18,566[a]		100.0

[a] Information on support services was not provided for approximately 1,600 students for whom regular classroom services were indicated.

One important component of the education of hearing-impaired children, regardless of whether they are in regular classes, in special education classes, or receive a portion of their daily instruction in each setting, is access to the systematic training of aided residual hearing or to speech therapy as needed. The range of possible services under these categories is, of course, broad, and it seems that most hearing-impaired students do receive some kind of auditory or speech training. In this regard, there is an interesting difference between the groups of students receiving at least some special education instruction and those who are receiving regular classroom instruction only: According to the 1981–82 Annual Survey data, about 84% of the special education students received speech therapy or auditory training, whereas these services were provided to fewer than 59% of the hearing-impaired children in regular education settings.

The different types of educational programs enroll hearing-impaired students with sharply differing characteristics, as reported by Karchmer and Trybus (1977) and Karchmer et al. (1979). Figures 3.2, 3.3, and 3.4 present updated information (using the 1981–82 Annual Survey data) by examining characteristics of students according to whether they were receiving: 1) instruction in special education classes only; 2) instruction in a regular classroom with hearing peers only; or 3) instruction in both settings.

Figure 3.2 illustrates clearly that the amount of time spent in a special education setting is closely related to the severity of the hearing loss. The percentage of hearing-impaired students with a profound hearing loss (91 dB, ANSI, or greater in the better ear) constituted 62% of the total number in a full-time special education setting, 32% of the students in a special education setting and a regular classroom for a portion of each day, and 14% of the students fully integrated in regular education classes only. Students with less than severe hearing loss (unaided thresholds of less than 71 dB) constituted approximately three-quarters of the totally mainstreamed group.

Other differences are also evident, according to the type of services received. As shown in Figure 3.3, white students comprised about 84% of the students receiving regular education only but 63% of the group in full-time special education classes. Also, according to the 1981–82 Annual Survey, about 31% of the total group of hearing-impaired students had other physical, learning, or emotional handicaps in addition to hearing loss. Figure 3.4 shows the percentage of students with additional handicaps, according to educational placement. The likelihood of a student's receiving regular classroom instruction is decreased greatly if that student has additional physical, learning, or emotional handicaps. Jensema and Mullins (1974) reported that children

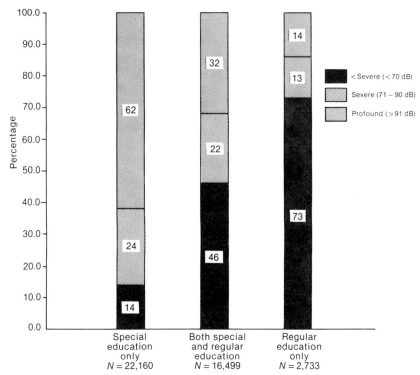

Figure 3.2.   Degree of hearing loss within different educational placements, according to 1981–82 Annual Survey.

with inherited hearing loss have significantly lower incidence of additional handicapping conditions than do children with illness-related hearing loss.

Finally, differences according to age at onset of hearing loss are evident for students receiving different types of service. Nearly all of the students receiving only special education services were identified as having a prelingual loss; only 3.3% lost their hearing after their third birthday. A slightly higher percentage of the students in both regular and special education classes during the school day, 8.2%, had a postlingual onset of hearing loss. Of the hearing-impaired students receiving regular classroom instruction only, 16.7% lost their hearing after the age of 3. Because the age at onset of hearing loss is a factor that has profound consequences for speech and language development, differences in the groups of students are worthy of note.

Taken together, these recent data strongly support the notion that hearing-impaired students who are partially or fully in mainstream ed-

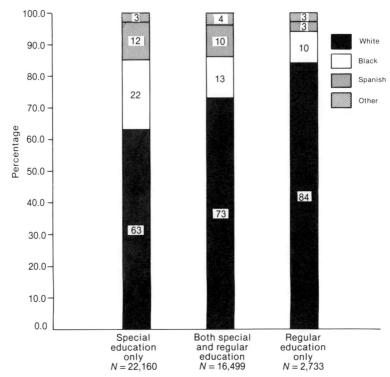

Figure 3.3.   Ethnic status within different educational placements, according to 1981–82 Annual Survey.

ucation differ from their hearing-impaired peers in special education classes according to many characteristics. The 1981–82 Annual Survey data confirmed earlier studies (Karchmer and Trybus, 1977; Karchmer et al., 1979; Wolk et al., 1982)—that hearing-impaired students being mainstreamed with students with normal hearing, in comparison with hearing-impaired students in special education settings, on average have less severe hearing losses, are more likely to be white, are less likely to be additionally handicapped, and are more likely to have a hearing loss incurred after the age of 3. The similarity of these findings to earlier findings suggests that differences among the groups remain great. The meaning of these data is that, when we compare types of programs and services, we must be careful also to take student characteristics into consideration. Different types of programs are basically serving different types of hearing-impaired students.

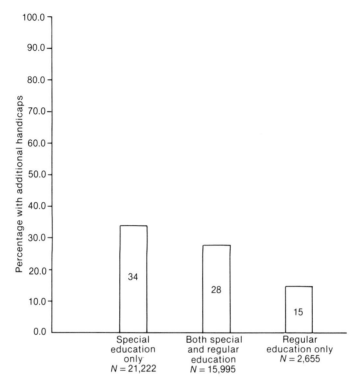

Figure 3.4.   Percentage of students with additional handicaps, according to educational placement in the 1981–82 Annual Survey.

COMMUNICATION PATTERNS

The hallmark of significant hearing loss is its influence on receptive and expressive communication. Hearing-impaired children use or are exposed to a variety of modes of communication at school and at home. The most comprehensive study of the communication patterns of hearing-impaired students in the United States was done in 1974, when survey data on communication were obtained from the parents and teachers of 657 students; these data were reported by Jensema and Trybus (1978). The information described the degree to which various means of communication (speech, signs, fingerspelling, writing, and gestures) were used between child and parent and child and classroom teacher. The results suggested that there was a great deal of variability in the patterns of communication used by and with hearing-impaired children. Virtually all combinations of modes were reported. Jensema and Trybus (1978) found that combinations of methods were the rule at school, but less so at home; while a combination of speech, sign, fingerspelling, writing, and gestures was the most common pattern at school, the use of speech alone was the most common pattern at home. Finally, relatively little consistency was found between the pattern of communication used at home and that used at school (Jensema and Trybus, p. 8).

In all four of the communication situations examined (parent to child and child to parent; teacher to student and student to teacher), a common pattern emerged: "When the use of speech is high, use of signs or fingerspelling is low, and vice versa."

Perhaps the most important aspect of the Jensema and Trybus study was its examination of the correlates of speech and sign use. The degree to which hearing-impaired students used sign or speech was found to be strongly related to student characteristics and their family backgrounds. The major variable related to sign and speech use was the child's unaided hearing threshold. Simply put, the greater the severity of hearing loss, the less use of speech was reported by or with the student; conversely, reported sign use increased with severity of hearing loss. The 70 dB threshold seemed to be a benchmark; when hearing level was at 70 dB or less, the emphasis was on speech with relatively little use of signs. Beyond 70 dB, there was a clear shift in emphasis away from speech and toward a greater reliance on signs (Jensema and Trybus, p. 11; also Chapter 2 in this volume).

Jensema and Trybus (1978) analyzed other characteristics of students and their families that related to communication patterns reported in the 1974 study, including:

1. *Family income level* Students from higher income groups were more likely to have speech used by and with them at home and at school. (The relationship between income and sign language use was less clear.)
2. *Ethnic status* Parents and teachers were reported to use more speech with white children than with ethnic minorities.
3. *Hearing status of the student's parents* In comparison with students who had normally hearing parents (91% in the study), students with hearing-impaired parents were characterized by different amounts of sign and speech use. Children with two hearing-impaired parents (3%) were reported to have a communication pattern with relatively more emphasis on signs and less on speech. However, students with one hearing-impaired and one normally hearing parent had practically the opposite result; as a group, families of these students were more likely to use speech and less likely to sign (p. 16).

Table 3.4.   Percentage of students with intelligible or very intelligible speech by program type and degree of hearing loss (from Jensema et al., 1978, p. 3)

Type of Program	Less than severe (≤70 dB)	Severe (71–90 dB)	Profound (≥91 dB)	Average by program type
Residential school, residential students	66.6	45.2	17.3	28.5
Residential school, day students	80.0	66.7	31.1	44.1
Day school	91.3	54.3	25.9	43.4
Full-time classes	84.9	62.4	23.5	52.0
All part-time services	89.9	56.6	39.1	74.2
Average by hearing loss	86.2	54.8	22.5	

4. *The relationship between academic achievement and communication mode*   The researchers analyzed achievement test outcomes according to speech and sign use, taking as a starting point the fact that different student characteristics are associated with different communication modes. The data suggest that once demographic factors are taken into account, higher levels of speech have only a modest positive relationship to academic achievement.

A primary point to be made here is that direct comparisons of the outcomes of particular communication methods are difficult at best. Given the reality of diversity within the field, questions of which is more appropriate must take into consideration the characteristics of the individual child.

One of the well-known concomitants of a significant, prelingual hearing loss is its effect on speech. In an attempt to characterize the *speech intelligibility* of hard-of-hearing and deaf students in the United States, the Office of Demographic Studies in 1974 obtained teachers' ratings of speech intelligibility for nearly 1,000 hearing-impaired students (Jensema et al., 1978). Teachers were asked to rate how intelligible they judged their students' speech would be to a hearing person not familiar with deafness. The results of the study indicated that the students' degree of hearing loss was the strongest correlate of rated speech intelligibility. As can be seen in Table 3.4, 86.2% of the students with less-than-severe hearing threshold in the better ear (≤70 dB) were judged to speak intelligibly. Beyond hearing levels of 70 dB, an abrupt drop in the percentage of students with intelligible speech was noted. Only 22.5% of the students with hearing levels greater than 90 dB were reported to speak intelligibly.

Although speech intelligibility related most strongly to degree of hearing loss, Jensema et al. identified other factors related to speech intelligibility. Family income correlated to some extent with intelligibility, as did ethnic status; black students were rated to be substantially less intelligible than students from other ethnic backgrounds. Use of a hearing aid (a variable also correlated with degree of hearing loss) was also found to be positively related to speech intelligibility.

> In summary, speech intelligibility appears to be related primarily to the extent and quality of auditory input as reflected by the degree of hearing loss, usage of hearing aids and the frequency of speech communication. (p. 5)

Examining the same data, Jensema and Trybus (1978) found that 52% of teachers surveyed were unable to identify the age at which a child first began to use a hearing aid. For the remainder of the group (48%):

> There is a fairly clear trend for a heavier speech emphasis to be associated with earlier first use of a hearing aid. Such early use is also associated with a general trend for less use of signs. (p. 15)

One interesting and somewhat disturbing finding from the 1974 study was that no overall differences in speech intelligibility were found by age. Thus, older students as a group were not found to speak more intelligibly than younger students. Although this is a cross-sectional finding, it strongly suggests that one of the primary goals of special education for hearing-impaired students is not being met, at least not when viewed from a nationwide perspective.

Finally, students in different kinds of educational programs were likely to have different degrees of speech intelligibility. Table 3.4 (right column) summarizes these differences. To a large degree, the results reflect the fact (noted before) that the different kinds of programs tend to enroll students of different hearing losses. When degree of hearing loss is taken into account, program differences were reduced sharply.

One exception is notable. Karchmer and Petersen (1980) examined information from the 1977–78 Annual Survey and from a special studies survey of 1974, concerning the similarities and differences between day and resident students at residential schools for the deaf. In a comparison of students with profound hearing loss ($\geq$91 dB) (Table 3.4), the percentage of commuter students who wore hearing aids and were rated as having intelligible speech (31.1%) was nearly double the corresponding percentage in the resident group (17.3%).

EDUCATIONAL ASSESSMENT

Educators of hearing-impaired students are often faced with the task of measuring students' academic progress using standardized achievement tests designed for normally hearing students. For individual students, results of these tests can be used to monitor school progress, to help make placement decisions, to identify areas of strength and weakness as a guide for instruction, and to provide a basis for reports to parents. Used appropriately, standardized achievement tests can help serve these and other functions. However, the testing of hearing-impaired children is an activity that has unique problems associated with it. Because most standardized tests designed for normally hearing students do not address these problems, they may not be appropriate for use with a great many hearing-impaired students. The following section describes some of the problems involved with the achievement testing of hearing-impaired students and the way these problems are being dealt with for a particular test. These issues are described in more detail by Allen et al. (1983). Although the discussion here relates to achievement tests in particular, many of the problems identified also exist in other kinds of testing situations.

Several major factors must be considered when determining the appropriateness of testing materials for hearing-impaired students, including: 1) whether test materials match the student's approximate level of skill (very little information of educational relevance can be obtained when tests are too difficult or too easy); 2) whether the student understands the task and how to respond to it; and 3) whether the specific contents and formats in which some test items occur are appropriate.

Appropriate Level of Test Materials

Achievement tests for hearing students are generally available as batteries—that is, they are collections of tests of various content areas at different difficulty levels. Achievement test batteries for normally hearing students are designed to be assigned on the basis of a student's age or grade placement. Ten-year-old students, for example, would be assigned a test that might have been designed around materials normally encountered by hearing students in approximately the fourth grade. Because the achievement of most hearing-impaired students in special education classes lags considerably behind that of their hearing peers (Trybus and Karchmer, 1977), assigning them to the level of the test used with their normally hearing peers may not be appropriate. Also, within a single age group, the range of observed academic abilities of hearing-impaired students varies considerably. There is no simple way to assign a test level to hearing-impaired students on the basis of grade or age alone. Another factor related to the assignment of hearing-impaired students to appropriate test materials is that hearing-impaired students' achievement levels tend to be uneven across different content areas. Generally hearing-impaired students' math skills outstrip their reading skills. Because test batteries are often designed to be of equivalent difficulty in terms of hearing students' performance, using conventional testing instruments for hearing-impaired students is often inappropriate because a test should be matched to the test-taker's ability level.

Degree to Which Students Understand What Is Being Asked

This issue, too, has multiple facets. It is clear that many young hearing-impaired children lack experience in the test-taking situation and thus may perform poorly.

In addition, a major consideration is communication. In order to do well on a standardized test, a person must understand what is being asked. Normal instructions do not take into consideration the diverse communication requirements that exist in the various programs for hearing-impaired students. Given the diversity that abounds in the field, it is not possible to prescribe a single specific method of communication. This poses a dilemma. On one hand, standardized procedures are needed to permit interpretable results; on the other hand, flexibility in the communication of the instructions is mandatory if hearing-impaired students are to understand what is being demanded of them.

Test Content and Format

There are many possible pitfalls in this regard; some items may be biased against certain hearing-impaired children to the degree that they are best answered by people with auditory experience. Some testing formats may be inappropriate. For example, a test requiring oral dictation of the items may be as much a test of a student's speech reception skills as a test of the particular content area. Finally, some tests designed for normally hearing students may not match well to the objectives employed in the curriculum for hearing-impaired students.

In the last several years, there has been considerable effort to address some of the problems outlined above. In 1974, the Office of Demographic Studies adapted the 6th Edition (1973) of the Stanford Achievement Test to make it more appropriate for use with deaf and hard-of-hearing students, then normed the test on a nationwide sample of nearly 7,000 hearing-impaired students. The Stanford as adapted for hearing-impaired students (SAT-HI) left the test items intact (to permit comparison with normally hearing students) while at the same time addressing some of the problems described above.

In the Spring of 1983, the Center for Assessment and Demographic Studies began developing new special procedures for administering the

7th Edition of the Stanford to hearing-impaired students. The intention of this project was to build on the strength of the SAT-HI while remedying its weaknesses.

The issues addressed included the following:

1. *The appropriate level of the battery to administer to the individual student*   The project developed short screening tests in reading and math so that students can be placed in different battery levels as individual needs require.
2. *Test instructions*   The project modified test instructions to make them adaptable to the variety of communication situations found in self-contained and integrated educational programs for hearing-impaired students.
3. *The use of Stanford subtests*   The project found that some of the Stanford subtests were not useful for many hearing-impaired students, either because they measured listening comprehension or because their format confounded the content being tested. Although these subtests will be available for regular or special education teachers who want them, they were not being adapted or normed for hearing-impaired students.
4. *Parallel forms*   Because the achievement growth of many hearing-impaired students is slow, many are given the same test materials 2 or more years in a row. This is not good measurement practice. Accordingly, current plans call for two parallel forms of this test to be made available for use with hearing-impaired students.

Assuming that hearing-impaired students can be tested with appropriate materials and that the difficulties described above can be solved, problems still remain in *interpreting test results*. Researchers are only now beginning to face questions of how hearing-impaired test-takers differ from normally hearing ones and to understand the implications these differences have for interpreting test scores. To say that a particular child with significant hearing loss scored on a particular reading test the same as an average hearing student in the third grade tells little about the factors that gave rise to the score. It is necessary to know whether the child primarily depended on the auditory channel or the visual channel for linguistic information. The hearing-impaired child may have an incomplete knowledge of English language structure in comparison with a normally hearing child of the same age. Recent research on hearing-impaired children's performance on a language arts test (Allen, in press) indicates that the relative difficulty of items may not be the same for them as it is for normally hearing children. Indeed, the underlying sequence of skill development in given academic areas may well be different for hearing-impaired and normally hearing children. Future study needs to focus on factors such as degree and etiology of hearing loss, educational history, and hearing aid usage to determine their influence on the sequence of skill development.

Another concern is the difference in the strategies used by hearing-impaired children in approaching the cognitive tasks involved in achievement testing. Specifically, do they attack the questions on an achievement test in the same way as most normally hearing children? Researchers are only now beginning to probe such questions, but evidence from several studies suggests that they sometimes approach the testing situation in a different way from normally hearing test-takers. In one example, Wilson et al. (1978) found evidence on a reading test that a sizeable minority of hearing-impaired students were using a particular visual matching strategy that was highly unlikely to be used by normally hearing children. The implication of this kind of analysis is that much more must be understood about the cognitive processing of students with severe or profound hearing loss if academic performance is to be fully interpreted.

REFERENCES

Allen, T. Test response variations between hearing-impaired and hearing students. J. Spec. Educ. In press.

Allen, T., C. S. White, and M. A. Karchmer. 1983. Issues in the development of a special edition for hearing-impaired students of the seventh edition of the Standard Achievement Test. Am. Ann. Deaf 128:34–39.

Jensema, C. J., M. Karchmer, and R. J. Trybus. 1978. The rated speech intelligibility of hearing impaired children: Basic relationships and a detailed analysis. Office of Demographic Studies, Gallaudet College, Washington, DC.

Jensema, C. W., and J. Mullins. 1974. Onset, cause and additional handicaps in hearing-impaired children. Am. Ann. Deaf 119:701–705.

Jensema, C. J., and R. J. Trybus. 1978. Communication patterns and educational achievement of hearing impaired students. Office of Demographic Studies, Gallaudet College, Washington, DC.

Karchmer, M. A., M. Milone, and S. Wolk. 1979. Educational significance of hearing loss at three levels of severity. Am. Ann. Deaf 124:97–109.

Karchmer, M. A., and L. M. Petersen. 1980. Commuter students at residential schools for the deaf. Office of Demographic Studies, Gallaudet College, Washington, DC.

Karchmer, M. A., and R. J. Trybus. 1977. Who are the deaf children in "mainstream" programs? Office of Demographic Studies, Gallaudet College, Washington, DC.

Resolution on interpreters in the classroom clarified. 1980. Newsounds 5(9):1.

Wilson, K., M. A. Karchmer, and C. Jensema. 1978. Literal vs. inferential analysis of reading achievement in hearing impaired students. In: H. Reynolds and C. Williams (eds.), Proceedings of the Gallaudet Conference on

Reading in Relation to Deafness, pp. 154–170. Gallaudet College Press, Washington, DC.

Wolk, S., M. Karchmer, and A. Schildroth. 1982. Patterns of academic and non-academic integration among hearing impaired students in special education. Center for Assessment and Demographic Studies, Gallaudet College, Washington, DC.

CHAPTER 4

INTERPRETER SERVICES: LEGAL RIGHTS OF HEARING-IMPAIRED PERSONS

Bonnie Poitras Tucker

CONTENTS

During the past several years, the issue of civil rights for handicapped persons has become increasingly prominent. Since 1974, when Section 504 was added to the Rehabilitation Act of 1973 to proscribe discrimination in all areas of the lives of handicapped people, society has publicly recognized that handicapped persons have the right to receive equal opportunities with respect to education, employment, social services, and government benefits. The legal right of hearing-impaired[1] (deaf or hard-of-hearing) persons to utilize the services of oral or sign language interpreters is a major aspect of this "handicapped civil rights" movement; nevertheless, this section of the law remains a

---

[1] Although the term "hearing-impaired" persons is the more common term today, and will be used frequently in this chapter, most federal and state statutes and all legal cases dealing with the rights of hearing-impaired persons use the term "deaf" rather than "hearing-impaired." When referring to such statutes and case law, therefore, the term "deaf" will be substituted in this chapter for the term "hearing-impaired."

"gray" area, rather than one where black-and-white "do's" and "don't's" are clearly outlined.

Several federal and state laws expressly provide for hearing-impaired persons to utilize the services of interpreters in certain settings, such as in the courtroom. Additionally, Sections 501, 503, and 504 of the Rehabilitation Act arguably permit hearing-impaired persons to use interpreters in other situations, although the scope of these statutes is constantly being reevaluated and the extent to which they authorize the provision or employment of interpreters is patently unclear. Although few will disagree with the need of hearing-impaired persons to have an interpreter present in many educational, employment, and service-related settings, the question of who bears the responsibility for paying for the interpreter's services is constantly being litigated and is really the heart of the matter. Unless the school, employer, or social service agency is required to bear that burden, hearing-impaired people will rarely be able to benefit from this expensive yet necessary service on a regular basis.

This chapter outlines laws that deal with the legal right of hearing-impaired persons to utilize the services of interpreters and discusses court decisions that impact on this subject. Additionally, the author cites various agencies that hearing-impaired people may contact for aid in locating an oral interpreter.

FEDERAL LAWS

Interpreters: Educational/Employment/Vocational Settings

Education For All Handicapped Children Act   This Act (20 U.S.C. § 1401 *et seq*) requires each participating state to provide handicapped children with a "free appropriate education." Parents are to be involved in all stages of the decision-making process with respect to determining the most appropriate education for their child. An individualized education program (IEP) must be established or revised annually for each handicapped child [20 U.S.C. § 1414(a)(5)], and the parents of the child must participate in the formulation of such a plan [20 U.S.C. § 1401(19)].

Section 121a 345(3)(e) of the Act provides that the public agency must take whatever action is necessary to ensure that the parent understands the proceedings at meetings that determine their child's appropriate mode of education, "including arranging for an interpreter for parents who are deaf."

Section 501 of the Rehabilitation Act of 1973   This section (29 U.S.C. § 791) requires each executive department and agency of the federal government, including the United States Postal Service, to implement an affirmative action plan for the hiring, placement, and advancement of qualified handicapped individuals.

The regulations implemented pursuant to Section 501 define a qualified handicapped individual as one who, with or without reasonable accommodations, is able to perform the essential functions of the position at issue without endangering the health and safety of the handicapped individual or other individuals and who meets the criteria for the particular position [29 C.F.R. § 1613.702(f)]. The federal employer must make "reasonable accommodations" for an employee's disability (e.g., deafness), unless the employer can demonstrate that such an accommodation would impose an "undue hardship" on the program's operation. "Reasonable accommodations" include the provision of interpreters [45 C.F.R. § 84.12(b)(2)]. Factors to be included in determining whether an undue hardship would result include the size and budget of the program in question, the nature of the program's operation, and the type and cost of the accommodation required [45 C.F.R. § 84.12(c)]. It would have to be argued that the deaf employee required the accommodation of an interpreter, and that such accommodation did not impose an undue hardship on the program's operation.

Section 503 of the Rehabilitation Act of 1973   This section (29 U.S.C. § 793) provides that any contract (including construction contract) in excess of $2,500 entered into by any federal department or agency for the procurement of personal property or nonpersonal services, or any subcontract in excess of $2,500 entered into by a prime contractor in carrying out any contract for the procurement of personal property or nonpersonal services, must contain a provision requiring that affirmative action be taken to employ and advance in employment qualified handicapped individuals.

The regulations implemented pursuant to Section 503 provide that a contractor must make "reasonable accommodations" for an employee's disability (e.g., deafness) unless the contractor can demonstrate that such an accommodation would impose an "undue hardship" in terms of "business necessity" and "financial cost and expenses" on the contractor's business [41 C.F.R. § 60–741.6(d)]. The regulations do not address the issue of interpreting services. As with Section 501, it would have to be argued that an interpreter was needed in a particular situation to accommodate an employee's deafness and that such accommodation did not impose an undue hardship on the employer.

Section 504 of the Rehabilitation Act of 1973   This section (29 U.S.C. § 794) provides that "no otherwise qualified handicapped individual" may be:

> . . . excluded from the participation in, denied the benefits of, or be subjected to discrimination under any program or activity receiving Federal financial assistance or under any program or activity conducted by any executive agency or by the United States Postal Service . . .

solely because of his or her handicap. This section primarily relates to education, employment, housing, health-related areas, and other social services and is intended to ensure handicapped persons "equal opportunity" under the law.

Section 504 was based on and modeled after the civil rights laws prohibiting sex and race discrimination and is often referred to as the "declaration of civil rights for handicapped persons." The Congressional Committee report with respect to Section 504 stated that:

> [S]ection 504 was enacted to prevent discrimination against all handicapped individuals regardless of their need for, or ability to benefit from, vocational rehabilitation services, in relation to Federal assistance in employment, housing, transportation, education, health services, or any other Federally aided program [U.S. Code Congr. & Adm. News 6373, 6388 (1974)]

The regulations implemented pursuant to Section 504 provide that "reasonable accommodations" should be made for known physical and mental limitations, unless the recipient can show that the "accommodation would impose an undue hardship on the operation of its program." The regulations suggest, but do not mandate, that such reasonable accommodations may include the provision of interpreters [45 C.F.R. §§ 84.12(a) and (b)].

The regulations mandate that health, welfare, and social service agencies with 15 or more employees must provide appropriate auxiliary aids to people with hearing impairments [45 C.F.R. § 84.52(d)(1)]. "Auxiliary aids" are defined as including interpreters [45 C.F.R. § 84.52(d)(3)]. Agencies with fewer than 15 employees may be required to provide auxiliary aids if such provision would not impair the agency's ability to provide its normal services [45 C.F.R. § 84.52(d)(2)].

The Department of Justice analyzed the regulations promulgated under Section 504 as requiring prisons to provide for the availability of qualified interpreters:

> . . . to enable hearing-impaired inmates to participate on an equal basis with non-handicapped inmates in the rehabilitation programs offered by the correctional agencies (e.g., educational programs). [45 Fed. Reg. 37,630 (1980)]

Title I of the Rehabilitation Act of 1973 [29 U.S.C. § 720(a) et seq]
This title authorizes the federal government to pay grants to the states
to assist them in meeting the current and future need of handicapped
persons so as to enable such persons to prepare for and engage in
gainful employment to the extent of their capabilities. Each state that
agrees to participate in the program must submit a plan for vocational
rehabilitation services for a 3-year period and must submit an individualized written rehabilitation program for each handicapped person
receiving vocational rehabilitation assistance. Pursuant to Section
103(a) of Title I [29 U.S.C. § 723(a)], the scope of rehabilitation services
to be provided to a handicapped person includes "any goods or services
necessary to render a handicapped individual employable." The list of
such "goods and services" includes "interpreter services for deaf individuals."

Interpreter Services: Training and Court Availability

28 U.S.C. § 1827   This section provides that the Director of the
Administrative Office of the United States courts shall establish a program to facilitate the use of interpreters in the courts of the United
States for hearing-impaired persons, as well as for persons for whom
English is not the primary language. The fees for such interpreter services are to be paid by the Attorney General from sums appropriated
to the Department of Justice, if the presiding judicial office does not
direct that such fees shall be apportioned among the parties or taxed
as costs in a civil action to be paid by the losing party.

28 U.S.C. § 1828   This section provides for interpreting services
in criminal and civil actions initiated by the United States in a United
States District Court. Fees for such interpreting services are to be paid
by the Director of the Administrative Office of the United States courts
out of sums appropriated to the federal judiciary, if the presiding judicial officer does not direct that such fees shall be apportioned among
the parties or taxed as costs in a civil action to be paid by the losing
party.

The Rehabilitation Comprehensive Services and Developmental Dis-
abilities Amendments of 1978   This section [29 U.S.C. § 774(d)] provides
for the establishment of an Office of Information and Resources for
the Handicapped and for grants to be awarded to a maximum of 12
programs for training interpreters for deaf persons. Ten centers were
awarded grants for the period of September, 1982 through August,
1983. The 10 centers include:

Community College of Denver
North Campus
3645 West 112th Ave.
Westminster, CO 80030

University of Wisconsin-Milwaukee
Dept. of Exceptional Ed.
P. O. Box 413
Milwaukee, WI 53201

Gallaudet College
800 Florida Avenue, NE
Washington, DC 20002

Johnson County Community College
College Boulevard at Quivira Rd.
Overland Parks, KS 66210

University of Tennessee
College of Education
Dept. of Spec. Ed. and Rehab.
Claxton Education Building
Knoxville, TN 37916

Ohlone College
Fremont-Neward Community
  College District
43600 Mission Blvd.
Fremont, CA 94538

Madonna College
36600 Schoolcraft Rd.
Livonia, MI 48150

Merrimack Valley College
Route 4, Hackett Hill Rd.
Manchester, NH 03102

Seattle Central Community College
Interpreter Training Prog.
1801 Broadway
Seattle, WA 98122

St. Paul TVI
Program for Deaf Students
235 Marshall Avenue
St. Paul, MN 55103

The purpose of this program is:

> . . . to train skilled manual and oral interpreters available for employment in public and private agencies involved in the provisions of health, education, welfare, rehabilitation, employment and related services to deaf people, . . . to assist in the training of a sufficient number of interpreters to meet the communication needs of deaf individuals. (U.S. Dept. of Education, DFDA No. 84, 129w, p. 3)

Department of Justice Analysis   The Department of Justice's analysis of the regulation promulgated under Section 504 (29 U.S.C. § 794) provides that:

> Court systems receiving Federal financial assistance shall provide for the availability of qualified interpreters for civil and criminal court proceedings involving persons with hearing or speaking impairments. (Federal Register, 1980)

and states that the recipient of federal financial assistance is obligated to pay for the interpreter's services. The Justice Department's analysis further provides that in circumstances where the courts appoint counsel for indigents, they must also assign qualified interpreters for hearing-impaired indigent defendants during all phases of the preparation and presentation of the defendant's case.

STATE LAWS

State Courts

Forty-eight states have enacted statutes providing that interpreters must be appointed for deaf parties, or for deaf parties or witnesses, in state court proceedings. The scope of these statutes vary. While some apply to both deaf parties and witnesses, others apply only to deaf parties. Some apply to all court proceedings, whether civil, criminal, probate, grand jury proceedings, administrative proceedings, or mental competency hearings; others apply only with respect to some judicial proceedings. Some provide that the interpreter must be certified by the state or the National Registry of Interpreters for the Deaf, Inc. (RID); others provide that the interpreter must be approved by the deaf client and/or by the National or State Association for the Deaf or that the interpreter must be able to readily communicate with and for deaf persons. At least one statute specifically refers only to sign language interpreters; Alabama's statute, for example, requires that interpreters utilized in criminal or probate proceedings must be fluent in sign language. In such cases, it will be necessary to explain the purpose and necessity for oral interpreters.

Some statutes provide for the county, court, or state to pay the cost of the interpreter; some provide for the interpreter's fee to be "taxed as costs," which generally means that the losing party will pay for the interpreter; some provide that the court or state will only pay for the interpreter if the deaf person is financially unable to do so; some provide that the court shall determine who is to pay for the interpreter; some provide that the state division of rehabilitation shall pay for the interpreter. Other statutes do not address the question of payment at all.

Jury Duty

Several states (California, Colorado, Massachusetts, Maryland, Oregon, and Washington) have recently permitted deaf persons to serve as jurors with the aid of an interpreter. In June of 1982, a hearing-impaired individual in Maryland became the first person in the United States to serve as a juror with court provision of an oral interpreter.

California and Colorado have enacted statutes that provide that no person shall be deemed to be incapable of jury service solely because of impaired hearing. These statutes further provide, however, that the existence of a defect in auditory functions may be grounds for either party's challenge and resultant dismissal of a potential juror if the court determines that the challenged person is incapable of performing the duties of a juror in a particular action.

Mental Patients

At least three states (California, Illinois, and North Dakota) have enacted statutes requiring that a mental patient be informed of his or her rights in a language that the patient understands. These statutes may be utilized to ensure a hearing-impaired person's right to an interpreter in certain mental health situations.

State Agencies

At least two states (New Mexico and Virginia) have laws requiring the provision of interpreters for hearing-impaired persons who seek services at state departments or agencies. The agencies in these states are required to pay for the interpreter's services.

CASE LAW

All court decisions that have dealt with the right of hearing-impaired persons to receive interpreting services have involved claims for sign language interpreters rather than oral interpreters. The same principles of law apply with respect to both types of interpreters, however, and these cases may be cited as authority with respect to hearing-impaired persons who seek to utilize the services of oral interpreters (the first group of whom were examined and certified by RID in St. Paul, Minnesota in October, 1979), as well as those who seek to utilize the services of sign language interpreters.

Education for All Handicapped Children Act

The United States Supreme Court recently held in *Board of Education* v. *Rowley* (1982), that the Education for All Handicapped Children Act does not require a Westchester, New York school district to provide a ten-year-old deaf student, Amy Rowley, with a sign language interpreter in the classroom. Although recognizing that the "free appropriate public education" that the Act mandates:

> . . . consists of education instruction specially designed to meet the unique needs of the handicapped child, supported by such services as are necessary to permit the child "to benefit" from instruction. [42 CCH S. Ct. Bull. at P. 4109]

the Court held that because Amy "perform[ed] better than the average child in her class and [was] advancing easily from grade to grade," she was able to "benefit from" the instruction, and was thus receiving a "free appropriate education" [*Id.* at p. 4131]. The Court specifically held that the Act does *not* require the state to provide services to handicapped children "sufficient to maximize each child's potential 'commensurate with the opportunity provided other children'" [*Id.* p. 4119].

Because *Board of Education* v. *Rowley* was not a class action and pertained solely to Amy Rowley's right to the services of an interpreter in the classroom, it is hopeful that, in a situation where a hearing-impaired child is not doing as well in school as Amy Rowley, it would be found that that child requires an interpreter in order "to benefit" from classroom instruction, and thus an interpreter would be required under the act. Undoubtedly, however, parents of hearing-impaired children would be more likely to succeed on a claim for an interpreter under this act if emphasis was placed on the deaf child's need to receive interpreter services in *general*, simply to understand what is being said, rather than on his or her need to rely on sign language help in particular.

In *Rowley*, the Supreme Court emphatically stated that it is not the Court's responsibility to choose whether total communication[2] or oral communication constitutes the most appropriate method of educating deaf children [42 CCH S. Ct. Bull. at 4128–29], and implicitly held that the Court's refusal to involve itself in such a determination was one factor behind its decision to deny Amy the right to an interpreter. During the trial to the district court, Amy's lawyers argued that total communication was the most effective means, and perhaps the *only* effective means, of educating deaf students and that Amy needed a sign language interpreter to receive the benefits of total communication rather than for simple purposes of understanding and receiving an education in general (see 483 F. Supp. at 535–36). The Supreme Court, therefore, was under the impression that the issue involved "sign language versus oral communication" rather than a determination of whether, in the first instance, Amy required *any* kind of an interpreter (sign language *or* oral) to benefit from classroom instruction.

Had Amy Rowley's lawyers educated the courts with respect to the RID certification of two classifications of interpreting specialists, the oral interpreter and the sign language interpreter, and that the preference of the hearing-impaired consumer would determine which type of specialist was utilized in classroom and related settings, and explained that the courts were not being asked to choose which type of interpreter Amy should use but were only being asked to recognize Amy's need for *some* type of an interpreter to understand more than 50% of what was being said in the classroom, a different result might

---

[2] The following definition of the term "total communication" was officially adopted at the 48th Meeting of the Conference of Executives of American Schools for the Deaf in Rochester, New York on May 5, 1976: "Total communication is a philosophy requiring the incorporation of appropriate aural, manual and oral modes of communication in order to ensure effective communication with and among hearing-impaired persons . . . ."

have been reached in this case. Unfortunately, the lawyers who represent hearing-impaired clients are often zealously protective of their belief in hearing-impaired persons' need to use sign language to communicate and tend to focus on the sign language aspect of the interpreter issue rather than on explaining that, regardless of a hearing-impaired person's chosen mode of communication, interpreters (oral or sign language) are usually necessary under certain circumstances.

Section 504 of the Rehabilitation Act

Section 504 is only applicable to programs or activities receiving federal funds. It has been held that where federal funds are expended generally in aid of an institution or agency but are not expended in aid of a particular program within that institution or agency, a deaf individual may not receive the services of an interpreter, at the institution's expense, for that program.

In *Omar Kunkel* v. *Orville B. Phing* (1981), a deaf inmate at the Minnesota Correctional Facility alleged that prison officials violated Section 504 of the Rehabilitation Act of 1973 by failing to provide him with sufficient services of a sign language interpreter to allow him to participate in and benefit from programs and activities accorded normally hearing inmates at the prison. Although the deaf inmate was being provided an interpreter for 2 hours a week for therapy sessions, he sought to have the prison provide him with an interpreter for *all* activities that he would participate in "but for" his hearing impairment. Because federal funding for the particular program in which the deaf inmate was enrolled within the prison had ceased as of June 30, 1981, even though the Minnesota Department of Corrections and the Minnesota Correctional Facility received federal funds for other programs, the court held that the deaf prisoner was not entitled to seek the services of an interpreter after July 30, 1981, although the inmate did have a claim based on the failure to receive an interpreter during the time spent in prison prior to that date.

The question of whether Section 504 requires an employer to pay for an interpreter for a hearing-impaired employee has not yet been litigated (or, at least, there are no reported decisions dealing with this topic). Although Section 504 is intended to prohibit employment discrimination by all recipients of federal funds, the majority of courts have held that a hearing-impaired individual may only sue for employment discrimination when the federal financial assistance was given to the employer recipient for the primary purpose of providing employment. Thus, a hearing-impaired person who is denied an interpreter in an employment setting and maintains that the provision of an interpreter would constitute a reasonable accommodation, would probably only be permitted to sue under Section 504 if his or her employer received federal financial assistance for the primary purpose of providing employment.

The question of whether a college is required to pay for interpreter services for a hearing-impaired student under Section 504 was answered in the affirmative in *Camenisch* v. *University of Texas* (1980), but that court's decision was vacated by the United States Supreme Court in *University of Texas* v. *Camenisch* (1980), and the case was remanded to the district court for a trial on the issue of who should bear the cost of an interpreter for Walter Camenisch, a deaf graduate student at the University of Texas in Austin. As of this writing, that case has not been resolved; however, a brief background of the *Camenisch* case serves to explain what is at issue in the court's resolution of this matter:

In *Davis* v. *Southeastern Community College* (1979), when deciding whether the college had to admit a deaf student to its nursing program, the United States Supreme Court held that:

> Section 504 by its terms does not compel educational institutions to disregard the disabilities of handicapped individuals or to make substantial modifications in their programs to allow disabled persons to participate. Instead, it requires only that an "otherwise qualified handicapped individual" not be excluded from participation in a federal funding program "solely by reasons of his handicap," indicating only that mere possession of a handicap is not a permissible ground for assuming an inability to function in a particular context. (442 U.S. at 405)

The Court found that only close, individual attention by a nursing instructor would suffice to accommodate Ms. Davis in the clinical portion of the nursing program and that, as a result, the college could only permit Ms. Davis to take academic courses but could not permit her to participate in the clinical phase of the program. The Court said:

> Such a fundamental alteration in the nature of a program is far more than the "modification" the regulation requires. Moreover, an interpretation of the regulations that required the extensive modifications necessary to include respondent in the nursing program would raise grave doubts about their validity. If these regulations were to require substantial adjustment in existing programs beyond those necessary to eliminate discrimination against otherwise qualified individuals, they would do more than clarify the meaning of § 504. Instead, they could constitute an unauthorized extension of the obligations imposed by that statute. (442 U.S. at 410)

The Supreme Court recognized, however, that it is difficult to distinguish between illegal discrimination and lawful refusal to extend unreasonable affirmative action. The Court summarized the difficulty of drawing that fine line as follows:

It is possible to envision situations where an insistence on continuing past requirements and practices might arbitrarily deprive genuinely qualified handicapped persons of the opportunity to participate in a covered program. Technological advances can be expected to enhance opportunities to rehabilitate the handicapped or otherwise to qualify them for some useful employment. Such advances may also enable attainment of these goals without imposing undue financial and administrative burdens upon a state. Thus, situations may arise where a refusal to modify an existing program might become unreasonable and discriminatory. Identification of those instances where a refusal to accommodate the needs of a disabled person amounts to discrimination against the handicapped continues to be an important responsibility of HEW. (442 U.S. at 412–13)

The Court concluded that Southeastern Community College's refusal to make the necessary adjustments in its nursing program to accommodate Ms. Davis did not constitute unlawful discrimination because in order to modify its program so as to permit full participation by Ms. Davis, the college would have to substantially lower its standards.

The question in *Camenisch* was whether *Davis* precluded a finding that the University was required to pay for Camenisch's interpreter. That involves answering two questions: 1) To what extent is affirmative action necessary to prevent discrimination? and 2) Where is the dividing line between an *unreasonable* refusal to modify an existing program, which constitutes illegal discrimination, and a *reasonable* refusal to modify an existing program, which constitutes a lawful refusal to extend affirmative action? Until *Camenisch* is resolved, it will remain uncertain whether colleges will be expected to bear the burden of paying for interpreter services for hearing-impaired students. The Supreme Court decision in *Board of Education* v. *Rowley* does not encourage success on the argument that colleges should be required to pay for such services, because it indicates the Supreme Court's extreme unwillingness to expand, or recognize at all, the concept of civil rights for hearing-impaired persons. In *Rowley*, however, the Court held that the Education for All Handicapped Children Act does *not* require that deaf children be given an opportunity to receive an education *equal* to the opportunity provided to nonhandicapped children. In sharp contrast, however, Section 504 of the Rehabilitation Act of 1973 has been repeatedly recognized as mandating that applicable services be provided to handicapped persons that are *equal* to those provided to nonhandicapped persons. This difference in the interpretation of the two statutes may warrant a finding that *Rowley* is irrelevant to a determination of whether Section 504 requires colleges to bear the burden of paying for interpreter services for hearing-impaired students.

Title I of the Rehabilitation Act

It has been held that under this act, a state vocational rehabilitation agency must pay for a hearing-impaired college student's interpreter.

In *Schornstein* v. *New Jersey Division of Vocational Rehabilitation Services* (1981), a deaf student attending Kean College, who was provided with financial aid by the New Jersey Division of Rehabilitation (NJDV), filed an action to require the NJDV and the college to provide her with an interpreter for her classes. The college claimed that the NJDV was responsible for financing the interpreting services, and the NJDV claimed that the college was responsible, under Section 504, for such payments. The NJDV maintained a blanket policy of refusing to provide interpreter services for deaf college students. The court held that NJDV's blanket policy violated Title 1 of the Rehabilitation Act. The court stated that

> . . . An agency which receives federal funds under Title 1 must provide its clients with at least those services enumerated in Section 103(a) which are necessary to the achievement of vocational goals. The inclusion of interpreter services in this list was neither casual nor incidental. (519 F. Supp. at 780)

The court noted, however, according to the regulations promulgated pursuant to Title 1, 45 C.F.R. § 361.45, the state would be free to establish a written uniform, economic test to be applied to consider the financial needs of handicapped persons to determine the extent of their participation in the costs of vocational rehabilitation services.

Similarly, in *Jones* v. *The Illinois Department of Rehabilitation Services* (1981), 504 F. Supp. 1244 (N.D. Ill. 1981), the court required the Illinois Department of Rehabilitation Services (IDRS) to pay for an interpreter for a deaf student at Illinois Institute of Technology (IIT), although IDRS claimed that IIT was responsible for the payment of such services.

SECURING INTERPRETER SERVICES

National Agencies and Organizations

The Registry of Interpreters for the Deaf, Inc. (RID)   RID, located at 814 Thayer Avenue, Silver Spring, Maryland 20910, is a national organization of sign language and oral interpreters for hearing-impaired persons. This agency will provide a regional directory for any of the 10 identified federal regions in the United States. The directory lists chapters of RID and names of certified oral or sign language interpreters in each region.

The RID is the only organization that formally evaluates and certifies oral and sign language interpreters according to standards established by the National Certification Board. The RID also functions as a service organization for professionally certified interpreters.

The Alexander Graham Bell Association for the Deaf The A. G. Bell Association is located at 3417 Volta Place, NW, Washington, D.C. 20007. This 98-year-old, nonprofit, international organization exists to encourage the teaching of speech, speechreading, and the dynamic use of residual hearing, in order to promote better public understanding of hearing loss and to work for better educational opportunities for hearing-impaired children. The A. G. Bell Association is able to direct inquiries for aid in finding an oral interpreter to major referral sources within many states.

For a further listing of national information and service organizations related to the hearing impaired (deaf and hard of hearing), see Appendix III on p. 270.

State Agencies and Organizations

Interpreter Referral Center (IRS) Many states have IRS centers, listed in the telephone directory, which coordinate consumers, interpreters (oral or sign language), and environments and maintain a current listing of RID certified interpreters within the state. The RID recommends that this be the first contact made when an agency, organization, or individual identifies the need for an oral or sign language interpreter for a hearing-impaired person.

Information and Referral Services Each state has a statewide information and referral service, listed in the telephone directory, which can refer persons to the proper state agency to contact for aid in finding an interpreter. The National Information and Referral Service, which publishes a booklet listing all state branches, is located at 12 East Exchange Street, Akron, Ohio 44309.

State Chapters of RID, National Association of the Deaf (NAD) or Other Associations for Hearing-Impaired Persons The state chapters of A. G. Bell Assoc., RID, and the NAD are valuable sources of information about area interpreters who may or may not be certified by the RID or who may be certified but not members of the RID. Additionally, many states have local associations or agencies for the deaf that may aid in finding interpreters for hearing-impaired persons. State vocational rehabilitation agencies may also be able to provide assistance in locating interpreters.

REFERENCES

Board of Education v. *Rowley*. 1982. No. 80-1002 (June 29).
Brill, R. C. 1976. Total communication definition adopted. Am. Ann. Deaf 121:358.
Camenisch v. *University of Texas*. 1980. 616 F. 2d 127 (5th Cir.).
Davis v. *Southeastern Community College*. 1979. 442 U.S. 397.

Jones v. *The Illinois Department of Rehabilitation Services*. 1981. 504 F. Supp. 1244 (N.D. III).

Omar Kunkel v. *Orville B. Phing*. 1981. Slip Op. No. 4-81-281 (D. Minn., Aug. 6).

Schornstein v. *New Jersey Division of Vocational Rehabilitation*. 1982. 519 F. Supp. 773 (D.N.J.); affirmed Slip Op. No. 81-3010 (3rd Cir., July 8).

CHAPTER 5

THE SYSTEM OF EVALUATION AND CERTIFICATION OF ORAL INTERPRETERS

Sandra G. Maronde, Winifred H. Northcott, and
Barbara Johnson Pulscher

CONTENTS

> Each honest calling, each walk of life, has its own elite, its own aristocracy based on excellence of performance.
>
> James Bryant Conant

There are multiple approaches to attainment of the competencies (knowledge or understanding, skills, and attitudes) required to become a formal candidate for evaluation and recommended certification as an oral interpreter by the Registry of Interpreters for the Deaf, Inc.

The acquisition of these proficiencies is an ongoing process for each individual. It is strongly influenced by constants such as the educational and work environment and the sociocultural setting in which each is a part, including the quality of interpersonal relationships within. In some instances, there may be intensive personal experience with deafness in a work-related way but minimal formal preparation. Other candidates may be sophisticated in the practice of oral interpreting, with refresher coursework and workshops as a supplement, although they are uncertified.

Parents and siblings who have a hearing-impaired speechreader in their family as well as teachers who operate in a pluralistic system of communicating with children and youth who have a significant hearing loss may seek to formalize the expertise they have gained in relating efficiently to auditory or visually-oriented speechreaders. Sign language interpreters may wish to supplement their professional skills and thereby gain additional certification in order to provide services to an increasingly diverse population of hearing-impaired (deaf and hard of hearing) persons, upon request.

In the *Testimony from Speechreaders* presented by the authors of Chapter 12 of this volume, still another classification of oral interpreter candidate surfaces: the "combination" interpreter (Federlin, 1979), who is employed as a dental assistant/interpreter; a tutor/interpreter or a secretary/interpreter, for example, and is formally prepared to incorporate interpreting skills as an adjunct to the basic skills that were originally required for employment.

Speechreaders who are hearing impaired themselves and are intimately familiar with the techniques that ease communication between hearing-impaired and hearing individuals (see Chapter 9 of this volume), may earn the Oral Interpreter Certificate: Visible to Spoken. It qualifies the hearing-impaired oral interpreter to interpret the remarks of another hearing-impaired person, who may or may not use understandable voiced speech, to a third party(ies).

Regardless of the source of motivation to complete workshops, coursework, and practicum in preparation for professional service as an oral interpreter, the challenge to a candidate to meet a panel of peers presiding at a formal evaluation leading to certification by the Registry of Interpreters for the Deaf, Inc. (RID) can be unsettling to contemplate.

What kind of questions are asked at the interview that follows a written test? What is the format of the test questions—are they essay-type or multiple choice? Will there be a warm-up time to become familiar with speakers presented on videotapes? How long will the entire demonstration of skills as an oral interpreter/transliterator go on? Will I know my score at the end of the day?

The purpose of this chapter is to describe the system of evaluation and certification of oral interpreters as established by the RID and to explain each step of the evaluation process.

THE REGISTRY OF INTERPRETERS FOR THE DEAF, INC. (RID)

RID is the only national professional organization in the United States providing evaluation and certification of two separate but equal classifications of specialists: the *oral interpreter* and the *sign language (manual) interpreter*. In many instances, one individual may hold both classifications of certification.

In the second year of its establishment, 1965, the RID (then known as the National Registry of Professional Interpreters and Translators for the Deaf) held a Workshop on Interpreting in Portland, Maine. A formal report of the meeting noted that in order to meet adequately the needs of any orally oriented adult requesting special communication services, such clients might be considered to be of three broad types:

Type 1: *Pure oralists*, who are likely to reject any form of manual communication perhaps to the point of excluding common gestures.

Type 2: *Conservative oralists*, who may permit some restricted use of manual communication in special situations or under specific circumstances.

Type 3: *Liberal oralists*, who are more inclined to use interpreters' services realistically according to their needs and communication limitations and may utilize the language of signs and fingerspelling when and where it is beneficial.

Currently, the "oral-manual" issue has been chastised (Castle, 1982; Francis, 1982; Gonzalez, 1982; Nelson, 1982; Northcott, 1977, 1979, 1981a, 1981b; Pachciarz, 1983) and has basically been laid to rest within the RID membership. In the 1980s, there is respect for individual differences in preferred mode of communication (Chapter 1 contains further clarification).

Resolution #2, approved by the RID membership at the Hartford Convention in June of 1982, was accepted by the Board of Directors of the RID at its November 18–21, 1982 meeting. It reads as follows:

WHEREAS the Deaf community has been burdened with a long standing and controversial debate concerning educational methodologies used with deaf children, and
WHEREAS the stated purpose of the RID is to serve all deaf people as communication facilitators,

BE IT, THEREFORE, RESOLVED that this convention of the RID re-affirm our purpose of service to all deaf persons, regardless of their personal communication preference, and

BE IT FURTHER RESOLVED that this convention memorialize the various chapters affiliated with the RID to the effect that it is not the duty of the interpreter to dictate the "official language" of deaf persons, lest interpreters lose sight of their true purpose in relation to the deaf community. (RID Board of Directors Actions, 1983)

Primary Purposes of the RID

RID's 1972 articles of incorporation list its goals and purposes as the following:

> To teach and educate persons to become interpreters . . . and transliterators; and to prepare, maintain, distribute a registry. . . . of certified interpreters and transliterators. (RID Primary Purposes, 1983)

The National Evaluation System

Later that same year, the National Evaluation System for sign language interpreters of the deaf was established by the RID to protect deaf individuals by assuring a high level of competency in interpreting services. Minimum-level standards for evaluation were established to determine a measure of the interpreter/transliterator's knowledge and ability in five areas (Dirst, 1980; Kirchner et al., 1980):

1. To use visible and spoken communication with the hearing-impaired individual.
2. To identify the communication mode of the deaf client(s) and to ensure the meaning of the message when communicated in the preferred mode as stated.
3. To render the hearing-impaired person's message in grammatically correct English.
4. To demonstrate understanding of the RID Code of Ethics and the application of high ethical standards as outlined in the Code.
5. To demonstrate awareness and ability to perform in these specialized areas of need: "religion, legal, medical, platform, educational, artistic, etc." (Dirst, 1980, p. 1).

In 1979, RID formally approved standards for basic competency in oral interpreting and an evaluation process as an integral part of the National Evaluation System. This led to several levels of certification for oral interpreters—a "parallel certification system for oral interpreters that is extant for sign language interpreters" (Castle, 1982, p. 9; Witter, 1979, p. 2). (A detailed history of the catalytic efforts of the Alexander Graham Bell Association for the Deaf, Inc. (AGBAD) in the mid-seventies, and later an interagency approach to the RID and AGBAD in requesting recognition and opportunities for professional growth for oral interpreters can be found in the Foreword and Chapter 1 of this volume.) Since 1979, hearing-impaired individuals whose stated preference in mode of communication is speechreading and speech, may request the services of an oral interpreter through a state Interpreter Referral Center, if available, or via the telephone directory under a different service agency title.

National Certification Board   In partial execution of its responsibility for the National Evaluation System for all interpreters/transliterators, the RID established a National Certification Board and underwrote the financial and professional support required in order for personnel to maintain the certification program (Dirst, 1980). The board is composed of five members and a chairperson: three hearing-impaired members holding Reverse Skills Certificates (RSC) (Sign to English) and two hearing members holding Comprehensive Skills Certificates (CSC) or Master Comprehensive Skills Certificates (MCSC). The Board is responsible for the development of evaluation forms, materials and certificates and the maintenance of consistency in the evaluation process. The Board is required to make periodic and/or requested bias checks.

National Review Board   The RID established a National Review Board to "maintain professional standards of the certification program" and act as a final arbitrator in reviewing questions related to an interpreter's professional behavior and work-related performance under a formal grievance procedure.

National Evaluation System Study Committee (NESSC)   In February of 1983, the President of RID, Judie Husted, selected the RID NESSC comprised of four members plus two consultants to the Committee. The committee met in April, 1983 to develop a timetable for the completion of a new RID National Evaluation System. The Committee will be responsible for final development, production, and marketing of the evaluation system and will work jointly with the National Office of RID to raise additional funds required to produce prototype National Evaluation System testing programs (NES Study Committee Selected, 1983).

This action dovetails with the proposed funding priorities for research activities to be supported by the National Institute of Handicapped Research (NIHR) in fiscal year, 1983. Under the classification Interpreters for the Deaf, it is pointed out that new opportunities have led to a demand for greater quality and quantity of interpreter services, not only for deaf persons but for service providers and institutions. Among the specific research and demonstration priorities listed are:

To identify characteristics of successful manual and oral interpreters
for deaf individuals for use in training, evaluating and certifying
new interpreters.

To evaluate current curricula used in training interpreters, measure
their effectiveness, and develop improved, tested and more uniform instructional packages for training both manual and oral interpreters for deaf individuals.

To study evaluation as a process that leads to appropriate certification
of interpreters for deaf persons, address the quality and content
of evaluation materials and consistency of evaluation procedures
among States, and establish reliability and validity measures for
the entire evaluation/certification process. (National Institute of
Handicapped Research, 1983, 21,573–21,574)

The Local Evaluation Team (LET): Oral Evaluations   According to
the RID system of checks and balances, the evaluation of candidates
is carried out in their local or regional geographical area. The scoring
evaluation team is composed of three members, each of whom must
be a member in good standing of the local affiliate RID chapter and
the RID, Inc. itself. The two hearing members must hold the Oral
Interpreter Certificate: Comprehensive (OIC:C). The single hearing-
impaired member of the team must hold the Oral Interpreter Certificate: Visible to Spoken (OIC:V/S). The LET Chairperson serves as a
coordinator/monitor of formal evaluations and can function as a scoring
evaluator only in case of emergency. An additional person interprets
or transliterates a candidate's spoken responses to the videotaped portion of any specific evaluation for the benefit of the hearing-impaired
rater, but does not participate when the three scoring members individually complete the Evaluation Rating Form (see Table 5.1) with
regard to the quality of professional performance and style of the candidate (Dirst, 1980, p. 13; NES Revisions, 1984, p. 1).

The local oral evaluation team does not issue certificates. Completed rating forms and the recommendations of each team member
are forwarded to the RID National Office for computer scoring (Motions acted on, 1980). Within seven or eight weeks the candidate is
notified about the evaluation results.

Evaluation dates are assigned to the LETs by the National RID
Office. The number of dates per year is based on previous demand.
Requests for additional dates or changes are negotiated with the National RID Office. A minimum of eight candidates must be scheduled
by the LET Chairperson, with written confirmation and applications
for evaluation and payment being received by the National RID Office
at least four weeks prior to the scheduled date of evaluation, before
materials are sent to the LET (NES, 1984, p. 1).

Table 5.1.   Evaluator's Rating Form (OIC:C, OIC:S/V, OIC:V/S), developed by RID.

Candidate's Name [□□□□□□□□□□□□□□□□□□□□]

Address [□□□□□□□□□□□□□□] [□□□□□□□□□□]
      Street   City

[□□]   [□□□□]   RID CHAPTER # [□□□]
State   Zip Code   Sponsoring

Date of Evaluation [□□□□□] Time [□□] [□□] Chapter # [□□□]

Evaluator [□□□□□□] Certificate Applied for: [□□□]

Certificate
Recommended: OIC:C □   OIC:S/V □   OIC:V/S □

Evaluators's Signature _____

I.   **INTERVIEW:** *Knowlege of Code of Ethics, Communication Skills*
    A.   Code of Ethics   **1 2 3 4 5**
        1. Manner   inappropriate □□□□□ appropriate
        2. Role and Function   inappropriate □□□□□ appropriate
        3. Confidentiality   inappropriate □□□□□ appropriate

    B.   Communication Skills
        1. Oral Skills   inappropriate □□□□□ appropriate
        2. Response Quality   inappropriate □□□□□ appropriate

II.   **PARAPHRASING FACTORS:** *(Spoken/Visible) Ability to convey a message from spoken English into a paraphrased visible message.*

		Left	Rating	Right
A.	Clarity	unclear	□□□□□	clear
B.	Non-spoken behaviors	inappropriate	□□□□□	appropriate
C.	Use of space	faulty	□□□□□	appropriate
D.	Speaker affect	inappropriate	□□□□□	appropriate
E.	Substitutions	inaccurate	□□□□□	accurate
F.	Fluency	slow/hesitant	□□□□□	fast/smooth
G.	Speed/time lag	inappropriate	□□□□□	appropriate
H.	Faithfulness	inaccurate	□□□□□	accurate
I.	Message conveyed	skewed	□□□□□	accurate
J.	Paraphrasing performance	transliterates	□□□□□	paraphrases

III.   **TRANSLITERATING FACTORS:** *(Spoken/Visible) Ability to convey a message from spoken English to visible message.*

		Left	Rating	Right
A.	Clarity	unclear	□□□□□	clear
B.	Non-spoken behaviors	inappropriate	□□□□□	appropriate
C.	Use of space	faulty	□□□□□	appropriate
D.	Speaker affect	inappropriate	□□□□□	appropriate
E.	Substitutions	inaccurate	□□□□□	accurate
F.	Fluency	slow/hesitant	□□□□□	fast/smooth
G.	Speed/time lag	inappropriate	□□□□□	appropriate
H.	Omission	frequent	□□□□□	infrequent
I.	Supportive mechanisms	inappropriate	□□□□□	appropriate
J.	Transliterating performance	paraphrases	□□□□□	transliterates

continued

Table 5.1.   (*Continued*)

IV.   PARAPHRASING FACTORS: *(Visible/Spoken) Ability to convey a visible message to a spoken message.*

A.	Decipher	inappropriate ☐☐☐☐☐	appropriate
B.	Message conveyed	skewed ☐☐☐☐☐	accurate
C.	English structure	inappropriate ☐☐☐☐☐	appropriate
D.	Speaker affect conveyed	inappropriate ☐☐☐☐☐	appropriate

V.   TRANSLITERATING FACTORS: *(Visible/Spoken) Ability to convey a visible English message to a spoken English message.*

A.	Decipher	inappropriate ☐☐☐☐☐	appropriate
B.	Message conveyed	skewed ☐☐☐☐☐	accurate
C.	Speaker affect conveyed	inappropriate ☐☐☐☐☐	appropriate

VI.   OVERALL PERFORMANCE: *Evaluator's general impression of the overall performance.*

A.	Message Comprehension	difficult ☐☐☐☐☐	easy
B.	Message accuracy	inconsistent ☐☐☐☐☐	consistent
C.	Comfort factor	uncomfortable ☐☐☐☐☐	comfortable
D.	Voice/Writing Intelligibility	unclear ☐☐☐☐☐	clear

ORAL INTERPRETER/TRANSLITERATOR CERTIFICATES

Currently, three oral interpreter certifications are awarded by the RID, Inc. through its National Evaluation System (Dirst, 1980; Oral Evaluation, 1981).

1. *Oral Interpreter Certificate: Comprehensive (OIC:C)* The "ability to paraphrase/transliterate a spoken message with or without voice and with natural lip movements with (sic) hearing-impaired persons and ability to understand the speech and/or mouth movements of a hearing impaired person and repeat it (sic) exactly or in essence for the benefit of a third person" (Dirst, 1980, p. 5; Oral Evaluation, 1981).

2. *Oral Interpreter Certificate: Spoken to Visible (OIC:S/V)* The "ability to paraphrase/transliterate a spoken message with or without voice and with natural lip movements with (sic) hearing-impaired persons and possess limited or minimal skills in ability to understand the speech and/or mouth movements of a hearing impaired person and repeat it (sic) exactly or in essence for the benefit of a third person" (Oral Evaluation, 1981, p. 5).

3. *Oral Interpreter Certificate: Visible to Spoken (OIC:V/S)* The "ability to understand the speech and/or mouth movements of a hearing impaired person and repeat it (sic) exactly or in essence

for the benefit of a third person." This can be done in a simultaneous (voice over) or consecutive manner (Dirst, 1980; Oral Evaluation, 1981).

The OIC:C is equated with the Comprehensive Skills Certificate (CSC) for sign language interpreters and requires the same level of accuracy during the evaluation process (Witter, 1979; Castle, 1980).

A hearing candidate can only apply for an OIC:C certificate. He or she must receive a score of 75% or above in all categories to be awarded the OIC:C certificate. If the candidate scores below 75% on the Visible to Spoken (V/S) portion only, an OIC:S/V certificate is awarded.

The OIC:V/S certificate is awarded only to hearing-impaired individuals; they must meet the minimum standards (75%) in basic competencies. Two skills are tested: the speechreading ability of the oral interpreter candidate and the ability to repeat verbatim or to paraphrase the remarks of the hearing-impaired speaker in spoken English.

Certification Maintenance Program

At the present time, this is available for certified sign language interpreters only, as approved by the RID Board of Directors at the annual meeting in Hartford, Connecticut in November, 1981 (Certificate maintenance program, 1981).

Compensation

The RID has taken the position that the oral interpreter should be compensated at an equivalent level to the sign language interpreter, i.e., OIC:C at the level of compensation for Comprehensive Skills Certificate (CSC). The 1980 survey of interpreter referral centers regarding compensation levels and a survey of the Southeast region of the United States conducted in 1981, showed that this was occurring (Dirst, 1981).

PRE-EVALUATION PROCEDURES

First Steps

An application for oral interpreter evaluation can be secured from the LET Chairperson or from the RID National Office. It requires an applicant to list the specific certificate being sought. Evaluation fees paid by candidates are written out to RID, Inc; the LET Chairperson collects these fees and mails the checks or money orders directly to the National Office. LETs then bill the National Office for their portion of the evaluation fee. The applicant will receive written information regarding the evaluation procedures, requirements for evaluation, fees, and an overview of the evaluation itself. A copy of the RID Code of Ethics will also be provided.

Applicants who do not meet the screening criteria for applications are eligible to take the test but will be scheduled after the candidates who do meet the criteria, if there is time available; otherwise, they need to reapply next time the test is offered, at which time priority is again given to those who do meet the screening criteria (NES Revisions, 1984, p. 1).

RID Membership

Active membership in the RID is highly desirable and should be an integral component of an oral interpreter's professional role and responsibilities. Although RID membership is not a prerequisite for evaluation and certification, it offers opportunities for not only professional growth experiences but also participation in the development of policies and procedures at the state, regional, and national levels which advance the quality control of the profession. An annual maintenance fee is required for both RID members and nonmembers, for each of the 5 years that a certificate remains in effect. However, no maintenance fee is required for members holding the Oral Interpreter Certificate: Visible to Spoken (OIC:V/S).

THE FORMAL EVALUATION

The original Guidelines (1979) for the professional preparation of oral interpreters are competency-based. They identify the knowledge or understanding, skills and attitudes that are required of an individual prior to formal RID evaluation for an appropriate level of certification. Certain criteria are seen as critical for successful completion of the evaluation (Castle, 1980). They include:

1. Personal, physical, and speaking characteristics of the applicant
2. Specific areas of knowledge and understanding relating to interpreting/transliterating and deafness
3. Specific skills relating to the direct service role of interpreter/transliterator

Warm-Up Session

In preparation for the formal evaluation, a separate, quiet room is provided for a maximum of 1 hour's practice in expressive (Spoken to Visible) and receptive (Visible to Spoken) interpreting and transliterating, as desired. A cassette audio tape (expressive practice) and ¾-

inch color cassette videotape (receptive practice) are provided along with scripts for use by the candidate (Dirst, 1980).

The evaluation consists of four parts, each of which must be completed satisfactorily in order for a candidate to be awarded certification. The same Evaluator's Rating Form is used for all certificates; appropriate sections are deleted if not germane to a specific evaluation.

The following descriptions are adapted or condensed from Dirst (1980), Information for Candidates (undated), and Caccamise et al. (1980).

Written Test (Short Essay; Multiple Choice)

This examination lasts approximately ½ hour and is administered and scored before the candidate is permitted to proceed for examination on the expressive and receptive interpreting skills portion of the evaluation. The topics on the written examination concern the RID Code of Ethics and the role, responsibilities, and function of the oral interpreter under varying circumstances and settings.

Interview

A candidate will be judged and rated on the basis of the following factors as listed on the Evaluator's Rating Form.

1. Code of Ethics
    a.   Manner (attitude, dress, behavior)
    b.   Role and function (responsibilities and conduct)
    c.   Confidentiality (the concept and its implications)
2. Communication Skills
    a.   Oral skills (clarity and fluency of self-expression; quality of ideas expressed)
    b.   Response quality (accuracy, confidence, and substance of responses

This examination lasts about 20 minutes.

Spoken to Visible Paraphrasing and Transliterating

The candidate paraphrases a spoken message from an audiotape, into a visible message, using natural lip movements, without voice, and then transliterates a spoken message from an audiotape (5 minutes) into a visible message, using natural lip movements, without voice, for the benefit of a hearing-impaired person.

Paraphrasing Factors

1. Clarity (of lip movements and discretion in rephrasing of key words)

2. Nonspoken behaviors (body language, body movement, and facial expression)
3. Speaker affect (faithful reproduction of the moods, emotions, feelings, and attitudes of the speaker)
4. Substitutions (match of consumer characteristics with selection of alternate wording)
5. Fluency (phrasing and smoothness of rate of paraphrasing/reproduction of original message)
6. Speed/time lag (degree of delay in keeping pace with the spoken message)
7. Faithfulness (retention of original message in mood and content)
8. Message conveyed (relates only to the production of the message, e.g., was the production paraphrased clearly and correctly?)
9. Paraphrasing performance (Did the candidate rephrase as appropriate, or give a verbatim repetition [transliterate]?)

Transliterating Factors   Factors 1 through 6 are the same as those listed above.
7. Omission (must be at a minimum and involve words not central to the intent of the speaker's message)
8. Supportive mechanisms (mirror-writing; pad-and-pencil writing; writing in the air for numbers or words difficult to speechread but which must be retained because of their importance)
9. Transliterating performance (as distinct from paraphrasing performance)

Visible to Spoken Paraphrasing and Transliterating

The candidate transmits a message from a hearing-impaired person, using voice or mouth movements only for the benefit of a third person(s).

Paraphrasing Factors

1. Decipher (accuracy of the interpreter's repetition of mood and content of the hearing-impaired individual's message; this involves the listening and speechreading skill of the candidate, including voiceover [simultaneous] and consecutive interpreting)
2. Message conveyed (ease of repetition in spoken or visible form; accuracy in rephrasing the speaker's remarks, retaining the meaning)
3. English structure (modification of original speaker's remarks to conform to standard grammatical structure, as appropriate)
4. Speaker affect conveyed (ability to convey the moods, feelings, emotions, and attitudes of the original speaker)

Transliterating Factors

1. Decipher (verbatim repetition of the speaker's remarks, retaining the moods, feelings, emotions, and attitudes faithfully)
2. Message conveyed (ease, accuracy, and intent preserved, in spoken or visible form)
3. Speaker affect conveyed (replication of the moods, feelings, emotions, and attitudes of the original speaker)

Overall Performance

1. Message comprehension (Did the evaluator understand the candidate's reproduction of the original message? Was it difficult to understand?)
2. Message accuracy (of information transmitted, via paraphrasing or transliterating)
3. Comfort factor (subjective judgment of evaluator; was the evaluator comfortable observing the candidate?)
4. Voice/writing intelligibility (enunciation and volume of voice used by the candidate; in the instance of a hearing-impaired candidate, was the written message conveyed from films or tapes a clear one, with intelligible English structure?)

A FORWARD GLANCE: UNMET NEEDS

Five years (1979–1984) is a scant period of time for the refinement of a system of evaluation and certification of oral interpreters. Yet, the groundswell of response to an appeal for interagency leadership in developing the National Evaluation System (NES) of the Registry of Interpreters for the Deaf, Inc. (RID) bodes well for the future.

Today, there is growing evidence of multi-disciplinary team interest and commitment to quality control of NES through refinement and expansion of its essential components. The active involvement of the ultimate consumer of oral interpreting services, the hearing-impaired speechreader is assumed as a pro-active team member alongside the sign language consumer in shaping the priorities established and the future actions taken.

The following "wish list" for RID is open-ended; it includes reference to the spheres of influence and the new populations on which the NES must have impact if the professional program is to become ultimately more than a paper exercise.

RID, Inc.

Extension of the availability of oral evaluation/certification to more states throughout the country   In 1982, 18 states were listed as having no certified oral interpreters (RID Printout, 1982)

Review of the RID 5-year plan of work (RID Inc., 1981) regarding the projected number of oral interpreters at all levels of certification

Recruitment of oral interpreters for RID membership in affiliate RID chapters and the national RID, Inc.

Examination of the RID by-laws to provide for representation by oral deaf consumers on the RID Board of Directors.

Appointment of representatives from the oral interpreter network to major committees and task forces of RID should include representatives from AGBAD, Oral Deaf Adults Section (ODAS), International Parents Organization (IPO), and International Organization of Educators of the Hearing Impaired (IOEHI)

Professional Preparation of Oral Interpreters—Preservice and In-service

Available long-term comprehensive programs of professional preparation of oral interpreters (degree and nondegree), which would lead, in turn, to evaluation and certification (see Chapter 8 of this volume)

Forums, papers, and invited speakers giving up-to-date lectures, role-play, demonstrations on oral interpreting techniques; hearing-impaired speechreaders as panelists and staff members; resource networks

Inter-Organization and Inter-Agency Activities and Research

Development of creative materials, films, tapes, library-based books, articles, pamphlets on oral interpreting

Implementation of a public education/awareness program about the availability and use of oral and sign language interpreters

Orientation of social service agencies and institutions and medical and business communities toward specialized support services for the hearing impaired, including the role and responsibilities of oral and sign language interpreters

Representation on task forces and action committees of the Department of Education, reflecting the heterogeneity of the hearing-impaired population (deaf and hard of hearing)

Research Priorities (Per-Lee, 1980)

Profile of the competent interpreter (number one priority, as voted by registrants at the Interpreter Research Conference (Per-Lee, 1980)

Study of evaluation of oral and sign language interpreters as a process that leads to certification (a Number 2 priority, as voted by registrants at the Interpreter Research Conference, 1980).

Orientation of the Public: General and Specialized Populations

Publicity/information shared between A. G. Bell Association and RID about major workshops on oral and sign language interpreting for exchange of speakers and orientation of membership. What is not understood is sometimes misunderstood.

Education of hearing-impaired individuals on how to use an oral or sign language interpreter.

The 1980s can mean the start of commitment to active improvement of the quality of interpreter services for hearing-impaired individuals, upon request, regardless of their preferred mode of communication.

REFERENCES

Caccamise, F., R. Dirst, R. DeVries et al. 1980. Introduction to Interpreting. RID Inc., Silver Spring, MD.

Castle, D. L. 1980. Certification of oral interpreters in the United States. Paper presented at the International Congress on Education of the Deaf, August 4–8, Hamburg, Germany.

Castle, W. E. 1982. Oral interpreting. RID Views VII(May/June):8.

Certificate maintenance program guidelines proposed. 1981. RID Views VIII(1):2.

Dirst, R. D. (ed.). 1980. Oral interpreter evaluation manual for evaluators. RID Inc., Silver Spring, MD.

Dirst, R. D. 1981. Memorandum, RID Oral evaluations—Update. RID, Inc., Silver Spring, MD.

Federlin, T. 1979. Sign language interpreters—The changing role. RID Views VII(October):4.

Francis, C. R. 1982. Letter to the editor. RID Views VII(May/June):11.

Gonzalez, K. A. 1982. Letter to the editor. RID Views VII(May/June):11.

Guidelines for the preparation of oral interpreters: Support specialists for hearing-impaired individuals. Volta Rev. 81:135–145.

Information for candidates—oral evaluation. Undated. RID Inc., National Evaluation System, Silver Spring, MD.

Kirchner, C., F. Caccamise, R. Dirst et al. 1980. The RID National Evaluation System (NES) and certification. In: F. Caccamise et al. (eds.), Introduction to Interpreting, pp. 100–112. RID Inc., Silver Spring, MD.

Motions acted on at the 1980 RID board meeting. Memo from James Stangarone, President, RID: Extract from minutes of meeting, November 7–9, Dallas, TX.

National Evaluation System Revisions. 1984. RID Views IX(May/June):1. (Special issue.)

National Institute of Handicapped Research. 1983. Proposed funding priorities for Fiscal Year 1983. (Research and Demonstration Projects: Interpreters for the deaf.). Fed. Reg. 47:21,573–21,574.

Nelson, D. J. 1982. Letter to the editor. RID Views VII(May/June):11.

NES Study Committee Selected. 1983. RID Views VIII(5):6.

Northcott, W. H. 1977. The oral interpreter: A necessary support specialist for the hearing impaired. Volta Rev. 79:136–144.

Northcott, W. H. 1979. Introduction. Guidelines for the preparation of oral interpreters. Volta Rev. 81:135–145.

Northcott, W. H. 1981a. The case for oral interpreting. Proceedings of the National Workshop for National Interpreter Training Consortium Members, October, 1981, St. Paul Technical Vocational Institute, St. Paul, Minnesota.

Northcott, W. H. 1981b. Freedom through speech: Every child's right. Volta Rev. 83:162–181.

Oral evaluation: Handout for mock oral evaluations. 1980. RID, Inc., Silver Spring, MD.

Oral interpreters: A communication dimension. 1982. RID Inc., Silver Spring, MD.

Pachciarz, J. 1983. Consumer column. RID Views VIII(5):2.

Per-Lee, M. S. (ed.). 1980. Interpreter research conference report: Targets for the eighties, October 6–10. The National Academy of Gallaudet College, Washington, DC.

Quigley, S. P. (ed.). 1965. Interpreting for deaf people. A report of a workshop on interpreting, Governor Baxter State School for the Deaf, July 7–27, Portland, ME.

RID Board of Directors Actions. 1983. RID Views VIII(5):4.

RID, Inc. 1981. Five year plan of work: July 1, 1980–July, 1985. RID Views VII (December):6–7.

RID Primary Purposes. 1983. RID Views VIII(4):1.

RID Printout. 1982. Certified oral interpreters: All classifications. RID Inc., Silver Spring, MD.

Witter, A. B. 1979. Oral interpreter certification. RID Views V(3):2.

EDUCATIONAL
CONSIDERATIONS AND
CURRICULUM CONTENT

CHAPTER 6

FACTORS INFLUENCING SPEECHREADING PERFORMANCE: RESEARCH FINDINGS

Richard G. Stoker and Marilyn French-St. George

CONTENTS

In spite of voluminous research, controversy still exists about almost everything thought to influence speechreading performance. Relative visibility conditions, speaking rate, information content, contribution of hearing, facial, and other gestures, and other more prosaic considerations (e.g., facial structure, dental hygiene, lip mobility, beards, and moustaches) must all be taken into consideration. The literature does not clearly indicate the bounds or essential components of visual speech perception (speechreading). This contention is supported by Conrad (1979), who called the situation "an open and challenging issue" (p. 191).

ISSUES IN SPEACHREADING RESEARCH

Farwell (1976) suggested three major problems facing researchers and consumers of research in the area of speechreading: 1) definitions, 2) test materials; and 3) sampling.

Definitions

Describing speechreading is difficult. Does speechreading include use of residual hearing? Does it include facial and other gestures? Is it produced with normal articulation, or should it be exaggerated or slowed down? Do normally hearing and hearing-impaired individuals have similar speechreading capacities? Unless such variables are precisely stated, the results cannot be accurately compared.

Test Materials

Because most conversational interactions cover a wide range of spoken material and take place in a variety of contexts, it is really not possible to sample all types of speech events in a single test. Tests that utilize isolated words or syllables seem to be unrepresentative of real-life situations (Goetzinger, 1978), and ongoing discourse presents problems of replicability and analysis, although some researchers (De Filippo and Scott, 1978; Rosen et al., 1981; Sparks et al., 1979) successfully utilized such material.

In the past 40 years, many attempts have been made to prepare standardized, reliable tests for speechreading (see Berger, 1972; Green and Green, in preparation, for a review). These efforts have enjoyed, at best, limited success. The Utley test (Utley, 1946a, 1946b) achieved probably the widest use, but few researchers and clinicians use it in the 1980s. Materials for tests of speechreading have included monosyllables, spondees (words with two syllables, equally stressed), forced-choice word tests, word pairs, phrases, isolated sentences, and short stories. Scoring of these tests has been conducted in various ways: percentage of total words identified, percentage of key words identified, correct identification of central thought, words transmitted per minute, percentage of correct phonemes, and percentage of correct visemes. No clear advantage has been shown for any of these materials or scoring methods.

The question of whether the test is to be live, filmed, or videotaped must also be considered. In general, a test presented live would seem to have so much uncontrolled variance as to be useless for research. Live tests are also susceptible to unconscious interference, e.g., the Clever Hans Effect (Sebeok and Sebeok, 1979), unless elaborate double-blind procedures are somehow devised. Several studies have compared the difference between film, video, and live presentation. When such things as background, illumination, border, and image size and quality are held constant, there seems to be no difference in performance (see McCormick, 1979, for a review). Many hearing-impaired persons report that live tests of speechreading are "easier" (Winkelaar et al., 1976), a fact that might be related to personal contact, emotional comfort, or perhaps to subception (subliminal perception). There is clearly a need for further research on this topic.

Sampling

Improper sampling can render data meaningless at best and misleading at worst. Few researchers, for example, have extensively studied congenitally deaf people who are expert speechreaders. Much of the body of knowledge on speechreading comes from studies done on hearing-impaired children with widely varying abilities or on 18 to 20-year-old normally hearing college students. In addition, researchers have rarely studied differences in speechreading scores caused by different speakers. A recent exception to this was a study by Kricos and Lesner (1982).

The research literature confirms that speechreading is an enormously complex process that can involve residual hearing, linguistic sophistication, and complex visual processing. These factors are laminated on an interpersonal continuum of emotions, intellect, communication skills, and maturity. Small wonder, indeed, that we do not have a perfect understanding of this wonderfully complex phenomenon.

ORGANIZATION OF THIS CHAPTER

The four major areas related to speechreading are 1) *organic factors*, 2) *phonetic factors*, 3) *linguistic factors*, and 4) *environmental factors*. Figure 6.1 diagrams the interrelatedness of these four areas. A fifth section covers research trends and suggestions for future investigation.

At the end of each section, there is a short practical summary of research related to the factor discussed. Significant points for the sender (speaker) are differentiated from findings that relate to the receiver (speechreader), thus distinguishing between the *expressive* and *receptive* aspects of speechreading.

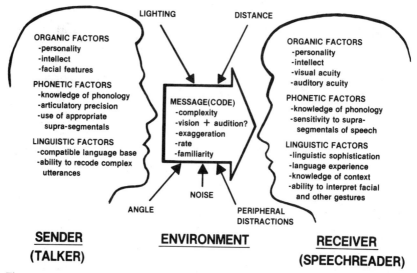

Figure 6.1.   The interrelatedness of the four factors in the speechreading process, from the points of view of the speaker, the receiver, and their environment.

ORGANIC FACTORS RELATED TO SPEECHREADING

Organic factors are those intrinsic characteristics of an individual that are not under direct physical control of either party in a communication pair (speaker/speechreader). Such factors include: *visual perceptual* abilities of speechreaders; *auditory perceptual* abilities of speechreaders; and *intelligence* and *personality* attributes of speechreaders.

Visual Perceptual Abilities of Speechreaders

Massaro (1975) stated that, "Visual perception involves the interaction of two sources of information available to the perceiver. The first is the visual stimulus available to the visual sensory system and the second is the knowledge of the perceiver" (p. 161). This interaction is illustrated in Figure 6.2. An individual with an intact visual system will detect a pattern of black and white shapes on a piece of paper. Applying worldly knowledge, the stimulus becomes a figure/ground problem in which a person sees alternately two black heads on a white background or a white vase against a black background. Similarly, for the speechreader, the visual perceptual task involves two phases: firstly, detecting temporally ordered visual stimuli and, second, relating them to knowledge obtained from previous encounters. Any assessment of the visual perceptual capabilities of a speechreader should, therefore,

Figure 6.2.   A Figure/Ground Problem in which, depending on the viewer's orientation, a person sees either two black faces on a white background or one white vase on a black background.

address both the subject's ability to detect visual stimuli and his or her ability to extract meaningful information from it.

Tests of the visual system may be divided into two groups: 1) tests that evaluate the peripheral physiological capabilities of the visual system; and 2) tests that evaluate the psychological processing capabilities of an individual (i.e., perceptual skills).

Peripheral Visual Function and the Speechreading Process   Several studies (Greene, 1978; Johnson et al., 1981; Levin and Erber, 1976) attempted to coordinate tests of physiological visual capabilities of hearing-impaired children and teenagers into screening protocols. Motivation for these efforts stemmed primarily from recognizing that the incidence of peripheral visual problems is higher among congenitally hearing-impaired individuals than their normally hearing peers. Opthamological evaluations cited in the above studies include: assessment of visual acuity in both the near and far distances, presence of myopia or hyperopia, assessment of color vision, assessment of peripheral vision, and assessment of binocular coordination.

Most studies comparing speechreading and the visual system have examined static visual acuity. The literature suggests that normally hearing individuals, with simulated hearing and visual deficiency, experience a significant reduction in speechreading ability when visual acuity falls below 20/40 (Hardick et al., 1970; Lovering, 1969). In contrast, hearing-impaired individuals demonstrated nonsignificant correlations between visual acuity and speechreading ability (Evans, 1960; Goetzinger, 1963). More recently, Erber (1979) and Romano and Berlow (1974) showed that hearing-impaired children have reduced speechreading ability under simulated reduced visual acuity conditions. Romano and Berlow (1974) suggested that the decrease is not sufficient to deny training in speechreading, provided visual acuity is better or equal to 20/80 and the distance between speaker and receiver is less than 5 feet. Caution is advised in interpreting their data, however, because their subjects were already assessed to be good speechreaders with normal visual acuity. Their experimental procedure also involved projecting the results of data obtained at an inter-speaker/receiver distance of 20 feet to that of 5 feet. Erber's data (1971) suggested that their extrapolation method may have overestimated the speechreading abilities of their subjects by approximately 30 percent.

Visual Perceptual Abilities and the Speechreading Process   Two perceptual strategies predominate the literature in the area of speechreading research (Hipskind, 1980): figure-ground patterning, demonstrated by detecting a target embedded in a similar stimulus; and 2) visual closure, demonstrated by identifying a target given incomplete visual information. A third factor is visual memory (De Filippo, 1981, 1982).

In a review of the experimental psychology literature, Massaro (1975) isolated two phenomena that bear directly on a subject's ability to separate figure from ground: *visual temporal integration* and *visual interruption*. Visual temporal integration refers to the phenomenon whereby the visual system averages the energy of a stimulus over time. Visual interruption occurs when visual stimuli, under certain circumstances, interrupt the visual processing of successive stimuli. How these factors relate to speechreading has yet to be determined. However, it can be speculated that the significant but weak correlations obtained in studies comparing speechreading ability to static visual figure-ground problems might have resulted from ignoring the temporal characteristics of the speechread stimulus (Armstrong, 1975; Blager and Alpiner, 1981; Bode et al., 1970; Sanders and Coscareili, 1970; Sharp, 1972). As an example, it was reported (Heider and Heider, 1940; Wozniak-Kaelin and Jackson, 1979) that visual recognition of vowels relates closely to speechreading ability, while recognition of consonants does not. These findings might have been, in part, a manifestation of a visual temporal integration process. Because the duration of vowels generally exceeds that of consonants, the visibility of the vowel will have the controlling influence on the effective detectability of a consonant vowel utterance.

Research comparing visual memory capabilities and speechreading was well reviewed by De Filippo (1981) and Green and Green (in preparation). Analysis of the research indicates that normally hearing individuals perform better on temporal memory tasks than hearing-impaired subjects. There are no obvious differences between the two groups on spatial memory tasks. Neyhus and Myklebust (1969) and Sharp (1972), using tests of visual sequential memory, demonstrated significant differences between groups of hearing-impaired children, who may be classified as either good or poor speechreaders. De Filippo (1981) further cited evidence (Costello, 1957; Risberg and Agelfors, 1978) that supports the notion of a positive correlation between visual spatial memory tasks and speechreading for hearing-impaired subjects.

De Filippo (1982) demonstrated markedly different patterns of behavior between hearing-impaired children and adults in a visual memory task. Visual memory performance was highly correlated with speechreading ability for the adult subjects, while the only predictor of the children's speechreading ability was element recognition performance, which was only weakly predictive.

Auditory Perceptual Abilities of Speechreaders

Tests of the auditory system may be divided into two groups: 1) tests that evaluate the peripheral capabilities of the auditory system (e.g., pure tone tests); and 2) tests that assess the more central auditory perceptual skills of an individual (e.g., speech discrimination tests, speech in noise tests, and competing message tasks).

Peripheral Auditory Function and the Speechreading Process   Assessment of tonal or speech stimuli detection levels for severely and profoundly hearing-impaired subjects with sensorineural hearing loss usually presents no particular problem. The relationship between auditory threshold values and speechreading ability has not been the subject of rigorous research. Clinical experience suggests that the best speechreaders are generally those individuals with severe and profound hearing losses of prelingual onset when other things, such as knowledge of the language base, are equal. The writers, however, do not suggest a causal relationship between severity of peripheral hearing loss and the speechreading process.

Auditory Perceptual Abilities and the Speechreading Process   A maximum word discrimination score of 10% might suggest that an individual has an extremely limited amount of residual hearing to integrate with the speechreading process. Practical experience and research tend to refute this point of view. Low frequency information, usually available to even profoundly deaf individuals, may often provide important prosodic cues to supplement the speechreading process. Risberg (1974), using normally hearing subjects, demonstrated that speechreading abilities improved from 32% to 46% when the visual stimuli were supplemented by low frequency acoustic information. The positive effects of audition upon speechreading performance has been demonstrated frequently (Carson and Goetzinger, 1975; Holmes et al., 1980; Keys et al., 1960; Ling et al., 1981; Nicholls, 1979; Stoker, 1980). Scores obtained from speech discrimination tests employing audition (A) and vision (V) are usually superior to tests addressing either A or V alone. Furthermore, scores obtained from the bimodal (A and V) presentation may even exceed the sum of the scores from A and V alone. There is, however, great individual variability, with some individuals demonstrating reduced scores in the A and V condition, compared to the V condition alone (Holmes et al., 1980; Nicholls, 1979).

Results from normally hearing subjects indicated that they, too, can combine auditory and visual cues to enhance receptive skills (Campbell and Dodd, 1980; Dodd, 1976, 1977, 1980; MacDonald and McGurk, 1978). Campbell and Dodd (1980) and Dodd (1977) performed a series of experiments to assess normally hearing subjects' ability to process A (under simulated hearing loss conditions), V, and combined (A and V) stimuli. They also introduced a fourth condition in their experiment: an asynchronous combined condition, in which audition lagged behind the visual stimuli. They found that both the synchronous and asynchronous conditions produced improved results compared to either the V or A mode alone, findings that merit further investigation with hearing-impaired subjects. For example, can hearing-impaired individuals incorporate auditory and visual stimuli that are out of synchrony? If they can, what effect, if any, will this have on oral interpreter training? There are also implications for electronic devices that might require a finite time interval to process auditory information before channeling it to the ear (Stoker, 1982).

Intelligence of Speechreaders

Most intelligence tests are heavily loaded with speech- and language-based items that may well bias the conclusions relating to the young hearing-impaired child. The trend recently has been to revise established tests by excluding the speech-based items (see Vernon and Ottinger, 1980, pp. 201–202, for recommended intelligence tests to be used with hearing-impaired individuals).

Berger (1972), O'Neill and Oyer (1981), and Green and Green (in preparation), in extensive reviews of the literature, found that, in general, research has not established any significant or meaningful relationship between speechreading ability and measurements of intelligence (using such tests as Standard Achievement Test, Goodenough Draw-a-Man Test, Wechsler-Bellevue Performance Scale, Stanford-Binet Test, Wechsler-Bellevue Adult Intelligence Test, and the Wechsler Intelligence Scale for Children (WISC). The consensus suggests that above normal intelligence does not significantly influence a person's speech-reading ability. There is, however, some evidence to suggest that intelligence as measured by the revised Stanford-Binet Test is a significant factor contributing to the speechreading ability of hearing-impaired, mentally retarded children (Smith et al., 1971).

Personality of Speechreaders

The measurement of personality is possibly even more complex than that of intelligence. For the individual with a significant hearing loss, personality assessments may well be biased by the teacher's perception of the individual's communication ability, particularly if the tester has little experience in working with the hearing impaired (for a complete review of personality assessment and interpretation within the hearing-impaired population, see Canestrari and Ricci-Bitti, 1978; Goetzinger, 1972; Goetzinger and O'Neill-Proud, 1975).

Traditionally, it has been assumed that individuals who are able to integrate information from a variety of sources make the best speechreaders (Kitson, 1915; Simmons, 1959); they have been termed "intuitive" as opposed to the "need to think" or "literal" individuals, referred to as "analytical" (Jeffers and Barley, 1978). Giolas et al. (1974) evaluated three personality variables (locus of control, evaluation style, and incentive orientation) and their relationship to speechreading among hearing-impaired fifth- and sixth-graders. The intrinsically oriented subjects, whose incentives were inner-directed, speechread significantly more words correctly than did the extrinsically oriented. It was hypothesized that the intrinsically oriented subjects were rewarded by the feelings of self-satisfaction and a sense of achievement on completion of a new and difficult task. Conversely, the extrinsically oriented subjects found little reward in the speech-reading task and, without tangible reward, performed less well.

Summary

Even though visual acuity is not a reliable predictor of speechreading ability, detection of visually transmitted speech may be difficult if the vision of the receiver (speechreader) is worse than 20/40. Intellectual capacities have not been found to be significantly related to speech-reading except within the mentally retarded, hearing-impaired population. Significant relationships have been established between speech-reading and the ability to solve static visual figure-ground problems. Further research is needed to determine what articulatory procedures, if any, the sender (speaker) should adopt to render the visual image optimally discernible as presented on the lips. The majority of hearing-impaired people find that speechreading is facilitated by the use of residual hearing. The sender (speaker) should, therefore, use appropriate levels of voice for maximum comprehension. (This would be impractical in some oral interpreting situations, however.) Further research is needed to determine the effect of the time lag introduced between the auditory message (from the speaker) and the visual image (from the interpreter) on the speechreading process. Finally, assessments of visual spatial memory have been found to correlate fairly well with speechreading abilities. Recent research (Dodd, 1980; Dodd and Hermelin, 1977) suggests an interaction between use of residual hearing and the coding of the visual stimuli. Some hearing-impaired individuals may code speechread material using a visual-spatial code, while others use a visual code more analogous to hearing that is coded temporally.

PHONETIC FACTORS RELATED TO SPEECHREADING

The phonetic aspects of speechreading are operationally limited to the movements and revelations occurring in the vicinity of the speech mechanism (the lips, tongue, teeth, jaw, cheeks, nares, and larynx).

Speech scientists commonly divide the phonetic consideration of speech into *segmental* (the basic elements—the vowels, diphthongs, and consonants) and *suprasegmental* features.

Segmentals

Vowels and Diphthongs   Fifteen vowels and diphthongs spoken by four individuals were filmed by Jackson et al. (1976), who made physical measurements of the lip shapes occurring during production of the vowels and diphthongs and identified perceptual features of the filmed stimuli based on a large number of observations made by speechreaders. These features were then correlated with the physical measurements. Two major perceptual features for vowel identification were noted: the *extension and rounding of the lips* feature and the *vertical lip separation* feature.

O'Neill and Oyer (1981) reported a study by Risberg and Agelfors (1978) that demonstrated that hearing-impaired speechreaders could identify vowels significantly better than a normally hearing group. Neither group could reliably detect fine differences in vowel length, however. The differences between hearing-impaired and normally hearing subjects are of interest, considering Heider and Heider's (1940) finding that vowel perception was significantly correlated with speechreading performance while consonant perception was not.

Consonants   Woodward (1957) and Woodward and Barber (1960) classified groups of consonants by a common point (place) of articulation and called members of such groups homophenes (sounds that look alike on the lips). For example, the visually similar bilabials /p/, /b/, and /m/ were classified as one group among the four identified:

Bilabials	/p,b,m/
Rounded labials	/w,r/
Labiodentals	/f,v/
Non-labials	/e,ð,t,d,n,l,s,z,ʃ,tʃ,ʤ,j,k,g,ŋ,h/

Fisher (1968) coined the term *viseme* to indicate the distinguishable visual characteristics of speech sounds. This, of course, was inspired by the use of the term, *phoneme,* to designate the smallest sounds of speech differentiated through audition. Fisher expanded Woodward and Barber's classifications to a total of five classes, while Binnie et al. (1974) identified nine homophenous consonant groups:

Group 1 /f,v/	Group 6 /r/
Group 2 /p,b,m/	Group 7 /θ,ð/
Group 3 /w/	Group 8 /t,d,s,z/
Group 4 /l,n/	Group 9 /k,g/
Group 5 /ʃ,ʒ/	

These data, indicating only two consonants (/l/ and /r/) capable of being uniquely identified through vision, spawned innumerable reports about the "impossibility" of speechreading as a reliable form of communication for the deaf (e.g., Denmark, 1978; Moores, 1982; Vernon, 1972). Such data were challenged recently by Scheinberg (1980), who used a sophisticated digitalization procedure to demonstrate that the sounds /p/, /b/, and /m/, previously characterized as belonging to the same homophene group (indicating that they were visually indistinguishable), were, in fact, visually different and were speechread accurately by competent speechreaders. These data were supported by Stoker (1980), who embedded the homophenous words "speed," "speedy," and "speedily" in the carrier phrase, "The boy walked _ home." The lexical problem of using "speed" and "speedy" in this context was overcome by illustrating the sentences using a dog named Speed or Speedy, respectively. Under these conditions, profoundly deaf speechreaders reliably detected the target words. Measurements showed considerable variation in the length of the target words, which Stoker hypothesized was the reason they could be accurately speechread, even though the visual revelation of each word was identical. These reports illustrate the value of research at the level of fluent speech rather than at the segmental level, a view poignantly supported by Gonzalez (1982), who asked, parenthetically, "Who would continue to use a communication system that only allowed 30% comprehension?"

Consonant clusters were the topic of research by Franks and Kimble (1972). They had 275 college students speechread 32 consonant cluster-vowel, nonsense syllables, spoken by three speakers. The clusters were incorrectly perceived 89% of the time. Clouser (1976) examined the vowel/consonant ratio of short and long sentences and the relationship between that ratio and speechreading difficulty among normally hearing and deaf subjects. He demonstrated no relationship between vowel/consonant ratio and speechreading performance. A significant finding of Clouser's study was the estimate that individual phoneme visibility scores accounted for only 5% of the amount of variability in lipreading performances.

Suprasegmentals

In general, the suprasemental aspects of speech relate to pitch, intensity, and rate (tempo). (For a more complete discussion of these features, see Lehiste, 1970, or Ling, 1976.) Suprasegmental characteristics of speech are highly influenced by exaggerated articulation and speaking without voice.

Speaking without Voice and with Exaggeration   O'Neill and Oyer (1981) reported research by Fulton (1964), which examined the physical effects of speaking without voice. The results indicated appreciable differences in size of lip opening, mouth width, and jaw movements, with more exaggeration occurring when words were not voiced. This is of concern because research (Vos, 1965, cited in O'Neill and Oyer, 1981) indicated that normal mouth movements are preferable to exaggerated mouth movements. These findings contradict those of Franks (1979), who found that somewhat exaggerated articulation facilitates sentence speechreading performance for both hearing-impaired and normally hearing speechreaders. Isolated spondee words or consonants were not rendered more speechreadable by exaggeration.

Rate of speech is closely related to exaggeration. Indeed, one form of exaggeration is a slowed rate of speech. Byers and Lieberman (1959) showed that artificial rate changes (caused by slowing the projection speed of a movie projector) had no effect on speechreading performance. Black et al. (1963) reported similar findings, indicating that moderate mechanical or electrical reduction of speaking rates tends to improve lipreading performance. It is possible that mechanical attenuation preserves crucial timing ratios, while merely speaking slower might distort them; there is no research on the effects of speakers slowing down their rate of speech. This is crucial, given the importance of suprasegmental information in auditory speech perception (Lehiste, 1970).

Pitch and Prosody   Little attention has been given to specific suprasegmental aspects of speechreading. One prominent exception is Fisher (1969), who found that speechreaders could reliably detect changes in meaning dependent upon pitch. Other research on lipreading and prosody (e.g., Risberg, 1974) generally considered residual audition the only reasonable perceptual channel for receiving prosodic information. Contradicting this was a report by Geers (1978), which demonstrated that visual phrase segmentation is dependent upon rhythm (visual perception of prosody). In order for the speechreader to reliably detect prosody, he or she must synthesize phonetic information presented via the suprasegmental features.

The serial processing limits of the visual system are well-known (Huggins, 1972; Julesz and Hirsh, 1972; Liberman et al., 1976). These data suggest that the vast number of individual elements contained in even a simple utterance must undergo some form of patterning or coding in the dynamic context of speechreading (Bever, 1970; Liberman et al., 1967).

A number of studies on rhythm and speechreading (Hannah, 1970; Heider, 1943; Heider and Heider, 1940; Simmons, 1959) assumed that awareness of rhythm is strongly related to the perception of speech by vision. As mentioned previously, Stoker (1980) presented evidence that demonstrates that perception of homophenous words by expert speechreaders can be predicted by examining the temporal pattern of the phrases in which the words are said. These findings, coupled with Erber's (1972) report that the visible opening of the oral cavity is directly proportional to the shape of the wave form envelope (time-intensity envelope), supports the notion that the visual channel can be used to reliably detect the suprasegmental characteristics of speech.

There is, therefore, more to speechreading than serial-phoneme analysis. It seems that higher-order perceptual organization, perhaps facilitated by temporal patterning, allows the skilled speechreader to grasp "gestalts," or "chunks," of meaning from the visual matrix presented.

Summary

The ability of speechreaders to understand speech will be enhanced if talkers remember when confusions occur to use phonemes most visibly distinct on the lips. Unfortunately, the great complexity introduced when vowels, diphthongs, and consonants are combined into syllables, words, and phrases makes it extremely difficult, if not impossible, to restructure running speech at the phonetic level in order to make it more speechreadable. Phonetic restructuring probably works best on isolated syllables and words where other strategies, such as contextual alteration, are not possible. Where such restructuring is desirable, it should be remembered that vowels are reliably read by most speechreaders, while many consonants and consonant clusters cause considerable difficulty.

The research suggests that slight articulatory exaggeration may facilitate speechreading. Speakers should probably be advised to speak somewhat slower than normal and to take precautions in order to preserve the normal relative prosody or rhythm of the utterance; such information has been shown to be extremely important in the perception of fluent speech by speechreaders.

LINGUISTIC FACTORS RELATED TO SPEECHREADING

The wide range of language-processing abilities of hearing-impaired individuals is well-known (Ivemey, 1976; Streng et al., 1978). The direct and discernible influence of hearing upon the development of language ensures language ability along a continuum within this population that ranges from minimal competence to fluency. This lack of homogeneity creates enormous problems for researchers and educators alike. It means that testing materials must often be adapted to the population at hand by changing the complexity or vocabulary of stimuli. Unfortunately, few researchers test or report the language level of their subjects. Many studies are performed on schoolchildren with widely varying language abilities; or, even less desirable, college students with normal hearing and (presumably) normal language are used to obtain information relative to general speechreading abilities. The net effect of the manifold procedures and practices embodied in research on language and speechreading is to make generalization from one study to another almost impossible.

Linguistic Complexity

Researchers have studied various aspects of linguistic complexity and speechreading performance. Morris (1944) investigated the effects of sentence length and the position of word groups within sequences of groups, reporting a decline in speechreading scores with increasing sentence length. No major effects for group position were reported. Clouser (1973), Beasly and Flaherty-Rintelmann (1976), Erber and McMahon (1976), and Green et al. (1981) also reported that speechreading performance decreases as a function of sentence length. This is interesting because increased sentence length implies increased linguistic redundancy and structure, which would theoretically lead to improved comprehension. Indeed, Clouser made this explicit, saying, in deference to effects of length on visibility, "Factors, such as syntactic structure, word familiarity, and knowledge of content probably become more important" (p. 35). Lloyd (1964) and Lloyd and Price (1971), in studies using the sentence as a unit of familiarity, found a significant relationship between familiarity and intelligibility. This was not consistent with much of the previous research, which failed to find familiarity as measured by letter, phoneme, and/or word frequency counts as significant factors in intelligibility. Most adult speechreaders seem to prefer connected discourse to one-word conversations. Indeed, sentential context seems to be a major help in fluent speechreading. Comparison of scores on isolated words versus those obtained on sentences is a tenuous business, at best. It cannot automatically be assumed that a score of, say, 55% on isolated words is better than a score of 50% on sentences. Sentences contain many small, often insignificant words that are difficult to speechread because of coarticulation. Because scores are usually computed on a strict percentage basis, sentence level material will often automatically be scored lower simply because of the scoring method.

Albright et al. (1973) investigated differences in lipreadability of English and Slurvian sentences. Slurvian sentences were matched with English sentences, for example, "Ah waits beep a light" in Slurvian, matched with "always be polite" in English. The investigators reported that the English sentences were speechread with a significantly higher degree of accuracy. These results suggest that fluent speech is easier to speechread than strings of isolated words organized in a sentence-like structure. As Albright et al. stated: "A semantic-syntactic hierarchy is necessary for speech perception" (p. 50).

Some of the data reported in the literature do not fairly represent the world of natural spoken communication. Because significant numbers of adult speechreaders have been shown to process sentences with an accuracy of 70% or better (De Filippo, 1982; Stoker, 1980), the external validity of research that claims a blanket reduction in speechreading acuity with increasing redundancy (length) is questionable.

In support of this point, consider a Russian study (Podmaryeva, 1974) which utilized expert hearing-impaired speechreaders and showed that sentences were perceived with 70% accuracy, while sounds were speechread with only 38% accuracy and individual words at 26% accuracy. Podmaryeva emphasized the importance of fluent speech for training, warning against the use of individual speech sounds.

Linguistic complexity in speechreading performance was addressed from a structural point of view by Hannah (1974), who analyzed the relative speechreading ability of several types of sentences organized according to the principles of transformational grammar. He found, in general, that higher-order transformations were more difficult to speechread. Similarly, Lowenbraun and Affleck (1970) demonstrated that deaf children tend to use syntactic cues to aid recall of speechread material. They found that the syntactic structure of an utterance affected the children's ability to speechread, with the more complex and longer structures being progressively more difficult. The data of Hanna (1974) and Lowenbraun and Affleck (1970) did not establish levels of linguistic competence for their hearing-impaired subjects (adults over 45 and children, respectively); therefore, it is impossible to separate the factor of general linguistic competence from the influence of linguistic complexity upon speechreadability. Normally, hearing subjects tested by Hannah experienced similar difficulties, although to a lesser degree, than those reported for the hearing impaired. It seems fair to surmise, therefore, that linguistically complex sentences are harder to speechread than less complex utterances and that hearing-impaired speechreaders sometimes have difficulty with complex sentence constructions.

Studies by Greene (1963) and Fisher (1969) showed that stress and intonation patterns, with the enormous linguistic information they convey, are available through speechreading. Corroborative evidence for this is reported by Geers (1978), who demonstrated that good speechreaders tend to parse visually presented sentences at phrase boundaries when presentation of such sentences is randomly interrupted by a flash of light. This is completely analogous to the auditory click migration phenomenon, which demonstrates intonation-syntax interaction in experiments involving normally hearing subjects (Wingfield, 1975).

Linguistic Competence

It is probable that skilled speechreaders are those with generally high levels of linguistic competence. Why, then, has relatively little research attempted to relate overall language facility with speechreading performance? Indeed, Farwell (1976) asked: "Where does speechreading leave off and language reading begin?" (p. 24).

De Filippo (1982) gave interesting insight into the problems of linguistic competence in speechreading research. She reported that receptive language (measured by a test of reading) accounted for 60% of the variance in speechreading scores achieved by a group of 39 deaf subjects, which indicates that a significant portion of the speechreading scores earned by her subjects could be predicted by reading scores alone. A contrasting conclusion was reported by Conrad (1977), who tested hearing-impaired and normally hearing teenagers of average non-verbal intelligence. He concluded that the relatively poor speechreading performance of the deaf subjects (which was not significantly different from the normal controls) was not caused by linguistic impairment. No other language measures were reported, the assumption being that the deaf subjects were similar to the normal controls.

Gestures and Facial Expressions

Gestures of the arms, hands, head, upper torso, and other body parts are universally utilized to punctuate and emphasize spoken language. Morris et al. (1979) emphasized the linguistic use of gestures, reporting that many gestures are practically universal across languages and can be traced to definite geographical origins. They also confirmed that gestures are capable of conveying complex meaning, in some cases more efficiently than the spoken word. Gestures and facial expressions have been well-investigated and formalized within the literature on American Sign Language (ASL) (Hoemann, 1978; Wilbur, 1979). The use of spatial orientation to indicate who is being talked about or when an event occurred plays an important role in the communication process involved in ASL. Changes in facial expression can convey both obvious and subtle cues to the mental state and semantic intent of the speaker. Drawing again from the ASL literature, sustained facial expressions can help in presenting related concepts within a particular phrase. It has been suggested that facial expression is equally useful in oral interpreting situations (Northcott, 1982).

The use of gestures and facial expressions as aids to the speechreading process has received little attention in the research literature. Popelka and Berger (1971) reported that speechreading performance increased an average of 20% with the use of appropriate gestures. An equally important finding was that inappropriate gestures reduced average speechreading scores by 20%. However, Lowell (1959) reported that the amount of visible facial expressions did not seem to affect speechreading scores. Berger et al. (1971) and Greenberg and Bode (1968) contradicted this, reporting that speechreading performance improves with increasing amounts of visible facial expression.

Summary

The linguistic sophistication of the receiver definitely influences his or her ability to speechread accurately. The message-sender is well-advised to match his or her utterances in length and complexity with the assessed degree of language competence of the recipient. Caution should be exercised to ensure that the language-processing capabilities of the speechreader are sufficient to comprehend the message, but no assumptions should be made regarding a lack of linguistic competence solely because hearing loss is present. Natural gestures should be used in abundance. Facial expressions will not hinder and might well materially assist speechreading. Effective facial expressions will, at the very least, make the speechreader's task more pleasant.

ENVIRONMENTAL FACTORS RELATED TO SPEECHREADING

Effects of Distance

The further a person is away from an object, the more difficult it is to visually discern the fine details. The question arises as to how great the inter-speaker/receiver distance can become before it begins to be detrimental to speechreading.

Neely (1956) and Berger et al. (1970) used normally hearing subjects to demonstrate no significant differences in speechreading scores at distances varying between 3 and 24 feet. Berger et al. (1970) did, however, notice that the 24-foot distance began to adversely affect the older subjects, which they attributed to diminished visual acuity.

Erber (1971), testing profoundly hearing-impaired teenagers at Central Institute for the Deaf, found a significant reduction in lipreading scores as distance from the speaker increased. The percentage of correct identification dropped at a rate of 0.8% per foot between 5 and 70 feet and at 0.5% per foot from 70 to 100 feet.

There is little evidence in the literature regarding the effect of very small inter-speaker/receiver distances on speechreading. Larr (1959) reported potential detrimental effects of close-range viewing. This finding is reasonable because there is a minimum distance at which the entire face is completely in focus during one visual fixation.

For a given visual fixation, there is a limited spatial range within which everything is in focus (Massaro, 1975). As the distance between objects and observer decreases, so does the range within which objects are in focus. At distances closer than approximately 5 feet, according to mathematical calculations, the receiver will be required to make multiple rapid adjustments in focusing in order to monitor the speaker's face. This would be possible, although probably very tiring, and not optimal for long-term viewing.

Effects of Lighting

The only comprehensive studies of the influence of lighting on the speechreading abilities of hearing-impaired individuals have evaluated children in classroom situations (Erber, 1974a, 1979; Jackson, 1967, cited by Berger, 1972). The results suggest that communication in many settings might be improved by altering lighting conditions. Erber (1974b, 1979) isolated the relative oral facial luminance as an important factor in determining the suitability of a given lighting situation. By proportionately increasing the light levels within the oral cavity, the articulators are rendered more visible. This may be achieved by introducing incandescent lighting from below and in front of the speaker (Erber, 1974b; Jackson, 1967). Erber (1979) pointed out, however, that such modifications may introduce other visual problems, including annoying brightness contrasts.

Effects of Angle

The effects of visual angle on the speechreading process, investigated by Erber (1974b) and Wozniak-Kaelin and Jackson (1979), involved profoundly hearing-impaired children and normally hearing adults, respectively. Erber found that the best horizontal angle for his subjects ranged from 0° to 45°. Mean scores dropped by 14 to 22% when the angle was increased to 90°. Wozniak-Kaelin and Jackson, however, found no differences in speechreading ability at 0° compared to 90°. Erber (1974b) also investigated the vertical angle and found no effect on speechreading for angles up to ± 30°.

It is inadvisable to generalize the results of these two studies because both employed optimal lighting conditions and the test stimuli were not typically those encountered in natural communication situations. Informal observations of experienced adult lipreaders made by the writers seem to confirm that horizontal visual angle does not become an important factor until angles exceed 90°. In fact, some individuals may be more speechreadable from angles exceeding 0° (head on). This would be a prime topic for further experimental work.

Effects of Noise

The ability to speechread, as stated earlier, is dependent to a great extent upon the use of residual hearing. Noise detracts from an acoustic signal and forces the speechreader to rely more heavily on the visual modality for speech reception. Noise also influences speech perception by the hearing impaired to a greater extent than for normal hearing individuals.

Data from unpublished masters' theses, cited by Berger (1972), demonstrated that significant reductions in speechreading scores were obtained upon introduction of various types of noise, including white noise, speech, and background noise. As an adjunct, the hearing-impaired individual may not be able to hear his or her own voice in situations with high background noise and thus will be unable to monitor his or her voice level; hence, he or she may not speak loud enough for communication to continue (Jacobs, 1981).

Noise has different effects on speakers. Most individuals instinctively raise their voice in the presence of noise (Lombard Effect). This has the general effect of creating exaggeration and distortion to the phonetic content of the message. Although it is speculation at this point, such distortions would tend to render speechreading more difficult.

Effects of Peripheral Visual Stimuli

Visual distractions assumed to be detrimental to the speechreading process include dark glasses, long hair, beards and moustaches, movements of the hands in front of the face, exaggerated lip movements, and a speaker with a pipe, cigarette, or cigar in his or her mouth (Berger, 1972; Jacobs et al., 1981; Popelka and Berger, 1971). Most of these factors reduce the visibility of the speaker, which has been shown by Stone (1957) to reduce speechreading scores.

A few studies have investigated the influence of background on the speechreading process. Keil (1968) employed various backdrops, ranging from static pictures to black-and-white moving pictures. Miller (1965, cited by Berger, 1972) used flashing lights and a red-on-white Archimedian spiral. Neither study showed any detrimental effect on speechreading ability; caution is advised, however, in reaching a conclusion here or applying it literally. In real-life situations, the speechreader's attention can be truly divided between the background and a speaker. It might be hypothesized that when the background is neutral, the speechreader's attention will be directed to the speaker. If the background relates to the speaker's topic, some facilitation might take place (Garstecki and O'Neill, 1980; Jacobs et al., 1981; Pelson and Prather, 1974). If, however, the background is competing for the speechreader's attention, some detrimental effects on speechreading ability may result from the subject's divided attention.

Summary

It has been shown that speechreaders can effectively understand the spoken word to a distance of approximately 24 feet if the conditions are ideal. The minimum distance at which a person can speechread has not been determined. However, distances closer than 5 feet would probably be very tiring. Evidence supports the value of supplying lighting from below and in front of the speaker. There is ample evidence to suggest that lipreading is reliably possible at angles ranging from 0° to 90° in the horizontal plane and from 0° to 30° in the vertical plane.

Speechreading is more likely to be facilitated in a quiet environment than a noisy one. Two major factors are possible; 1) residual hearing is affected by noise; and 2) speakers adjust their speaking mode (usually by increasing the effective volume) accordingly. Objects that interfere with the visibility of the lips are detrimental to speechreading and should be avoided. Speakers who are intent upon being optimally speechreadable should avoid smoking, wearing facial hair, chewing gum, and moving hands in front of the face. The negative effects of poor backgrounds have not really been proven by research. It seems logical, however, that any background that materially interferes with visual perception (such as psychedelic art) will negatively affect speechreading capacity.

RESEARCH TRENDS AND SUGGESTIONS FOR FURTHER RESEARCH

It is obvious from earlier suggestions for further research in this chapter that there is much still to be learned about facilitation of speechreading. Several exceptionally promising areas of research in this field bear special mention here.

The complexity of the speechreading process lends itself to complex mathematical modeling. It will be possible at some point to specify a mathematical formula within a computer that could answer, in a theoretical way, almost any question about speechreading. One attempt at computer modeling of speechreading was reported by Argila (1979). It is likely that others will follow. Another application of computer technology to speechreading research could be the perfection of a visual speech synthesis device that would use computer graphics or possibly videodisc graphics to synthesize, by rule, a facial image to accompany any spoken discourse desired. Operation of such a device would closely parallel auditory speech synthesis devices already available. A visual speech synthesis device would allow a precision and replicability currently lacking in studies on the speechreading process. It would also, for the first time, permit truly replicable clinical procedures.

The expanding use of professionally trained and certified oral interpreters creates a whole field of research; information is desperately needed to provide a data base for these specialists in their professional work. Perhaps in time, we may be able to accurately describe and agree on the characteristics of a model oral interpreter.

The area of training also lacks a solid empirical base. Teachers have very little reliable information on how to teach hearing-impaired children to be good speechreaders. A few researchers (e.g., Cronin, 1979, and Johnson and Kaye, 1979) have taken the lead here. Cronin described a computer-assisted system (DAVID) that uses prepared video-taped segments to teach speechreading to students at the National Technical Institute for the Deaf.

Many people claim that speechreading is an art form and thus cannot be taught. However, many artists fervently believe that art can be taught as well as music and other "intuitive" subjects. Only time and future research will help to reveal whether effective speechreading is a tool potentially available to all or a special skill reserved for a few. It is hoped that the information presented here will hasten the day when educators and researchers feel confident in routinely working as a team to provide this valuable skill to all who may benefit from it.

REFERENCES

Albright, P., N. M. Hipskind, and G. H. Schuckers. 1973. A comparison of visibility and speechreading performance on English and Slurvian. J. Commun. Disord. 6:45–52.

Anderson, R., and G. Faust. 1973. Educational Psychology: The Science of Instruction and Learning. Harper & Row, New York.

Argila, C. A. 1979. A computer simulation of lip-reading. Doctoral dissertation. University of Santo Tomas, Manila, Phillipines.

Armstrong, M. B. S. 1974. Visual training in aural rehabilitation. Doctoral dissertation. University of Illinois, Urbana-Champaign.

Beasly, D. S., and A. K. Flaherty-Rintelmann. 1976. Children's perception of temporally distorted sentential approximations of varying length. Audiology 15:315–325.

Berger, K. W. 1972. Speechreading and principles and methods. National Educational Press, Baltimore.

Berger, K. W., R. A. DePompei, and J. L. Droder. 1970. The effect of distance on speechreading. Ohio J. Speech Hear. 5:115–122.

Berger, K. W., M. Garner, and J. A. Sudman. 1971. The effect of degree of facial exposure and the vertical angle of vision on speechreading performance. Teach. Deaf 69:322–326.

Bever, T. G. 1970. The comprehension and memory of sentences with temporal relations. In: G. B. Flores-D'Arcais and W. J. M. Leveit (eds.), Advances in Psycholinguistics, pp. 33–54. North Holland Publishers, Amsterdam.

Binnie, C. A., A. A. Montgomery, and P. L. Jackson. 1974. Auditory and visual contributions to the perception of consonants. J. Speech Hear. Res. 17:619–630.

Black, J. W., P. P. O'Reilly, and L. Peck. 1963. Self-administered training in lipreading. J. Speech Hear. Dis. 28:183–186.

Blager, F. B., and J. G. Alpiner. 1981. Correlation between visual spatial ability and speechreading. J. Commun. Disord. 14:331–339.

Bode, D. L., G. P. Nerbonne, and L. J. Sahlstrom. 1970. Speechreading and the synthesis of distorted printed sentences. J. Speech Hear. Res. 13:115–121.

Byers, V. W., and L. Lieberman. 1959. Lipreading performance and the rate of the speaker. J. Speech Hear Res. 2:271–276.

Campbell, R., and B. Dodd. 1980. Hearing by eye. Q. J. Exp. Psychol. 32:85–99.

Canestrari, R., and P. E. Ricci-Bitti. 1978. Psychology of the hearing impaired and differential psychological reactions to prosthetic rehabilitation. Audiology 17:32–42.

Carson, P. A., and C. P. Goetzinger. 1975. A study of learning in deaf children. J. Aud. Res. 15:73–80.

Clouser, R. A. 1973. Relationships between visual speech reception and linguistic features of sentences. Doctoral dissertation. The Pennsylvania State University, State College.

Clouser, R. A. 1976. The effect of vowel-consonant ratio and sentence length on lipreading ability. Am. Ann. Deaf. 121:513–518.

Conrad, R. 1977. Lipreading by deaf and hearing children. Br. J. Educ. Psychol. 47:60–65.

Conrad, R. 1979. The Deaf School Child. Harper & Row, London.

Costello, M. R. 1957. A study of speechreading as a developing language process in deaf and in hard of hearing children. Doctoral dissertation. Northwestern University, Chicago.

Cronin, B. 1979. The DAVID system: The development of an interactive video system at NTID. Am. Ann. Deaf. 124:616–618.

De Filippo, C. L. 1981. Memory for articulated sequences and lipreading performance of deaf observers. Doctoral dissertation. Washington University, St. Louis.

De Filippo, C. L. 1982. Memory for articulated sequences and lipreading performance of hearing impaired observers. Volta Rev. 84:134–146.

De Filippo, C. L., and B. L. Scott. 1978. A method for training and evaluating the reception of ongoing speech. J. Acoust. Soc. Am. 63:1,186–1,192.

Denmark, J. C. 1978. Early profound deafness and mental retardation. Br. J. Ment. Subnorm. 24:81–89.

Dodd, B. 1976. The phonological systems of deaf children. J. Speech Hear. Disabil. 41:185–198.

Dodd, B. 1977. The role of vision in the perception of speech. Perception 6:31–40.

Dodd, B. 1980. Interaction of auditory and visual information in speech perception. Br. J. Psychol. 71:541–549.

Dodd, B., and B. Hermelin. 1977. Phonological coding by the prelingually deaf. Percept. Psychophys. 21:413–417.

Erber, N. P. 1971. Effects of distance on visual perception of speech. J. Speech Hear. Res. 14:848–857.

Erber, N. P. 1972. Speech envelope cues as an acoustic aid to lipreading for profoundly deaf children. J. Acoust. Soc. Am. 51:1224–1227.

Erber, N. P. 1974a. Visual perception of speech by deaf children: Recent developments and continuing needs. J. Speech Hear. Dis. 39:178–185.

Erber, N. P. 1974b. Effects of angle, distance, and illumination on visual reception of speech by profoundly deaf children. J. Speech Hear. Res. 17:99–112.

Erber, N. P. 1979. Auditory-visual perception of speech with reduced optical clarity. J. Speech Hear. Res. 22:212–223.

Erber, N. P., and D. A. McMahon. 1976. Effects of sentence context on recognition of words through lipreading by deaf children. J. Speech Hear. Res. 19:112–119.

Evans, L. 1960. Factors related to listening and lipreading. Teach. Deaf 58:417–423.

Farwell, R. M. 1976. Speechreading: A research review. Am. Ann. Deaf. 121:19–30.

Fisher, C. G. 1968. Confusions among visually perceived consonants. J. Speech Hear. Res. 11:796–800.

Fisher, C. G. 1969. The visibility of terminal pitch contour. J. Speech Hear. Res. 12:379–382.

Franks, J. R. 1979. The influence of exaggerated mouth movements on lipreading. Audiol. Hear. Educ. 5:12–16.

Franks, J. R., and J. Kimble. 1972. The confusion of English consonant clusters in lip reading. J. Speech Hear. Res. 15:474–482.

Fulton, R. M. 1964. Comparative assessment of visible difference between voiced and unvoiced words. Master's thesis. Michigan State University, East Lansing.

Garstecki, D. C., and J. J. O'Neill. 1980. Situational cue and strategy influence on speechreading. Scand. Audiol. 9:147–151.

Geers, A. E. 1978. Intonation contour and syntactic structure as predictors of apparent segmentation. J. Exp. Psychol. 4:273–283.

Giolas, T. G., E. C. Butterfield, and J. S. Weaver. 1974. Some motivational correlates of lipreading. J. Speech Hear. Res. 17:18–24.

Goetzinger, C. P. 1963. A study of monocular vs. binocular vision in speechreading. Proc. Int. Congr. Educ. Deaf 326–333.

Goetzinger, C. P. 1972. The psychology of hearing impairment. In: J. Katz (ed.), Handbook of Clinical Audiology, pp. 666–693. Williams & Wilkins, Baltimore.

Goetzinger, C. P. 1978. Word discrimination testing. In J. Katz (ed.), Handbook of Clinical Audiology, 2nd Ed., pp. 149–158. Williams & Wilkins, Baltimore.

Goetzinger, C. P., and G. O'Neill-Proud. 1975. The impact of hearing impairment upon the psychological development of children. J. Aud. Res. 15:1–60.

Gonzalez, K. A. 1982. Speechreading: Do we or don't we? Paper presented at the convention of the Conference of Interpreter Trainers, February 17-20, Tucson.

Green, K. W., W. B. Green, and D. W. Holmes. 1980. Speechreading abilities of young deaf children. Am. Ann. Deaf 125:905–908.

Green, W. B., and K. W. Green. Speechreading: Theory and Application. University Park Press, Baltimore. In preparation.

Green, W. B., K. W. Green, and D. W. Holmes. 1981. Growth of speechreading proficiency in young hearing-impaired children. Volta Rev. 83:389–393.

Greenberg, H. L., and D. L. Bode. 1968. Visual discrimination of consonants. J. Speech Hear. Res. 11:869–874.

Greene, D. 1963. An investigation of the ability of unskilled lipreaders to determine the accented syllable of polysyllabic words. Master's thesis. Michigan State University, East Lansing.

Greene, H. A. 1978. Implications of a comprehensive vision—Screening program for hearing impaired children. Volta Rev. 80:467–475.

Hannah, E. P. 1970. Nuclear stress variation as a factor in speechreading. Paper presented at the convention of ASHA. November 20–23, New York.

Hannah, E. P. 1974. Speechreading: Some linguistic factors. Acta Symbolica 5:57–66.

Hardick, E. J., H. J. Oyer, and P. E. Irion. 1970. Lipreading performance as related to measurements of vision. J. Speech Hear. Res. 13:92–100.

Heider, F. 1943. Acoustic training helps lipreading. Volta Rev. 45:135–138.

Heider, F., and G. M. Heider. 1940. An experimental investigation of lipreading. Psychol. Monogr. 52:124–133.

Hipskind, N. M., 1980. Visual stimuli in communication. In: R. L. Schow and M. A. Nerbonne (eds.), Introduction to Aural Rehabilitation, pp. 111–135. University Park Press, Baltimore.

Hoemann, H. W. 1978. Communicating with Deaf People. University Park Press, Baltimore.

Holmes, D. W., B. Groccia, K. Johnson, and W. Green. 1980. Deaf children's processing of auditory, visual, and combined stimuli. Ear Hear. 1:126–129.

Huggins, A. W. F. 1972. On the perception of temporal phenomena in speech. J. Acoust. Soc. Am. 51:1,279–1,290.

Ivemey, G. 1976. The written syntax of an English deaf child: An exploration in method. Br. J. Disabil. Commun. 11:103–120.

Jackson, P. L., A. A. Montgomery, and C. A. Binnie. 1976. Perceptual dimensions underlying vowel lipreading performance. J. Speech Hear. Res. 19:796–812.

Jackson, W. D. 1967. Effects of lighting condition and mode of presentation on speechreading accuracy of deaf children. Ed.D. dissertation. Indiana University, Indianapolis.

Jacobs, M. A. 1981. Speechreading Strategies, 3rd Ed. Rochester Institute of Technology, Rochester, NY.

Jacobs, M. A., E. W. Clymer, M. Buckley, et al. 1981. Associational Cues. Rochester Institute of Technology, Rochester, NY.

Jeffers, J., and M. Barley. 1978. Speechreading (Lipreading), 6th Ed. Charles C Thomas, Springfield, IL.

Johnson, C. M., and J. H. Kaye. 1979. Behavioral contrast during the acquisition of speech reading. Percept. Motor Skills 49:171–180.

Johnson, D. D., F. Caccamise, A. M. Rothblum, L. F. Hamilton, and M. Howard. 1981. Identification and follow-up of visual impairments in hearing-impaired populations. Am. Ann. Deaf 126:321–360.

Julesz, B., and I. J. Hirsh. 1972. Visual and auditory perception—An essay of comparison. In: E. E. David and P. B. Denes (eds.), Human Communication: A Unified View. McGraw-Hill, New York.

Keil, J. M. 1968. The effects of peripheral visual stimuli on lipreading performance. Doctoral dissertation. Michigan State University, E. Lansing.

Keys, J. W., R. F. Krug, and H. E. Spushler. 1960. Effects and interactions of auditory and visual cues in oral communication. Publication no. EDO 02887. U. S. Dept. of Education, Washington, DC.

Kitson, H. D. 1915. Psychological tests for lipreading ability. Volta Rev. 17:471–476.

Kricos, P. B., and S. A. Lesner. 1982. Differences in visual intelligibility across talkers. Volta Rev. 84:219–225.

Larr, A. L. 1959. Speechreading through closed circuit television. Volta Rev. 61:19–22.

Lehiste, I. 1970. Suprasegmentals. MIT Press, Boston.

Levin, S., and N. P. Erber. 1976. A vision screening program for deaf children. Volta Rev. 78:90–99.

Liberman, A. M., F. S. Cooper, D. P. Shankweiler, and M. Studdert-Kennedy. 1967. Perception of the speech code. Psychol. Rev. 74:431–461.

Liberman, A. M., P. W. Nye, and M. Studdert-Kennedy. 1976. On the perception of phonetic features: Or what do we know about speech which is relevant to the deaf? Paper presented at the convention of the A. G. Bell Assoc., June 18–24, Boston.

Ling, D. 1976. Speech and the Hearing Impaired Child. A. G. Bell Assoc., Washington, DC.

Ling, D., D. Leckie, D. Pollack, J. Simser, and A. Smith. 1981. Syllable reception by hearing-impaired children trained from infancy in auditory-oral programs. Volta Rev. 83:451–457.

Lovering, L. J. 1969. Lipreading performance as a function of visual acuity. Doctoral dissertation. Michigan State University, E. Lansing.

Lowell, E. L. 1959. Research on speechreading: Some relationships to language development and implications for the classroom teacher. Proceedings, 39th meeting of the Convention of American Instructors of the Deaf, pp. 68–73. U. S. Government Printing Office, Washington, DC.

Lowenbraun, S., and J. Q. Affleck. 1970. The ability of deaf children to use syntactic cues for immediate recall of speechread material. Except. Child. 36:735–741.

Lloyd, L. L. 1964. Sentence familiarity as a factor in visual speech reception (lipreading). J. Speech Hear. Dis. 29:409–413.

Lloyd, L. L. and J. G. Price. 1971. Sentence familiarity as a factor in visual speech reception (lipreading) of deaf college students. J. Speech Hear. Res. 29:291–294.

McCormick, B. 1979. A comparison between a two-dimensional and a three-dimensional lipreading test. IRCS Medical science: Biomedical technology 7:324.

MacDonald, J., and H. McGurk. 1978. Visual influences on speech perception processes. Percept. Psychophys. 24:253–257.

Massaro, D. W. 1975. Experimental psychology and information processing. Rand McNally College, Chicago.

Miller, C. A. 1965. Lipreading performance as a function of continuous visual distractions. Master's thesis. Michigan State University, E. Lansing.

Moores, D. F. 1982. Educating the Deaf, 2nd Ed. Houghton Mifflin, Boston.

Morris, D. M. 1944. A study of some of the factors involved in lipreading. Master's thesis. Smith College, Northampton, MA.

Morris, D., P. Collett, P. Marsh, and M. O'Shaughnessy. 1979. Gestures. Stein and Day, New York.

Neely, K. K. 1956. Effects of visual factors on intelligibility of speech. J. Acoust. Soc. Am. 28:1,276–1,277.

Neyhus, A. I., and H. R. Myklebust. 1969. Speechreading failure in deaf children. Final Report. Project No. 6-2582. U.S.O.E, Bureau of Education for the Handicapped, Washington, DC.

Nicholls, G. 1979. Cued speech and the reception of spoken language. Master's thesis. McGill University, Montreal.

Northcott, W. H. 1982. The professional oral interpreter. A. G. Bell Assoc., Washington, DC.

O'Neill, J. J., and H. J. Oyer. 1981. Visual communication for the hard of hearing. Prentice-Hall, Englewood Cliffs, NJ.

Pelson, R. O., and W. F. Prather. 1974. Effects of visual message-related cues, age and hearing impairment on speechreading performance. J. Speech Hear. Res. 17:518–525.

Podmaryeva, N. L. 1974. The comparative discriminability of elements of speech during auditory and visual perception. Defektologiya 3:14–18.

Popelka, G. R., and K. W. Berger. 1971. Gestures and visual speech reception. Am. Ann. Deaf 116:434–436.

Risberg, A. 1974. The importance of prosodic speech elements for the lipreader. In: H. Birk Nielsen and E. Kaupp (eds.), Visual and audio-visual perception of speech, pp. 153–164. The Almquist and Wiksell Periodical Co., Stockholm, Sweden.

Risberg, A., and E. Agelfors. 1978. Information extraction and information processing in speechreading. Speech Transmission Laboratory, Q. Prog. Stat. Rep. (Stockholm) 2–3:62–82.

Romano, P. E., and S. Berlow. 1974. Vision requirements for lipreading. Am. Ann. Deaf 119:383–386.

Rosen, S. M., A. J. Fourcin, and B. C. J. Moore. 1981. Voice pitch as an aid to lipreading. Nature 291:150–152.

Sanders, J. W., and J. E. Coscarelli. 1970. The relationship of visual synthesis skills to lipreading. Am. Ann. Deaf 115:23–26.

Scheinberg, J. S. 1980. Analysis of speechreading cues using an interleaved technique. J. Commun. Dis. 13:489–492.

Sebeok, T. A., and J. V. Sebeok. 1979. Performing animals: Secrets of the trade. Psychol. Today 13:78–91.

Sharp, E. Y. 1972. The relationship of visual closure to speechreading. J. Except. Child. 38:729–734.

Simmons, A. A. 1959. Factors related to lipreading. J. Speech Hear. Res. 2:340–352.

Smith, R. C., J. W. Hillis, and D. W. Kitchen. 1971. The relationship between lipreading and intelligence. J. Acad. Rehab. Audiol. 4:23–31.

Sparks, D. W., L. A. Ardell, M. Bougeois, B. Wiedmer, and D. K. Kuhl. 1979. Investigating the MESA (multipoint electrotactile speech aid): The transmission of connected discourse. J. Acoust. Soc. Am. 65:810–816.

Stoker, R. G. 1980. Temporal pattern recognition and speech perception by the hearing impaired. Doctoral dissertation. McGill University, Montreal, Canada.

Stoker, R. G. 1982. Telecommunications technology and the hearing impaired: Recent research trends and a look into the future. Volta Rev. 84:147–155.

Stone, L. 1957. Facial cues of context in lipreading. John Tracy Clinic Research Papers V. John Tracy Clinic, Los Angeles.

Streng, A. H., R. R. Kretschmer, and L. W. Kretschmer. 1978. Language Learning and Deafness. Grune & Stratton, New York.

Utley, J. 1946a. Factors involved in the teaching and testing of lipreading through the use of motion pictures. Volta Rev. 38:657–659.

Utley, J. 1946b. A test of lipreading ability. J. Speech Hear. Dis. 11:109–116.

Vernon, M. 1972. Mind over mouth: A rationale for total communication. Volta Rev. 74:529–540.

Vernon, M., and P. J. Ottinger. 1980. Psychosocial aspects of hearing impairment. In: R. L. Schow and M. A. Nerbonne (eds.), Introduction to Aural Rehabilitation, pp. 181–205. University Park Press, Baltimore.

Vos, L. J. 1965. The effects of exaggerated and non-exaggerated stimuli on lipreading ability. Master's thesis. Michigan State University, East Lansing.

Wilbur, R. B. 1979. American Sign Language and Sign Systems. University Park Press, Baltimore.

Wingfield, A. 1975. The intonation-syntax interaction: Prosodic features in perceptual processing of sentences. In: A. Cohen and S. G. Nooteboom (eds.), Structure and Process in Speech Perception. Springer-Verlag, Heidelberg.

Winkelaar, R. G., J. Arnold, and E. Johnson. 1976. A comparison of speechreading abilities using live and recorded presentations. Communication Humane (Human Communication) 1(Summer):43–48.

Woodward, M. F. 1957. Linguistic methodology in lipreading research. John Tracy Clinic Research Papers IV. John Tracy Clinic, Los Angeles.

Woodward, M. F., and C. G. Barber. 1960. Phoneme perception in lipreading. J. Speech Hear. Res. 3:212–222.

Wozniak-Kaelin, V. D., and P. L. Jackson. 1979. Visual vowel and diphthong perception from two horizontal viewing angles. J. Speech Hear. Res. 22:354–365.

CHAPTER 7

THE PROCESS OF SPEECHREADING

Walter B. Green and Kathleen W. Green

CONTENTS

VISION IN COMMUNICATION

The role of vision in the communicative process assumes increased importance for individuals who are hearing impaired. The specific aspects of habilitative/rehabilitative programs that seek to enhance various visual skills encompass what is commonly referred to as *speechreading*.

We have perhaps chuckled at the statement, "I can't hear you; I don't have my glasses on." Well, there seems to be truth in the statement. Visual cues are used by the normally hearing person in communicative situations. Everyone can acknowledge the affective tone added to messages by being able to observe facial expressions and hand motions. Experts in the area of interpersonal communication place considerable emphasis on the role of nonverbal (observable) cues. Under adverse listening conditions, normally hearing persons experience an enhancement in speech recognition scores when allowed visual cues (Erber, 1975). Training for the hearing-impaired person will teach him or her to make optimum use of this visual information.

Because language was clearly intended to be learned and understood most efficiently through the auditory channel, the visual sense cannot be expected as a perfect substitute in the presence of hearing loss. It can, however, be developed to supplement residual hearing. For example, when considering the visibility of speech sounds, the clearest information available to the speechreader is place of production (for example, lips closing as with /p/ versus tongue between the teeth as with *th* (Erber, 1972). Because "place" information is often not available auditorily to most hearing-impaired persons (heavy concentration of acoustic energy in the frequency region most often affected by hearing losses), vision can clearly be of assistance (Ling, 1978). Furthermore most people are not aware of the degree to which they use nonverbal cues. By bringing these cues to a conscious level, the hearing-impaired person can discover a wealth of information to supplement his or her residual hearing.

DEFINITIONS OF SPEECHREADING

An understanding of the basic tenets thought to comprise the speech-reading process should initially include a discussion of the now outdated concept of "reading the lips," implicit in the original term, "lipreading." Early attempts to define the nature of speechreading were often viewed in conjunction with the teaching of articulatory skills (Jeffers and Barley, 1971; Green and Green, in preparation); that is, speechreading training was thought to be most efficient when it followed an approach similar to that used for the acquisition of speech sounds. Clinicians stressed the recognition of the movements associated with individual speech sounds, which could then be practiced in words and eventually combined to form sentences. The philosophy that the process was attributable almost entirely to the recognition of movements of the speech mechanism led to the predominant use of the term, lipreading. Inherent in formal definitions of lipreading was the assumption that the peripheral visual mechanism became an acceptable substitute for hearing.

Hearing-impaired persons who engage in speechreading utilize visual information and processes that are much more complex than observing data available only from lip movements. Information can be gained from facial expressions, hand gestures, and body movements as well as the environment. Thus, the term, speechreading, implies not only the recognition of lip movements but the use of other visual cues combined with sufficient synthetic ability to "size up" the communicative situation.

A definition of speechreading should also consider the processes that underlie the skill. The initial activity in the process of speechreading centers on the peripheral coding of visual events by the eye. It is here that physical events are resolved in such a way that higher neurological centers can act on the code in a perceptual fashion. The perceived events must then be associated with language comprehension in order for speechreading to occur.

Speechreading is, indeed, a complex set of skills, developed from the interaction of the visual mechanism with our language base. It is much more than closely watching the lip movements of a given speaker!

SPEECHREADING METHODOLOGIES

The Individual with Postlingual Hearing Loss

The foundation of speechreading instruction, as it has been practiced in this country, can be traced to the early 20th century (Green and Green, in preparation). During this period, several individuals developed philosophies and subsequently published formal instructional procedures and materials for use in teaching postlingually hearing-impaired youth and hard-of-hearing or deafened adults to speechread. The methodologies that developed as a result can be basically classified as *analytic* and *synthetic*.

Analytic   The proponents of an analytic approach advocate that the speechreader "analyze" the individual speech components that comprise words, sentences, and longer utterances. The premise is that recognition of the whole is dependent on recognition of the component parts. The philosophy is reflected in training materials, which place considerable emphasis on syllable recognition.

Mueller-Walle Method   Martha Bruhn (Bruhn, 1955) is credited with introducing the Mueller-Walle method of speechreading in this country in the early 1900s. This analytic approach was developed in Hamburg, Germany, where Miss Bruhn took speechreading lessons. This method consists of grouping sounds on the basis of their visible characteristics. For example, /f/ and /v/ look the same to the speechreader because both require contact between the upper teeth and lower lip. A lesson centers around one of these groups, pairing consonants with different vowels (e.g., fa, fo, foo, fa, and fe). In subsequent lessons, different consonant-vowel syllables are practiced in combination (e.g., *fa-ma; so-fa*). Combining these syllables rapidly and rhythmically is the basis of the practice. These nonsense syllable combinations form the basis for eventual sentence practice.

Jena Method   Developed in Jena, Germany by Karl Brauckmann, the Jena Method was introduced in the United States by Anna Bunger in the mid-1920s (Bunger, 1961). In this approach, speech sounds are classified on the basis of how they are formed rather than how they appear (e.g., one group is "lips" consisting of /b, p, v, f, m, w, wh/).

This is unusual for a speechreading method but consistent with the considerable emphasis placed upon increasing the speechreader's kinesthetic awareness of speech movements by repetition of syllables in unison with the instructor. Basically, the thinking is that self-aware-ness of how a sound is produced facilitates its visual recognition. Consonants are paired with different vowels and practiced in rhythmic drills, stressing different syllables (e.g., "Peter, Peter, pumpkin eater" has the accent on the first syllables with second syllables unaccented). Longer passages are also provided for practice.

Synthetic   At the other end of the continuum are those subscribing to the philosophy that speechreading involves predicting or "filling in" the content of a message from having seen perhaps only some of the parts. The speechreader should be able to "synthesize" the communicative intent of a message from having observed some of it and complete the thought by using personal knowledge of the speaker, situation, and context. It was recognized that language is redundant and that not all information must be received visually (or auditorily) for the meaning to surface. Emphasis is placed on the comprehension (not repeating word-for-word) of sentences and longer passages.

Edward Nitchie (Nitchie, 1912) is generally credited with the de-velopment of the synthetic approach in the early 1900s and with laying the foundation for "modern" speechreading. Nitchie was the first to recognize that the information available to the analytic speechreader is limited "due to the obscurity of many of the movements and, sec-ondly, the rapidity of their formation" (p. 16) and that he or she is more likely to be successful by using intuition and aiming to grasp the essential meaning or gestalt of the sentence or paragraphs. Nitchie believed that speechreading consisted of two skills, the analytic *and* the synthetic, but he placed considerably more emphasis on the latter. Lessons consisted of introducing a movement (the one associated with /p/, /b/, and /m/, for example—lips open from a shut position) and using word drills to contrast that movement with others (e.g., bell; fell; well; shell). Visual recognition of the movement was then practiced in sen-tences and longer passages, in which emphasis was placed on quick perception of visible movements and the use of an intuitive mind (with training) to fill in (e.g., "Did you hear the doorbell ring?" "The bowl broke when it fell on the floor."). Although Nitchie did introduce and advocate the role of synthesizing in speechreading, his materials also reflected some emphasis on analyzing, i.e., recognizing specific move-ments.

The approach developed by Cora and Rose Kinzie (Kinzie, 1920) is generally classified as *synthetic* but could just as accurately be called "eclectic." The Kinzies used the Mueller-Walle sound classification method and the philosophical emphasis on synthesizing developed by Nitchie. Lessons centered around a particular movement, such as /f, v/, with practice at the word, sentence, and story level. Some consider the Kinzies' most significant contribution to be a series of lessons prepared for preschool and school-age hearing-impaired children.

In the 1980s, an emphasis on communication is slowly beginning to replace *formal* instruction in speechreading and/or the dynamic use of residual hearing (Alpiner, 1982; Giolas, 1982; Green and Green, in preparation). Briefly, emphasis is placed on interacting in real communicative settings with pre- and post-discussions of the variety of cues that are available to the hearing-impaired person, who is given knowledge of the many limitations of speechreading as well as strategies to compensate for them. This training includes the opportunity to develop visual awareness, along with any available residual hearing for use in natural conversations.

Factors Affecting Speechreading Performance

The factors that influence speechreading performance have traditionally been categorized into three groups, those related to: 1) the speaker; 2) the environment; and 3) the speechreader (O'Neill and Oyer, 1981; Green and Green, in preparation). A speaker who talks rapidly with minimal lip and jaw movement or in a darkened room will unfavorably affect the speechreader's performance. Similarly, a speechreader who rigidly concentrates on deciphering every word will probably not be as successful as one whose approach is to derive the gist of the message. These groups of variables are discussed in detail in Chapter 6 of this volume, but one aspect deserves attention here.

Experimental investigation concerning speechreader characteristics has probably received the most attention and, unfortunately, has yielded the fewest definitive answers (Davis and Hardick, 1981; Green and Green, in preparation; Oyer and Frankmann, 1975). We still are not certain why some people seem to be naturally good speechreaders and others can only achieve minimal performance following years of training. Although it is known that good speechreaders handle visual tasks well and can synthesize well, there still seem to be other factors, and combinations thereof, that are not understood.

One point does seem to be clear. The speechreading task confronting the prelingually hearing-impaired child is different in nature and scope from that facing the postlingually hearing-impaired child or the adult with an acquired loss. The key to the difference is that speechreading traditionally refers to the visual comprehension of a *known* language. The child with a prelingual hearing loss is likely to have serious language deficits and, therefore, may be using speechreading as one of the facilitators in the language learning process. In this instance, the role of speechreading in the therapeutic plan is understandably unique.

Language knowledge is central to the process of speechreading. There are several limitations involved in the visual recognition of speech (discussed in the next section) and the speechreader must, therefore, avail himself or herself of other cues. Structural and contextual cues are primary among these. Structural cues refer to our knowledge of predictable morpheme ordering in the construction of sentences. For example, "-ly" appears at the end of a word and "the" does not appear at the end of a sentence. This knowledge, albeit unconscious, assists the speechreader. Similarly, language knowledge enables us to predict information if we are familiar with the context. If we successfully speechread "throw," we could pretty safely predict that the other word would be "ball" and not "mall." The greater a person's quantitative and qualitative experience with the language, the better his or her position in being able to fill in what was missed or might not have been visually available. Given this situation, the prelingually hearing-impaired child is at an obvious disadvantage.

The Individual with Prelingual Hearing Loss

Boothroyd (1982) addressed the speechreading difficulty experienced by the hearing-impaired child who is not linguistically competent, and others have supplied evidence to confirm this difficulty. The speechreading performance of the young hearing-impaired child seems to parallel (and is limited by) his or her knowledge of the language. Words are more easily speechread by the prelingually hearing-impaired child than are phrases or sentences (Erber and McMahon, 1976; Green et al., 1980). This probably reflects the typical emphasis on formal vocabulary development and on "words the child must know," found in the training of too many young hearing-impaired children.

Furthermore, nouns are more easily speechread than are verbs or adjectives (Green et al., 1980). This, too, is in accord with the vocabulary training for the hearing-impaired child, i.e., concrete, naming words are often taught first. This type of approach to vocabulary development is currently being replaced with one that has greater emphasis on *function* words in full sentences (including many parts of speech) that will facilitate the child's interaction with his or her environment (Kretschmer and Kretschmer, 1978). Another investigation (Green et al., 1981a) indicated that, after a 1-year period, significant improvement occurred in the speechreading of words and sentences but not phrases, with performance on words remaining best. It can be hypothesized that coarticulation effects (see next section for explanation of coarticulation) render words in longer utterances more difficult to speechread than when they are in isolation and the contextual information in phrases is insufficient to be useful (Erber and McMahon, 1976; Green et al., 1980). Finally, it has been shown that young normally hearing children with no speechreading training performed significantly better on tasks involving the speechreading of words, phrases, and sentences than young hearing-impaired children enrolled in a program that stressed the development of visual skills. The normally hearing children had age-appropriate language skills, which probably contributed to their superior performance (Green et al., 1981b).

Aural Habilitation

The objective of auditory training of very young children is frequently identified as *comprehension* of natural language flowing from natural listening, with careful attention given to the development of aided residual hearing. Listening is a *learned* behavior, a complex skill involving audition, auditory memory, auditory sequencing, and monitoring of one's own voice. Informal speechreading is a natural supplement in many instances. It is "caught," not "taught" (Northcott, 1977).

Ling (1981) cited Erber's (1979) review of seven word recognition studies, in which gains of 1% to 15% were reported when audition was added to speechreading, in support of the value of early, initial auditory-oral programming at the preschool level for children with severe and profound hearing losses. *Auditory-oral* children demonstrate superiority in language usage (spoken, written, and read), compared to *visual-oral* children (Luterman, 1976; Hanners, 1977; Pollack, 1974; Rister, 1975). The assumption is that careful monitoring of a child's performance and progress under any method/mode of communication will ensure continuation or change of setting as deemed appropriate (for discussion, see Chapter 2 of this volume).

In summary, knowledge of the language and use of any remnant of hearing can facilitate its visual recognition. This should be borne in mind when training linguistically delayed, hearing-impaired children.

LIMITATIONS OF SPEECHREADING

Regardless of the level of speechreading performance that has been attained, a person is confronted with certain limitations concerning the amount of information that can be perceived visually. These limitations can be categorized into two classes: *extrinsic* and *intrinsic*. Extrinsic limitations refer to such factors as distance from speaker, which may vary from several feet in normal communicative encounters to one spanning an entire auditorium. The latter would, of course, limit, if not totally obliterate, the amount of available visual information. The intrinsic limitations refer to those associated with the inherent nature of speech production. One example is that many speech sounds are not visually available to the speechreader simply because they are produced in the oral cavity with the teeth obstructing the view.

Extrinsic Limitations

These factors fall into two general groups: 1) factors related to the environment; and 2) factors related to the speaker. Angle, distance, and lighting seem to be the most critical environmental factors. When the angle between the speaker and speechreader is 90° (side view) or greater, considerable visual information that would be available with a 0° angle (frontal view) is lost (Oyer and Frankmann, 1975). Similarly, speechreading the stage actors on Saturday night or the preacher on Sunday morning is not possible when a person is seated in (or toward) the rear of a large room. A darkened room, a shadow on the speaker's face, or sunshine in the viewer's eyes also decrease the amount of information available to the speechreader. However, these environmental factors are, to some extent, under the control of the speechreader. Examples include positioning the speechreader at a reasonable distance from the speaker and, in less formal settings, requesting that the speaker reposition himself or herself if overhead lighting is casting a shadow on his or her face.

Speaker characteristics are also considered to be extrinsic limitations. As discussed in Chapter 7 in this volume, adequate articulatory gestures, facial expressions, and a relatively normal speaking rate create a favorable condition for the speechreader. Speechreaders who mumble and/or speak "a mile a minute" make the speechreader's task frustrating. Under most conditions, the speaker's characteristics are more difficult to change than environmental conditions. Years of habituation have probably contributed to the mumbler's speech pattern, for example, and a request from the speechreader to modify such a pattern will probably not meet with success.

Intrinsic Limitations

Low Visibility of Most Speech Sounds   Many consonants (/l/, /t/, /d/, /s/, (n), /k/, /g/, for example) and all vowels are made by tongue movements in the mouth, with teeth obstructing visibility to varying degrees. Although some of these sounds are reasonably visible when produced in isolation and some have associated visible lip movements (/u/ as in "boot," for example) recall once again that the speechreader is concerned with connected speech. Movements in connected speech are rapid, and when joined with movements of preceding and following sounds, they make a sound that is readily distinct in isolation difficult to identify.

Homophenous (or Viseme) Grouping of Consonants   A group consists of those consonants which share an articulatory movement and, hence, look similar to the speechreader. Examples of homophenous groups include: /p/, /b/, and /m/ (bilabial) and /f/ and /v/ (labiodental). Therefore, although there are 25 consonants having distinct acoustical characteristics, the number is dramatically reduced for the speechreader. The reported number of homophenous groups ranges from 4 to 9 and as high as 12 when a theoretical classification (rather than one based on viewer responses) is used (Binnie et al., 1976; Fisher, 1968; Kricos and Lesner, 1982; Woodward and Barber, 1960). The variability is probably related to the vowel with which the consonant is paired, lighting conditions, and speaker differences among other variables (Binnie et al., 1976; Kricos and Lesner, 1982).

Rapidity of Connected Speech   Articulatory gestures that are highly visible when produced in isolation become obscured in normally rapid connected speech. The *th* as in "thumb" would be classified as a visible sound; the tongue moving between the teeth is clear when the sound is produced in isolation. However, when "thumb," is produced in the context of a sentence, the tongue is rarely protruded to the point of being readily visible. Our aim is to have speech acoustically, not visually, clear, and this can be accomplished without marked tongue protrusion.

Coarticulation Effects   Phonemes that might be visually identifiable in isolation are rendered more obscure when produced in connected speech. Coarticulation refers to the fact that in ongoing speech, phonemes are not produced as distinct units but are strung together with varying degrees of overlapping between adjacent sounds. That is, each sound is influenced by those preceding and following it. This influence affects the acoustical spectrum of the sound as well as its visible characteristics. To illustrate the latter, consider the word, "spoon." If each phoneme is produced in isolation, only the vowel is characterized by lip-rounding. However, lip-rounding appears throughout in the coarticulated word (Daniloff et al., 1980). During the production of the initial consonant blend, the articulatory mechanism is readying itself for the vowel and is still returning from that position during the production of the final consonant.

Consider the impact of these intrinsic variables on the speechreader. First, many sounds are not visible; second, many visible sounds look the same as other sounds; third, the rapidity of normal speech obscures sounds.

Extrinsic and particularly intrinsic limitations illustrate that speech is much less distinct visually than it is acoustically. This, in turn, suggests that the speechreader should and must rely on additional cues in order to be successful. These cues include facial gestures, audition when available, the context of the message, and the situation.

PROGRAM DEVELOPMENT: INDIVIDUAL NEEDS

The emphasis placed upon speechreading in aural habilitation/rehabilitation programs is determined by a number of factors and can only be clearly specified after a careful assessment of individual needs. The primary factors to consider are: 1) age of onset of hearing loss; 2) degree of hearing loss in the speech range; and 3) personal factors, such as educational or vocational needs. An emphasis on visual speech recognition training (analytic) might be appropriate for the adult with an acquired loss but not for a prelingually hearing-impaired child whose speech and language skills are only developing. The severity of the loss and functional residual hearing determine the extent to which speechreading can be aided by auditory cues and consequently influences the form of training initiated (perhaps bisensory—audition and vision); obviously, the more residual hearing to supplement speechreading, the better. Finally, a school-age child may present specific educational problems that speechreading instruction can address as one dimension of supportive service during the school day.

ASSESSMENT OF PREPROGRAM STATUS

A number of formal measures over the years have attempted to measure speechreading proficiency. Such measures are important in planning therapeutic programs as well as in assessing speechreading skill. Generally, tests of speechreading contain items ranging from words to sentences and, in some cases, story material. Many formal speechreading tests are available on film to ensure a degree of objectivity in the presentation of test items (Green and Green, in preparation).

A formal test of speechreading that has proven to be both valid and reliable does not seem to exist (Berger, 1972; Chermak, 1981; Green and Green, in preparation; O'Neill and Oyer, 1981). Utley (1946) developed a filmed measure that included words, sentences, and stories. The Utley Test (1946) (How Well Can You Read Lips?), the most widely used test in the last 30 years, is in limited use in the 1980s. Barley (Jeffers and Barley, 1971) reported a measure that utilized groups of sentences developed at the Central Institute for the Deaf (CID). More recently, CID sentences were employed as a speechreading measure at the National Technical Institute for the Deaf (NTID) (Johnson, 1976). The Diagnostic Test of Speechreading (Myklebust and Neyhus, 1970) was standardized on hearing-impaired children between the ages of 4 and 9 years. This filmed test contains word, phrase, and sentence stimuli. A screening test of speechreading comprised of 100 consonant-vowel syllables was developed by Binnie et al. (1976). A more detailed discussion of available tests can be found in O'Neill and Oyer (1981), Jeffers and Barley (1971), Berger (1972, p. 159), and Green and Green, (in preparation).

There may be times when formal testing may not be possible. In these instances, it is important to realize that informal tests are almost never as accurate as would be desirable and probably cannot be duplicated with any degree of precision. Every effort should be made to employ standardized tests.

Treatment Goals

Following formal assessment, the establishment of realistic treatment goals that identify an individual's specific needs are always subject to revision or changes as the direct service program progresses. (See Table 7.1 for sample treatment goals for a speechreading lesson that is appropriate for adult clients.)

Speechreading programs usually include some training in the so-called analytical area; such as in the recognition of basic movements involved in speech production. In Table 7.1, for example, the goal in Goal 1 is to improve visual identification. The speechreader learns to recognize specific movements associated with speech. For example, he or she can be taught that moving the upper teeth to the lower lip characterizes the /f, v/ sound and then trained to identify words that contain this movement. Ideally, the speechreader acquires the visual perceptual skills necessary to not only recognize various speech movements but also to do so rapidly. A skilled speechreader is thought to have a high degree of visual identification proficiency if he or she shows the ability to shift focus rapidly from far to near and vice versa. He or she is able to use the peripheral visual system to gather detailed information while sustaining visual attention for lengthy periods of time (Jeffers and Barley, 1971). Because speech is often visually ambiguous, training in the recognition of the more visible consonants and vowels may increase the speechreader's visual awareness in general as well as facilitate the recognition of key content words that, in turn, may allow him or her to fill in and understand the remainder of the message.

The second area in speechreading programming involves the development of synthetic, or inductive, skills (see Table 7.1, Goal 2). The goal is to develop the speechreader's willingness to take guesses and/

Table 7.1.   Treatment goals for speechreading lesson appropriate for adult clients

Goal 1	*To improve visual identification: "tongue between the teeth" movement associated with (th)* *Procedure:* Several four-word sets of words are presented—the words are similar except for the initial consonant. The task is to identify the position of the (th) word—first or second, etc. Example: *f*in, *s*in, *th*in, *b*in. *Note:* This activity can also be used by varying the final consonant and can be made more or less difficult by varying the speed of presentation.
Goal 2	*To improve synthetic ability* *Procedure:* Instructor presents an article from a weekly news magazine, which the adult reads regularly. Questions concerning main points follow the presentation. *Note:* Familiarity with the magazine should facilitate the speechreader's task. An additional way to make the task easier is to provide the title of the article and/or key words.
Goal 3:	*To demonstrate usefulness of observing facial expressions and other nonverbal cues* *Procedure:* Instructor presents the same article/story twice—the first time without facial expression and hand/body gestures and the second time including them. *Note:* The adult should perceive a dramatic difference between the two presentations and begin to be more observant of such cues.

or form decisions based on often limited visual information. This is accomplished in two general ways: 1) information-giving; and 2) providing practice material.

First, the speechreader is given certain information and/or demonstrations concerning the predictability of messages. This information centers on knowledge of the topic, the relationship between speakers, the situation, and the context of the message. In order, consider the following four examples:

1. A person attending a lecture on ecology *expects* certain vocabulary words to appear and not others.
2. A student and a professor might be discussing performance in a course and probably not Saturday night activities.

3. Household budget and economic recession are not likely topics to surface when attending a football game (unless a topic shift is made).
4. Words that are likely to follow "I heard the weather report" include "rain," "sun," or "snow."

When the speechreader realizes that in most, if not every, communicative encounter, certain words are predictable and others can be eliminated, he or she can form an appropriate mental set that will better enable him or her to induce the whole message from an often incomplete set of visible clues. Second, practice material for this type of training should, in general, consist of longer passages (not words or phrases), with no emphasis on individual speech sounds or comprehension of every word—only the entire thought or gestalt of the passage matters.

An integral component of synthetic training is describing and/or demonstrating the wealth of information available in facial expressions, hand gestures, and body movements (see Table 7.1, Goal 3). Animated speakers are typically easier to speechread because they provide so much nonverbal information. Although not all speakers fall into this category, the proficient speechreader is alert to any, even minimal, cues of this nature.

Erickson (1978) provided strategies for the speechreader: relax, don't be afraid to guess, and be flexible (be prepared to guess wrong and quickly revise). These three important positive suggestions effectively summarize the role of synthesis or induction in the speechreading process.

Special Consideration

The method and content of speechreading instruction assume different forms, depending upon the premise of meeting the individual's specific needs. There are three common categories of persons with hearing loss: the prelingually hearing-impaired child; the postlingually hearing-impaired child; and the adventitiously hearing-impaired adult. As is apparent, age of acquisition of hearing loss is an important determiner of the content of any individualized program.

Prelingually Hearing-Impaired Child   The critical point concerning this group is that speechreading instruction cannot take precedence over other habilitative procedures, nor can it be conducted in isolation from them. The development of functional language associated with the child's daily activities and the natural times of adult-child interactions should be the focal point around which other procedures revolve. Amplification, preferably binaural, is vital to developing auditory capabilities for language acquisition—the natural method for learning. Informal speechreading is used in conjunction with residual hearing to facilitate language learning (Northcott, 1977). Early attempts should be made to increase the child's auditory attentiveness. Even the very young child should be encouraged to "listen" when spoken to and reinforced when he or she responds appropriately. The message can be repeated if the child looks at the speaker questioningly. Although the very young child with developing language will not be able to associate speech motor patterns with meaningful words, he or she is laying the foundation for formal speechreading instruction if required as he or she matures. Furthermore, the child may, at this early stage, gain information from facial expressions and other visual cues that will facilitate his or her cognitive/language development.

As the child develops a level of competence with language, a more formal approach to speechreading can be used if necessary, with the restriction that it be at the child's functional receptive language level. For example, if recent language stimulation has centered on wh- question comprehension in connection with family pets or a recent vacation, a speechreading lesson can be based on simple, short "who, what, when, and where" questions and the child requested to respond appropriately.

Postlingually Hearing-Impaired Child   The school-age child with an acquired hearing loss may require traditional speechreading instruction designed to develop his or her inductive (predictive or guessing) skills and increase his or her awareness of related (phonemes) and nonspeech-related sentence cues (facial expressions, gestures, etc.) This child is typically a candidate for speechreading training that coordinates with academic subject matter. The increased number of hearing-impaired children being assimilated into the regular classroom has made speechreading instruction a valuable adjunct service. Speechreading lessons can focus on learning to recognize visually new, difficult, or technical vocabulary that the classroom teacher is planning to introduce in lessons as well as supplemental teaching of the concepts such words convey. In addition to preferential seating and classroom amplification, the hearing-impaired child or adolescent is given one more aid to help prevent educational failure. This is most appropriate for children who are middle-school aged and older because they are exposed to sciences, more advanced mathematics, and social studies. It may be supplemented by the services of an oral interpreter as specified in an individual education program (IEP).

Adventitiously Hearing-Impaired Adult   Withdrawal from social activities and frustration and anxiety in communicative settings are common problems faced by an adult as a consequence of hearing loss; yet, such feelings are directly counter to those the successful speechreader brings to communicative encounters. Counseling in the form of information-giving, developing the art of being a good listener, and ensuring some immediate success for the person is beneficial. Group discussions among hearing-impaired persons taking speechreading instruction are also particularly valuable. Knowing others have similar problems and how they have resolved them boosts morale and confidence. Serious and resistant problems of this nature should be referred to appropriate personnel.

Finally, adults often complain of difficulties with a soft-spoken or mumbling spouse and job situations that make speechreading difficult. A relative, friend, or colleague can be given tips concerning communication with the hearing impaired, including a clear light on the speaker's face; a slower rate if speech is very rapid; rephrasing rather than exact repetition if he or she is not understood, etc. Practice in speechreading at a mock board meeting and/or occasional use of an oral interpreter can help with employment situations. The speechreader should be reminded that there will be times when he or she will not succeed, but a confident attitude will enable him or her to ask for a repetition without fear or embarrassment.

In summary, instruction in speechreading can be an effective rehabilitative procedure for both children and adults with varying kinds and degrees of hearing loss. The effectiveness of instruction is likely related to recognition of individual needs and recognition of the limitations of speechreading so that realistic goals are established.

REFERENCES

Alpiner, J. G. 1982. Handbook of Adult Rehabilitative Audiology, 2nd Ed. Williams and Wilkins, Baltimore.

Berger, K. W. 1972. Speechreading Principles and Methods. Herald Publishing, Kent, Ohio.

Binnie, C. A., P. L. Jackson, and A. A. Montgomery. 1976. Visual intelligibility of consonants: A lipreading screening test with implications for aural rehabilitation. J. Speech Hear. Disabil. 41:530–539.

Boothroyd, A. 1982. Hearing Impairments in Young Children. Prentice-Hall, Englewood Cliffs, NJ.

Bruhn, M. E. 1955. The Mueller-Walle Method of Lip-Reading for the Hard of Hearing. The Volta Bureau, Washington, DC.

Bunger, A. M. 1961. Speechreading—Jena Method. Interstate Press, Danville, IL.

Chermak, G. D. 1981. Handbook of Audiological Rehabilitation. Charles C Thomas, Springfield, IL.

Daniloff, R., G. Schuckers, and L. Feth. 1980. The Physiology of Speech and Hearing. Prentice-Hall, Englewood Cliffs, NJ.

Davis, H. (ed.). 1965. The young deaf child: Identification and management. Acta Otolaryngol. Suppl. 206.

Davis, J. M., and E. J. Hardick. 1981. Rehabilitative Audiology for Children and Adults. John Wiley and Sons, New York.

Erber, N. P. 1972. Auditory, visual and auditory-visual recognition of consonants by children with normal and impaired hearing. J. Speech Hear. Res. 15:413–422.

Erber, N. 1975. Auditory-visual perception of speech: A survey. J. Speech Hear. Disabil. 40:481–492.

Erber, N. P. 1979. Speech perception by profoundly hearing-impaired children. J. Speech Hear. Res. 44:255–270.

Erber, N. P., and D. A. McMahon. 1976. Effects of sentence context on recognition of words through lipreading by deaf children. J. Speech Hear. Res. 19:112–119.

Erickson, J. G. 1978. Speech Reading: An Aid to Communication. The Interstate Printers & Publishers, Danville, IL.

Fisher, C. G. 1968. Confusions among visually perceived consonants. J. Speech Hear. Res. 11:796–801.

Giolas, T. G. 1982. Hearing-Handicapped Adults. Prentice-Hall, Englewood Cliffs, NJ.

Green, K. W., W. B. Green, and D. W. Holmes. 1980. Speechreading abilities of young deaf children. Am. Ann. Deaf 125:906–908.

Green, K. W., W. B. Green, and D. W. Holmes. 1981b. Speechreading skills of young normal-hearing and deaf children. Am. Ann. Deaf 126:505–508.

Green, W. B., and K. W. Green. Speechreading: Theory and Application. University Park Press, Baltimore. In preparation.

Green, W. B., K. W. Green, and D. W. Holmes. 1981a. Growth of speechreading proficiency in young hearing-impaired children. Volta Rev. 83: 389–393.

Hanners, B. A. 1977. A study of language skills in 34 hearing-impaired children for whom remediation began before age three. Unpublished doctoral dissertation. Vanderbilt University, Nashville.

Jeffers, J., and M. Barley. 1971. Speechreading (Lipreading). Charles C Thomas, Springfield, IL.

Johnson, D. D. 1976. Communication characteristics of a young deaf adult population: Techniques for evaluating their communication skills. Am. Ann. Deaf 121:409–424.

Kinzie, C. E. 1920. The Kinzie method of speech reading. Volta Rev. 22:909–919.

Kretschmer, R., and L. Kretschmer. 1978. Language Development and Intervention with the Hearing Impaired. University Park Press, Baltimore.

Kricos, P. B., and S. A. Lesner. 1982. Differences in visual intelligibility across talkers. Volta Rev. 84:219–225.

Ling, D. 1978. Aural Rehabilitation. A. G. Bell Assoc., Washington, DC.

Ling, D. 1981. A survey of the present status of methods in English-speaking countries for the development of receptive and expressive oral skills. In: A. M. Mulholland (ed.), Oral Education Today and Tomorrow. Proceedings: First International Symposium on Oral Education, Sint Michielsgestel, Holland, 1979. A. G. Bell Assoc., Washington, DC.

Luterman, D. M. 1976. A comparison of language skills in hearing impaired children trained in a visual/oral method and an auditory oral method. Am. Ann. Deaf 121:389–393.

Myklebust, H. R., and A. I. Neyhus. 1970. Diagnostic Test of Speechreading. Grune and Stratton, New York.

Nitchie, E. B. 1912. Lip Reading Principles and Practice. Frederick P. Stokes, New York.

Northcott, W. H. (ed.). 1977. Curriculum Guide: Hearing-Impaired Children, Birth to Three, and Their Parents. Rev. Ed. A. G. Bell Assoc., Washington, DC.

O'Neill, J. J., and H. J. Oyer. 1981. Visual Communication for the Hearing Impaired. Prentice-Hall, Englewood Cliffs, NJ.

Oyer, H. J., and J. P. Frankmann. 1975. The Aural Rehabilitative Process: A Conceptual Framework Analysis. Holt, Rinehart and Winston, New York.

Pollack, D. 1974. Denver's acoupedic program. Peabody J. Educ. 51:180–185.

Rister, A. 1975. Deaf children in mainstream education. Volta Rev. 77:279–291.

Utley, J. 1946. A test of lipreading ability. J. Speech Hear. Disabil. 11:109–116.

Woodward, M. F., and C. G. Barber. 1960. Phoneme perception in lipreading. J. Speech Hear. Res. 3:212–222.

CHAPTER 8

CURRICULUM CONSIDERATIONS FOR THE INSTRUCTION OF ORAL INTERPRETERS

Linda A. Siple

CONTENTS

Communication between hearing and hearing-impaired (deaf and hard-of-hearing) persons has existed for as long as these two populations have had the need to express and share ideas. Over the centuries, this receptive interchange has been assisted by interpreters who are skilled in understanding the various methods of communication used by hearing and hearing-impaired persons. Prior to the 1960s, the individuals providing this assistance often acquired their skills through involvement with hearing-impaired family members or as educators or clergy serving hearing-impaired persons (Dirst and Caccamise, 1980). Some of these individuals were highly competent and provided a much needed service, but their numbers were few. Others recognized the need for professional education but found no established programs (Babbini, 1965).

    In the 1980s, the education of sign language and/or oral interpreters for the hearing impaired is being addressed by more than 50 educational institutions in 31 states and the District of Columbia. The scope of these programs extends from short-term preparation to a degree at the Associate or Baccalaureate level (Siple, 1982).

In addition, single courses in sign language and/or oral interpreting are currently being offered in speech and hearing centers and other direct service agencies for the hearing impaired. State-affiliated Registry of Interpreters for the Deaf (RID) chapters also periodically offer workshops on sign language or oral interpreting.

Federal legislation has had a significant impact on the profession of interpreting, highlighting the rights of hearing-impaired persons to interpreting services under certain conditions. This, in turn, increased the demand for qualified interpreters and expanded formal educational opportunities for students of interpreting. The Vocational Rehabilitation Act Amendments of 1965 (PL 89-333) state that interpreting services can be authorized as part of the services extended to hearing-impaired clients (Dirst and Caccamise, 1980). The Rehabilitation Act of 1973 (Section 504, PL 93-112) and the Education for All Handicapped Children Act of 1975 (PL 94-142) each address interpreting services as one possible auxiliary aid that may be required to make the educational environment accessible for hearing-impaired students (Hurwitz and Witter, 1979) (see Chapter 4 for a detailed discussion). These laws highlighted the need to ensure the availability of qualified interpreters, which was addressed in part by the establishment of the National Interpreter Training Consortium (NITC) (see Chapter 5 in this volume for additional information).

This consortium was funded by the Rehabilitation Services Administration in 1973 and consisted of six institutions located across the United States (Witter-Merithew, 1980). To "increase the supply of skilled manual and oral interpreters available throughout the country" (Office of Human Development Services, 1980, p. 1), 10 annual interpreter training grants ($50,000 to $100,000 each) were authorized in 1978 under the legislative authority of the Comprehensive Rehabilitative Services Amendment (PL 95-602) to establish new training sites or expand existing interpreter training programs. They were designed to provide short-term preparation and therefore could not meet the entire demand placed on institutions or organizations offering programs of interpreter preparation.

However, as Hurwitz and Witter (1979) identified: ". . . It has often been assumed that interpreting means sign language or that a deaf student must learn sign language to use an interpreter . . ." (p. 144). This realization sparked a new demand for the education and preparation of oral interpreters in order that every hearing-impaired consumer, upon request, may receive interpreting services regardless of his or her preferred mode of communication (Castle, 1982; Dirst and Caccamise, 1980; Northcott, 1979, 1980).

In turn, this awareness prompted many administrators of educational programs for interpreters to provide not only instruction in interpreting American Sign Language and the various English-based forms of sign language but also to expand the existing curriculum to include the formal preparation of oral interpreters. This eclectic approach to the education of interpreters will afford some program graduates broader knowledge and skills, thus leading to increased employment opportunities. Equally important, the graduate will possess a greater appreciation of the heterogeneity and individuality to be found among hearing-impaired persons.

INSTRUCTION IN ORAL INTERPRETING: CURRICULAR DESIGN

Educators of interpreters for the hearing impaired are faced with a very difficult task when designing instruction. The older and more well-established disciplines have a myriad of resources to draw from when designing curriculum. The field of formal preparation of interpreters (sign language and oral) is a very young discipline, and documented methods and resources are meager. The designing process is plagued with a never-ending search for materials and appropriate methods for presenting content areas.

One content area that has received little curricular attention is that of oral interpreting. The relative newness of formal preparation programs coupled with the lack of identified specialists in content areas, materials, methods, and resources have posed many curricular development problems for the multidisciplinary team of coordinator(s), instructors, adjunct lecturers, and hearing-impaired speechreaders required to implement a comprehensive program. The remainder of this chapter addresses the curricular development of a program in oral interpreting and offers an open-ended set of resources and materials to aid in the instructional process.

Instructional Goals and Objectives

Within a comprehensive curriculum, the designer needs to state the purpose of each course or, more specifically, what the student is expected to accomplish as a result of the instruction provided (Dick and Carey, 1978). This purpose can be communicated through the use of instructional goals.

The development of instructional goals for any one course in a comprehensive program designed to prepare professional oral interpreters can be accomplished through an analysis of the actual task to be performed. Each oral interpreter needs to demonstrate proficiency in certain competencies (such as knowledge, skills, and attitudes) in order to function effectively. Contained within the "Guidelines for the Preparation of Oral Interpreters: Support Specialists for Hearing Impaired Individuals" (1979) is an example of one type of task analysis for oral interpreting. It has been used in the following instructional development process. The identified tasks can be grouped into specific content areas related to the coursework required of students in a comprehensive program. Within this analysis, there are eight major content areas that need to be addressed when establishing instructional goals:

1. *Educational Management Systems*   The body of knowledge related to alternative educational environments; aural habilitation/rehabilitation; the process of speechreading; support services and personnel; telecommunication systems; resource networks

2. *Psychosocial Aspects of Deafness*   The body of knowledge related to hearing impairment (mild to profound loss) and hearing-impaired consumers, which includes cultural, psychological, social, and audiological aspects of individual adaptation to hearing loss; attitudes toward oralism

3. *Theory and Practice of Interpreting*   The body of knowledge related to the oral interpreting process (Spoken to Visible (S/V); Visible to Spoken (V/S)), which includes communication assessment (receptive and expressive); adaptive interpreting techniques; and situational and environmental considerations and modifications

4. *Professional Aspects of Interpreting*   The body of knowledge related to oral interpreting, which includes inter/intrapersonal communication skills; ethical behavior; professional credentials; materials and resources; career options; professional growth opportunities; and resource networks

5. *Oral Transliteration (Spoken-to-Visible)*   The psychomotor task of receiving an auditory message from a speaker and reproducing it verbatim, with or without voice, using clear lip movements and natural gestures

6. *Oral Interpretation (Spoken-to-Visible)*   The psychomotor task of receiving an auditory message from a speaker and reproducing it with occasional or substantial rephrasing of the speaker's remarks, presented with or without voice and always with natural lip movements

7. *Oral Transliteration (Visible-to-Spoken)*   The psychomotor task of receiving an auditory and/or visual message from a hearing-impaired (deaf or hard-of-hearing) speaker who may or may not use understandable voiced speech, standard inflectional patterns and grammatical constructions, with vocal repetition of his or her exact words

8. *Oral Interpretation (Visible-to-Spoken)*   The psychomotor task of receiving an auditory and/or visual message from a hearing-impaired speaker who may or may not use understandable voiced speech, standard inflectional patterns and grammatical construction, and verbally rephrasing the message while retaining its meaning

Once instructional goals have been formulated in the eight major content areas, a decision can be made on how the student will reach these goals. Course objectives, which are measurable, communicate what must be specifically done in order to satisfy the more global instructional goals. In addition to presenting statements of expected performance to the student, these objectives also assist the instructor in determining the relevance of planned instruction within a particular course (Dick and Carey, 1978).

The following instructional goals and related objectives offer a framework for a comprehensive program in oral transliteration and interpretation (Bishop, 1979; Cassell, in preparation; Guidelines, 1979; Northcott et al., 1980; Ross, 1978; Siple, in preparation):

Content Area: Educational Management Systems
Goal 1.0
   Given class discussions, readings, and site visitations, the student will demonstrate with 75% accuracy knowledge of major considerations affecting educational programming and supplemental services for hearing-impaired children and youth.
Objectives:
   1.1   Given lectures and class discussions, the student will identify with 90% accuracy six alternative educational placements (settings) that are currently available to accomodate to individual differences in school-age children and youths with hearing loss.
   1.2   Given instruction and demonstrations of various types of individual hearing aids, the student will demonstrate knowledge of the range of functional usage—their benefits and limitations.
   1.3   Given panel demonstrations, lectures, and readings, the student will describe the primary focus of three major educational methods of instruction in use with hearing-impaired children in the United States: Oral Method (Auditory/Verbal or Visual/Oral); Rochester Method; and the Simultaneous (or Combined) Method.
   1.4   Given panel discussions and readings involving recent federal legislation affecting the handicapped, the student will de-

scribe the impact on the philosophy of mainstreaming and the profession of interpreting.

1.5   Given lectures and opportunities for a variety of direct contacts with speechreaders, the student will identify six major factors involved in the process of speechreading.

1.6   Given three different telecommunication devices (standard teletype, digital display, e.g., MCM, and screen display, e.g., C-Phone) the student will demonstrate knowledge of operational procedures.

Content Area: *Psychosocial Aspects of Deafness*
Goal 2.0

Given readings, lectures, class discussions, and observations of hearing-impaired individuals that relate to cultural, psychological, social, and audiological aspects of adaptation to hearing loss, the student will identify labels and generalizations that interfere with the recognition of hereterogeneity of personality characteristics of individuals with significant hearing loss.

Objectives

2.1   Given a list of acronyms of the major organizations and associations of and for the hearing impaired, the student will identify with 80% accuracy the full name, purpose, major activities, and publication (if any) of each.

2.2   Given statements related to the psychosocial aspects of deafness, the student will identify overgeneralizations or inaccuracies, rewrite the statements to be accurate, then state any evidence, including references to support each rewritten statement.

2.3   Given lectures, readings, and firsthand contact with individuals from three basic classifications of population with significant hearing loss, based on etiology and age of onset of deafness, the student will be prepared to discuss the heterogeneity of individuals within each classification and some predictable generalizations about each group as distinct from others.

2.4   Following readings, observation, and volunteer role play, the student will participate in group discussions to analyze his or her feelings and attitudes about oralism and oral persons known by class members.

Content Area: *Theory and Practice of Interpreting*
Goal 3.0

Given class discussions and readings, the student will demonstrate with 75% accuracy knowledge of accurate communication assessment (prior to and during the assignment), principles of interpreting in various situations, and principles of managing the physical environment.

Objectives:

3.1 Given videotapes of various hearing-impaired individuals, the student will generate a recommendation of the most appropriate communication techniques to be used while oral interpreting, e.g., verbatim or paraphrased presentation of message; mirror-writing (air-writing); occasional use of pad and pencil; use of gestures; or use of fingerspelling to clarify words or phrases.

3.2 Given class discussions and readings, the student will identify and demonstrate the principles of oral transliteration (verbatim repetition) and oral interpreting (paraphrased repetition) as they apply to various specialized situations (e.g., telephone, classroom, medical, legal, or religious).

3.3 Given class discussions and readings, the student will identify the principles of dress as they apply to the task of oral interpreting.

3.4 Given class discussions and reading, the student will identify in various diagrams of typical interpreting environments, the most appropriate position for an oral interpreter and indicate adaptions of the physical environment to facilitate oral interpreting (e.g., lighting or background) and voice inflection that reflects the mood and intent of the speaker.

Videotape Criteria:

Ten minutes in length

Conversational pace (120–140 wpm)

   speech patterns that are approximately 50% discernible to the average hearing individual

A message that contains a minimum of 15 grammatical errors in the message

A message that contains a minimum of 15 errors in pronunciation

A message that reflects inverted English syntax

Content Area: *Professional Aspects of Interpreting*

Goal 4.0

Given written examinations, role play situations, and written projects, the student will demonstrate with 75% accuracy, knowledge and application of the four major dimensions of professional interpreting.

Objectives:

4.1 Given role-play situations or descriptions of situations that challenge the concepts contained within the RID Code of

Ethics, the student will generate a recommendation describing the most appropriate action to be taken (Note: Appropriate as deemed by the instructor).

4.2   Given class discussions and readings, the student will generate a written professional development plan that includes options for continued education within the field of oral interpreting; knowledge of professional organizations and potential benefits from membership; techniques for self-critique and evaluation of technical skills; an explanation of the RID Certification Evaluation System; and rationale for seeking formal certification.

4.3   Given class discussions and readings, the student will generate a written project that demonstrates knowledge of career opportunities and business practices in the profession of oral interpreting. The project will include a resumé and letter of introduction; name and location of industrial and professional environments; agencies and institutions that commonly utilize interpreting services; current range of salary/hourly rate for interpreters; billing procedures; record-keeping procedures; and considerations in filing federal and state income taxes.

4.4   Given class discussions and readings, the student will identify and demonstrate the principles of inter/intrapersonal communication skills (hearing and hearing-impaired individuals).

Content Area: *Spoken-to-Visible Oral Transliteration (S/V)—Verbatim*

Goal 5.0

Given a spoken message recorded on audiotape at 140 words per minute, the student will give a verbatim repetition of the speaker's remarks, demonstrating 75% accuracy in each of the following major skill areas (objectives):

Objectives—Given spoken messages recorded on audiotape at 90, 100, 120, 130, and 140 words per minute, the student will repeat the precise words of the speaker, demonstrating his or her ability to:

5.1   Produce inaudible and audible speech, which demonstrates the principles of clear speech production and articulation

5.2   Produce facial expressions that reflects the mood and intent of the speaker

5.3   Produce natural gestures and body language to support the intent of the message

Content Area: *Spoken-to-Visible Oral Interpretation (S/V)—Paraphrase*

Goal 6.0

Given a spoken message recorded on audiotape at 140 words per minute, the student will interpret (paraphrase) with or without voice, demonstrating 75% accuracy in employment of adaptive techniques and nonverbal behavior to increase consumer comprehension.

Objectives—Given spoken messages recorded on audiotape at 90, 100, 120, 130, and 140 words per minute the student will demonstrate 75% accuracy in his or her ability to:

6.1 Repeat the message, with and without voice, utilizing the principles of clear speech production and articulation
6.2 Identify and clarify low visibility words or phrases
6.3 Apply paraphrasing techniques of oral interpreting, which maintain the intent of the message
6.4 Produce facial expressions that reflect the mood and intent of the speaker.
6.5 Produce natural gestures and body language that support the intent of the message.

Audiotape Criteria (for Transliteration and Interpretation):

Ten minutes in length

A message that contains a minimum of 60 words or phrases in context that are considered to have low visibility or ambiguity to an average speechreader

A message that contains the remarks of a minimum of two speakers

Voices of speakers that convey a variety of emotions

A message that contains numbers or letters, names of people/organizations, information which is conducive to visual representation, and questions.

Content Area: *Visible-to-Spoken Oral Transliteration (V/S)—Verbatim*

Goal 7.0

Given a videotape of a hearing-impaired individual who is presenting a lecture orally, the student will vocally repeat the message verbatim demonstrating 75% accuracy in the following three major skill areas:

Objectives—Given videotapes of one or more hearing-impaired individuals presenting lectures orally in which they use speech patterns that range from clear to difficult to discern, the student will vocally repeat the message verbatim, demonstrating 75% accuracy in his or her ability to:

7.1   Speechread and/or auditorily receive the message of a hearing-impaired individual, who may demonstrate a variety of deviations from average speech patterns.

7.2   Convey the original message verbatim

7.3   Employ public speaking skills, including appropriate volume, pronunciation, articulation, and voice inflection that reflect the mood and intent of the speaker

Videotape Criteria:

Ten minutes in length

Conversational pace (120 to 140 words per minute)

Speech patterns that are approximately 50% comprehensible to the average hearing individual

A message that contains a minimum of 15 grammatical errors

A message that contains a minimum of five errors in pronunciation

A message that reflects appropriate English syntax

Content   Area: Visible-to-Spoken   Oral   Interpreting   (V/S)—Paraphrasing

Goal 8.0

Given a videotape of a hearing-impaired individual who is presenting a lecture orally, the student will vocally interpret (paraphrase) the message, demonstrating 75% accuracy in the following three major skill areas.

Objectives—Given videotapes of one or more hearing-impaired individuals presenting a lecture verbally, in which speech patterns range from clear to difficult to discern, the student will vocally interpret (paraphrase) the message, demonstrating 75% accuracy in his or her ability to:

8.1   Speechread hearing-impaired individuals, who may demonstrate a variety of deviations from average speech patterns

8.2   Demonstrate paraphrasing techniques and appropriate English grammatical construction while accurately conveying the message content

8.3   Employ public speaking skills that demonstrate appropriate rhythm and tone of voice, pronunciation, articulation, and natural gestures

Videotape Criteria:

Ten minutes in length

Conversational pace (120 to 140 words per minute)

Speech patterns that are approximately 50% discernible to the average hearing individual

A message which contains a minimum of 15 grammatical errors in the message

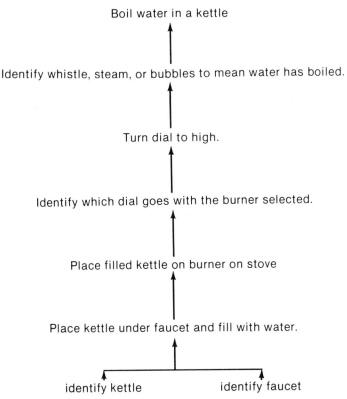

Figure 8.1   Representation of a goal and an instructional hierarchy of skills.

A minimum of 15 pronunciation errors
A message that reflects inverted English syntax

Instructional Analysis

One of the major elements of instructional design is the identification or analysis of the precise skills and knowledge needed to achieve stated instructional goals. This analysis assists the instructor in making the transition from goals to objectives and can also identify the possible sequence of instruction; the method of analysis can vary, depending on the complexity of the tasks stated in the instructional goals (Dick and Carey, 1978). When the central question, "What does the student need to already know before he or she can learn this skill?" is asked each time a new task is identified, a list of subordinate skills can be generated and shaped into a hierarchy or sequence of instructional events. For example, Figure 8.1 shows what the hierarchy would be if the instructional goal is for the student to "boil water in a kettle." As indicated, the breakdown of skills is not always linear. The act of placing the kettle under the faucet does require the student to first identify a kettle and a sink, but the order of identification does not affect the outcome.

The creation of instructional hierarchies can: 1) help the instructor to identify subordinate skills which were initially overlooked and can offer a possible explanation as to why a previously taught skill was not demonstrated at an acceptable level; 2) determine the entry behaviors of the potential student population; or 3) continue the hierarchy until it matches the entry behaviors of the identified student population. This will ensure that the student receives all the instruction necessary in order to reach the instructional goals.

Hierarchies do not identify the amount of time required for a student to achieve a specific level of instruction, however. For example, it will probably take much less time for a student to *memorize* a list of 10 terms and their definitions than to *generate* a recommendation regarding communication assessment. The verbs used to describe the desired skills should reflect the complexity of a task and suggest a possible timeline (Kemp, 1977).

To utilize the instructional goals for Spoken-to-Visible Oral Transliteration—Verbatim and Spoken-to-Visible Oral Interpretation—Paraphrasing, the hierarchy depicted in Figures 8.2 through 8.5 shows one possible instructional analysis in which each instructional goal breaks down into major objectives. This analysis does not suggest that any one of the four goals must be achieved first before moving to the next. Instruction directed toward all four goals can occur simultaneously as long as the student possesses the prerequisite knowledge or skill first.

ENTRY CHARACTERISTICS

One of the fundamental mistakes that occurs when instructional curriculum is designed (although it may seem to be very effective on the surface) is the failure to analyze the characteristics of students who are newly enrolled. The result is often either overestimation of the students' abilities, which can create a very frustrating learning environment, or underestimation, which can lead a student to feel bored or lack the motivation to learn.

Unfortunately, many times the target population is analyzed for prerequisite skills and knowledge after the instruction has been developed and tested on a group of students. This type of "buckshot" approach to instruction becomes very costly and can have a serious negative impact on the educational potential of individual students.

1.1   Given spoken messages recorded on audiotape at 90, 100, 120, 130, and 140 words per minute, the student will transliterate, demonstrating his or her ability to reproduce inaudible speech that utilizes the principles of clear speech production and articulation.

↑

Demonstrate the principles of articulation and natural speech rhythm while inaudibly reproducing a lecture verbatim (externally generated message).

↑

Demonstrate the principles of articulation and natural speech rhythm while inaudibly reproducing sentences and paragraphs (externally generated message).

↑

Demonstrate the principles of articulation and natural rhythm of speech while audibly and inaudibly producing words, phrases, and sentences (self-generated message).

↑

Demonstrate the proper placement of the tongue, lips, teeth, etc., when audibly and inaudibly producing isolated vowels, consonants, and diphthongs.

Figure 8.2   Spoken-to-Visible Oral Transliteration—Verbatim: Goal and major objectives to demonstrate principles of clear speech production and articulation.

An early analysis of the target population leads to a listing of entry behaviors that the student must possess in order to participate in a particular instructional activity and reach the instructional goals (e.g., a student must be able to identify elements of speech that "look alike" on the lips, such as *p, b,* and *m,* before being able to recognize and label homophenous words, such as "*pat,*" "*bat,*" "*ban,*" and "*bad*").

In the 1980s, individuals who seek formal preparation in the area of oral interpreting seem to come from widely varying backgrounds and, therefore, possess very different entry skills and knowledge. A review of the characteristics of individuals who have participated in oral interpreter preparation programs at the National Technical Institute for the Deaf at the Rochester Institute of Technology reveals three major student populations:

1.2   Given spoken messages recorded on audiotape at 90, 100, 130, and 140 words per minute, the student will orally interpret, demonstrating his or her ability to identify and clarify words and phrases that have low visibility.

Demonstrate the ability to combine techniques to clarify words and phrases that have low visibility while inaudibly reproducing a lecture.

| Demonstrate the technique of word substitution through script analysis. | Demonstrate the technique of adding word clarifiers through script analysis. | Demonstrate the technique of using sentence reorganization (placing main idea first) through script analysis. |

Identify synonyms that are highly visible.

Identify strategies for dealing with words/phrases that have low visibility.

Identify the common characteristics of words/phrases that have low visibility.

Identify words/phrases that have low visibility.

Identify the various articulatory positions of the elements of speech.

Figure 8.3   Spoken-to-Visible Oral Interpretation—Paraphrasing: Goal and major objectives to demonstrate adaptive techniques for purpose of clarification.

Figure 8.4   Spoken-to-Visible Oral Transliteration—Verbatim: Goal and major objectives to demonstrate nonverbal support techniques (natural gestures and body language).

1.3   Given spoken messages recorded on audiotape at 90, 100, 120, 130, and 140 words per minute, the student will transliterate with or without voice, demonstrating his or her ability to produce natural gestures and body language that support the intent of the message.

↑   ↑   ↑

Demonstrate natural gestures that convey words or concepts while orally transliterating, e.g., "farewell", "come here!" (externally generated).

Demonstrate natural gestures that convey numbers or letters while orally transliterating, e.g., air-writing, finger-spelling, indication of number of fingers (externally generated).

Demonstrate natural gestures that convey word separations while orally transliterating, e.g., acronym of organization (externally generated).

↑

Demonstrate natural gestures that convey the above three categories (self-generated).

↑

Identify natural gestures that do not interfere with speechreading.

↑

Identify natural gestures used in everyday conversations.

↑

Differentiate between a natural gesture and a sign.

↑   ↑   ↑

Demonstrate natural gestures that convey the organization of concepts while orally transliterating, e.g., vertical listings, categories (externally generated).

Demonstrate natural gestures that convey change in speaker or location of information source while orally transliterating, e.g., "on the board..." (externally generated).

Demonstrate natural gestures and facial expressions that convey questions, emotions, etc., while orally transliterating (externally generated).

↑

Demonstrate natural gestures and body movements that convey the above three categories (self-generated).

↑

Identify body shifts/movements that are distracting to a speechreader, e.g., head-bobbing.

↑

Identify body shifts/movements that supplement natural gestures.

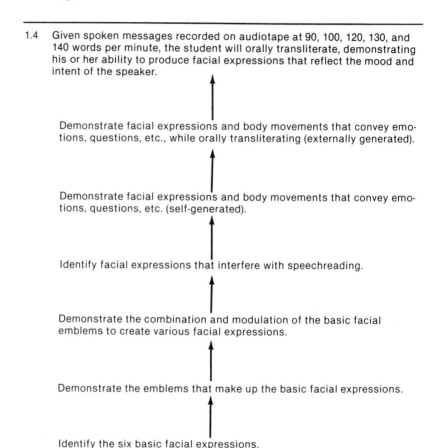

1.4   Given spoken messages recorded on audiotape at 90, 100, 120, 130, and 140 words per minute, the student will orally transliterate, demonstrating his or her ability to produce facial expressions that reflect the mood and intent of the speaker.

Demonstrate facial expressions and body movements that convey emotions, questions, etc., while orally transliterating (externally generated).

Demonstrate facial expressions and body movements that convey emotions, questions, etc. (self-generated).

Identify facial expressions that interfere with speechreading.

Demonstrate the combination and modulation of the basic facial emblems to create various facial expressions.

Demonstrate the emblems that make up the basic facial expressions.

Identify the six basic facial expressions.

Figure 8.5   Spoken-to-Visible Oral Transliteration—Verbatim: Goal and major objectives to demonstrate nonverbal support techniques (facial expressions).

1. Professional Sign Language Interpreters, who hold various levels of sign language certification from the RID, most of whom have participated in a formal Sign Language Interpreter preparation program
2. Professionals working in the field of hearing impairment, e.g., speech pathologists, audiologists, and instructors of the hearing impaired
3. Professionals or individuals who do not possess formal education in the field of hearing impairment but who do draw from an experiential base, e.g., parents/siblings of hearing-impaired individuals

The widely varying amounts of sustained contact with and knowledge related to hearing-impaired speechreaders and the task of interpreting makes each group discrete from the other two.

One way of dealing with this potential problem is to seek a homogeneous group of students based on formal criteria for entrance into a comprehensive program.

Another possible solution would be to individualize instruction and assign varying amounts of practicum, observation, and/or interaction with hearing-impaired speechreaders. This would allow the student to progress at his or her own pace.

The entry characteristics of the student population coupled with the ultimate educational goal of the institution greatly influence the length of an educational program. Appendices A and B suggest entry criteria and content for a 1-week course and a 2-year academic degree (AAS) program in oral interpreting, respectively.

Testing

Testing instruments designed to measure instructional objectives are important; they evaluate the progress of a student and supply the instructor with information about the effectiveness of instruction. For this reason, test items need to match the stated performance and criterion (Dick and Carey, 1978).

Instructors can utilize four basic types of tests (Dick and Carey, 1978):

1. Entry behavior tests, which measure the skills and/or knowledge that are critical for entering the instructional activity
2. Pretests, which measure the amount of skill and/or knowledge the students already possess about the topic to be taught
3. Post-tests, which are given after instruction and measure all of the specified objectives
4. Embedded tests, which are given throughout instruction and measure small sets of objectives.

When embedded tests are given immediately following instruction they serve as an extension of it, thus helping a student to transform the information into what will be required later on the post-test and to increase the conditions of recall (Anderson and Faust, 1973).

Testing for the knowledge components of oral interpreting can be accomplished by reviewing the stated performance in each objective. The actual type of test item to be used (fill-in-the-blank, true/false, etc.) depends on the performance required. Dick and Carey (1978) provided a helpful graph to match performance with the type of test items that should be used.

The testing instrument designed to measure the psychomotor skills involved in oral interpreting requires special attention and implementation. The area of oral transliteration—verbatim, or interpretation—paraphrasing, needs a carefully written script that addresses the performance criteria stated earlier. For example, one test item might be the use of a body shift and/or pointing with the index finger to indicate a change of speaker. If the script only presents this opportunity once and the student does not perform the expected behavior, it cannot be assumed that the behavior was not learned. However, if the script allows for this behavior to occur five times and the student performs the behavior four out of the five, or 80% of the time, he or she has satisfied the objective.

Each item to be tested and the expected behavioral outcome should be identified on the script. For example, the following sentence might be used to assess facial expression for questions and the use of adaptive techniques:

DO YOU	ENJOY SKIING?
_____ yes _____ no	_____ yes _____ no
(Question shown) i.e., raised eyebrows	(Adaptive technique used?) i.e., added, "in the wintertime" or "downhill or cross country"

When this script is given to the student, it not only shows how well he or she did but also suggests possible improvements.

Field tests can be conducted by having the script presented orally to several hearing-impaired speechreaders utilizing a minimum of support mechanisms. Analyzing which words or phrases were clear because of their context, which were not, and seeking answers to appropriate ways in which such words and phrases can be clarified can help the instructor to gain insight for designing an effective testing instrument.

When administering an audiotaped script, it is useful to videotape the student so that when feedback is given, strengths or areas in need of improvement can be readily pointed out.

It is helpful to select a qualified hearing-impaired individual who can help to evaluate the students' abilities during testing because a hearing individual, although skilled in the task of oral interpreting or having an extensive background in speech production, does not need to depend on speechreading as his or her means of receiving communication and might possibly overlook or overemphasize specific content areas.

The creation of a script for the task of Visible-to-Spoken oral interpreting can be accomplished by utilizing the criteria stated earlier. Again, a carefully written script should be used, and the student should be audiotaped for the purpose of feedback. Given the nature of this task, a qualified hearing individual will need to be present to evaluate the student's performance.

Instructional Team

The implementation of a comprehensive program requires careful orchestration of an instructional team. The program coordinator should identify a team of highly qualified professionals and instructional assistants who will provide the student with new perspectives and current knowledge and practices within the field of oral interpreting and related areas. An effective instructional team consists of individuals functioning in four major roles:

1. *The Permanent Faculty*   These individuals should possess not only academic credentials in communication sciences (speech-language and hearing) and educational psychology, but also extensive experience and professional certification in oral interpreting, i.e., OIC:C for hearing faculty members and OIC:V/S for hearing-impaired faculty members. These individuals need to address the major responsibility for the design and instruction of curriculum, development of media resources, and the coordination and supervision of practicum.
2. *Instructional Assistants*   Several of these individuals are needed to provide support to the program faculty. Hearing and hearing-impaired assistants may function as self-instruction lab coordinators, media specialists, and/or supervisors of the instructional and critique processes. Local hearing and speech centers or audiology clinics are excellent resources for obtaining additional instructors.
3. *Adjunct faculty*   Speechreading instructors, speech pathologists, and audiologists can provide instruction that will greatly enhance the student's body of knowledge and theory.
4. *Guest Lecturers*   These community resource specialists provide the student with the opportunity to gain new insights. Suggested guest lecturers may include members of the local ODAS chapter; chairperson for the local RID Evaluation Committee; certified oral interpreters; potential normally hearing and hearing-impaired consumers; and local experts in telecommunication systems and signaling devices, public speaking techniques, stress management, resumé-writing, and drama/mime techniques.

Evaluation and Revision

Once a comprehensive educational curriculum has been fully developed, it is important to determine how well the curriculum is serving its objectives. A *formative evaluation* should take place during the developmental stages of each course where an instructor identifies weaknesses in the instruction or areas that need to be revised. A formative evaluation, as Kemp (1977) stated

> . . . should relate not only to the suitability of objectives, subject content, learning methods, and materials, but also to the roles of personnel, the use of facilities and equipment, schedules, and other factors that all together affect the optimum performance for achievement of the objectives. (p. 98)

After the formative evaluation is completed and the necessary revisions are made, it is then important to determine the effectiveness of each course when it is in full use. This process is called a *summative evaluation* (for an in-depth analysis of how to conduct both forms of evaluation, see Dick and Carey, 1978).

CONCLUSION

In the current field of formal preparation of oral interpreters for service to hearing-impaired speechreaders, the instructor not only lectures and demonstrates, but also functions as the curriculum designer, resource person, media specialist, evaluator, and reviser. Only after all of the above roles have been effectively accomplished can the instructor become the implementer. The instructional design suggestions presented in this chapter are designed to assist instructors in meeting each of their multi-role responsibilities.

ACKNOWLEDGMENTS

The materials herein were produced in the course of an agreement between the Rochester Institute of Technology and the U.S. Department of Education.

REFERENCES

Anderson, R., and G. Faust. 1973. Educational Psychology. Harper and Row, New York.
Babbini, B. 1965. Program for training interpreters. In: S. P. Quigley (ed.), Interpreting for Deaf People, pp. 105–127. U.S. Department of Health, Education, and Welfare, Washington, DC.
Bishop, M. E. (ed.). 1979. Mainstreaming: Practical Ideas for Educating Hearing-Impaired Students. A. G. Bell Assoc., Washington, DC.
Cassell, D. Aspects of Professional Interpreting. National Technical Institute for the Deaf at Rochester Institute of Technology. Rochester, NY. In preparation.
Castle, W. E. 1982. Oral interpreting. RID Views. VII (May/June): 8.
Dick, W., and L. Carey. 1978. The Systematic Design of Instruction. Scott, Foresman and Company, Glenview, Il.

Dirst, R., and F. Caccamise. 1980. Introduction. In: F. Caccamise, D. Dirst, R. D. DeVries et al. (eds.), Introduction to Interpreting, pp. 1–9. RID, Silver Spring, MD.

Gonzalez, K. 1981. Why oral interpreting? RID Views VII:6.

Guidelines for the preparation of oral interpreters: Support specialists for the hearing impaired. 1979. Volta Rev. 81:135–145.

Hurwitz, T., and A. Witter. 1979. Principles of interpreting in an educational environment. In: M. E. Bishop (ed.), Practical Ideas for Educating Hearing-Impaired Students, pp. 135–149. A. G. Bell Assoc., Washington, DC.

Kemp, J. 1977. Instructional Design: A Plan for Unit and Course Development, 2nd Ed. Fearon Publishers, Belmont, CA.

Northcott, W. H. 1977. The oral interpreter: A necessary support specialist for the hearing impaired. Volta Rev. 79:136–144.

Northcott, W. H. 1979. Introduction. In: Guidelines for the Preparation of Oral Interpreters, pp. 135–138. Volta Rev. 81:135–145.

Northcott, W. H. 1980. Implications of mainstreaming for the education of hearing-impaired children in the 1980's. A. G. Bell Assoc., Washington, DC.

Northcott, W. H. 1982. The professional oral interpreter: A support specialist for the speechreader (lipreader). A. G. Bell Assoc., Washington, DC.

Northcott, W. H., R. Carlson, D. Flack, H. Draving, and M. Schommer. 1980. Oral interpreting. In: F. Caccamise et al. (eds.), Introduction to Interpreting, pp. 32–36. RID, Silver Spring, MD.

Office of Human Development Services. 1980. Program information for training program for interpreters for deaf individuals. Division of Manpower Development, Rehabilitation Services Administration, Department of Health, Education and Welfare, Washington, DC.

Ross, M., and T. G. Giolas (eds.). 1978. Auditory Management of Hearing-Impaired Children. University Park Press, Baltimore.

Siple, L. 1982. Resource Guide: Interpreter Training Programs. RID and Conference of Interpreter Trainers, Silver Spring, MD.

Siple, L. Theory and Practice of Interpreting. National Technical Institute for the Deaf at Rochester Institute of Technology. In preparation.

Wells, J. Aspects of Deafness. National Technical Institute for the Deaf at Rochester Institute of Technology. In preparation.

Witter-Merithew, A. 1980. Training of interpreters: Interpreter preparation—past, present, and future. In: F. Caccamise et al. (eds.), Introduction to Interpreting. RID, Silver Spring MD.

APPENDIX A

Suggested Curriculum Content: One-Week Course on Oral Interpreting

ENTRY CRITERIA

The following criteria have been developed by the Alexander Graham Bell Association for the Deaf, Committee on Oral Interpreting for the regional Volta Series courses designed for the instruction and preparation of oral interpreters (Summer, 1983):

1. a. A minimum of 250 hours of experience with hearing-impaired persons who primarily use spoken language for expressive and receptive communication.

    or

    b. A minimum of 25 hours interpreting experience
2. Two years of college
3. Commitment to completion of the entire course
4. Commitment to pursue further instruction and practicum experience after completion of the Volta Series course.
5. Three letters of reference and recommendation: two from hearing-impaired speechreaders and one from an employer, instructor, or associate in the field of hearing impairment.

Day One

Morning

Introduction to Oral Interpreting
> Pretest on knowledge and attitudes
> Why the need for oral interpreters?
> Classifications of hearing-impaired speechreaders
> Historical overview of oral interpreting
> Definitions of current terminology

Panel Discussion with Hearing-Impaired Speechreaders
> Educational backgrounds and personal philosophies
> Employment status and coping mechanisms
> Perspectives on oral interpreting
> Etc.

Afternoon

Introduction to Speech Production and Articulation
> Place of articulation
> Process of speechreading; factors influencing performance (research findings)

Individual evaluation of participants' speech production (with and without voice)

Evening

Reception
Interaction of all participants and instructors
Interaction of local hearing-impaired speechreaders; local ODAS chapter

Day 2

Morning

Introduction to the Task of Oral Interpreting
Words or phrases with low visibility when in context; words that look alike on the lips (homophenes)
Verbal/nonverbal adaptive techniques
Script analysis
Demonstration/modeling of oral interpreting
Practice with paragraphs recorded at 90 to 110 words per minute

Afternoon

Environmental Considerations
Placement or distance with regard to hearing consumer(s), hearing-impaired consumer(s), and/or media
Lighting
Clothing
Verbal/Nonverbal Adaptive Techniques—Continued
Demonstration/modeling of oral interpreting
Practice and critique while using audiotaped lectures recorded at 90, 100, 110, 125, and 135 words per minute

Evening

Self-Instructional Lab and Individualized Assistance
Audiotaped lectures varying in difficulty and speed
Videotape recording equipment available for self-critique

Day 3

Morning

Oral Interpreting: Visible to Spoken (Voicing Techniques)
Public speaking techniques
Consecutive voicing; simultaneous (voiceover)
Practice and critique while using videotapes of hearing-impaired

speechreaders presenting lectures (speech quality of varying difficulty)

Afternoon

Aspects of Professionalism
Characteristics of professional interpreters
Twelve elements of RID Code of Ethics
Application of Code of Ethics within role-play situations

Evening

*Telecommunication Systems, Signaling Devices, and Hearing Aids
Used by the Hearing Impaired*
Hands-on session
Simulated deafness experience

Day 4

Morning

Oral Interpreting in Specialized Settings
Knowledge and application of telephone, medical, classroom, etc.
Practice and critique

Afternoon

Practicum: Visible to Spoken and Spoken to Visible
Mock lecture situations with hearing-impaired speechreaders providing feedback

Evening

Self-Instruction Lab and Individualized Assistance

Day 5

Morning

Resource Networks
Professional organizations
Formal in-service training opportunities
Informal professional growth opportunities
Employment opportunities
RID Evaluation System
Description of system and five major evaluation areas

Afternoon

Mock RID Evaluation Post-test
Closing Remarks

CURRICULAR RESOURCES

Dirst, R. D. (ed.). 1980. Oral interpreter evaluation manual for evaluators. RID, Inc., Silver Spring, Maryland.

Guidelines for the preparation of oral interpreters: Support specialists for hearing-impaired individuals. 1979. Volta Rev. 81:135–145.

APPENDIX B

Two-Year Oral Interpreter AAS Degree Program: Suggested Curriculum (Total: 64 Semester Credits)

FIRST SEMESTER

Introduction to Oral Interpreting	2
Educational Management Systems for the Hearing Impaired	2
Auditory/Oral Communication (Amplification Systems; Auditory Training; Hearing Aids; Language; Speech Production; and Maintenance)	3
Speechreading Systems	3
Dynamics of Human Communication	3
English Composition	3
	16

SECOND SEMESTER

Expressive Oral Interpreting (Spoken-to-Visible)	3
Expressive Oral Interpreting—Laboratory	2
Psychosocial Aspects of Deafness	3
Aspects of Professional Interpreting	3
Public Speaking	3
Humanities Elective	3
	17

THIRD SEMESTER

Expressive Oral Interpreting in Specialized Settings	3
Expressive Oral Interpreting in Specialized Settings: Laboratory	2
Receptive Oral Interpreting (Visible-to-Spoken)	3
Receptive Oral Interpreting (Visible-to-Spoken)—Laboratory	2
Introduction to Manual Communication and Sign Systems	3
Social Science Elective	3
	16

FOURTH SEMESTER

Seminar: Oral Interpreting	2
Oral Interpreting Practicum	7
Science Elective	3
Literature Elective	3
	15

CHAPTER 9

EFFECTIVE ORAL INTERPRETERS: AN ANALYSIS

Diane L. Castle

CONTENTS

The oral interpreter is a facilitator for the transmission of information to hearing-impaired or normally hearing consumers. To be effective, the oral interpreter cannot simply imitate the speaker in a mechanical, routine manner but must use a variety of skills and techniques to convey the message. These skills and techniques are delineated in this chapter in order that others may see the complex process more clearly. The process of oral interpreting is described within the framework of a communication loop: The oral interpreter as facilitator is the sender, the hearing-impaired speechreader or hearing consumer is the receiver, the content from the speaker is the message to be transmitted, and the conditions under which the interpreting takes place constitute the environment.

Much of the literature that deals with research on or the development of speechreading skills (as discussed in other chapters) can serve as a resource for the formal preparation of oral interpreters. Publications from the Registry of Interpreters for the Deaf, Inc. (RID) also provide information about the interpreting process and the evaluation/certification of interpreters. This chapter applies knowledge from those areas, along with information from the disciplines of education of the deaf, linguistics, phonetics, experimental psychology, audiology, and speech pathology, to the role of the oral interpreter.

THE ORAL INTERPRETER: THE MEDIUM FOR THE MESSAGE

Physical Characteristics

People are born with certain characteristics that cannot be changed easily (e.g., facial and body structures) and other characteristics that may be modified if there is the need or desire (e.g., speech, facial expressions, body mobility, posture, dress, and hairstyle). An oral interpreter should possess definite characteristics that will enhance ease of speechreading for the hearing-impaired consumer and ensure understanding of the hearing-impaired person's message for the normally hearing consumer. A person who wishes to become an effective oral interpreter must, in most instances, be willing to modify certain speech habits and other personal characteristics. Such modifications occur through preservice training and a great deal of practical experience.

Apparently, speakers who are the easiest to speechread are also the most intelligible to a listener (Berger, 1972), which suggests that precise articulation is important for understanding the message either through vision or audition. The speechreader depends on certain visible movements of the articulators (lips, tongue, teeth, jaw, and palate) to help identify spoken language. Appropriate lip, tongue, and jaw movements offer visible cues to certain vowel and consonant speech sounds and rule out other groups of sounds. If certain speech movements are not produced conventionally, they may not be recognized by the speechreader. Any malformation of the facial structure that interferes with conventional speech production could affect the success of the oral interpreter and, in turn, the speechreader.

People vary in their ability to communicate. Careless, indistinct, or exaggerated speech tends to interfere with effective speechreading (Berger, 1972). The wide variations in speech production are easily demonstrated by watching different speakers on television newscasts when the sound is turned off. After a short period of attempting to speechread these persons, the necessity for clear articulatory movements, mobility of lips and jaw, normal rhythm and stress patterns, and good facial expression on the part of the oral interpreter is apparent. Fortunately for the prospective oral interpreter, speech habits and nonverbal communication can be improved with training.

Certain prosodic features (Borden and Harris, 1980) embedded in spoken language can indicate attitudes, feelings, and changes in meaning. These features are conveyed nonverbally to the speechreader by the facial expressions, body language, and natural gestures of the oral interpreter. For example, various moods, feelings, and attitudes can be expressed through movements of the forehead, eyebrows, nose, mouth, cheeks, eyes, head, and neck as well as eye contact. Similarly, natural gestures and body language can convey familiar expressions (hello, goodbye, shh, hot, cold, etc.) and situations (scolding, a private conversation, a choice, a different speaker, etc.). Thus, hair that obscures movements of the forehead, eyebrows, or cheeks and a beard or moustache that hides the mouth or upper lip, cheeks, and/or jaw can become barriers to full comprehension by the speechreader.

Receptive-Expressive Verbal Skills

The oral interpreter plays a crucial role in the transmission of the message from the speaker to the hearing-impaired or normally hearing consumer. The speaker determines such factors as the message content and its meaning, the word order, grammatical structure, rate, and intonation. The oral interpreter, selectively attending to the message, rapidly decodes and then restructures the message appropriately for the consumer. For the oral interpreter, the process of understanding the speaker involves a knowledge of the language and its redundancies, which help to anticipate and verify what is being said by narrowing down possible choices and ruling out unlikely possibilities. The process of perceiving the message while it is spoken, placing chunks of the message in memory in order to check its accuracy from the pattern of sounds yet to come, and then correctly representing the message for the consumer may require several seconds (Caccamise et al., 1980; Jacobs, 1982; Jeffers and Barley, 1971; Sanders, 1977). The brief time lag between speaker presentation and oral interpreter presentation is necessary for analyzing and restructuring the message and is inherent in oral, foreign language, and sign language interpreting. The accuracy of this process depends in part on the verbal skills, listening skills, and attention span of the oral interpreter. The ability of the oral interpreter to attend to the message and process it while ignoring competing auditory and/or visual distractions is an important competence.

Some persons seem to have a natural aptitude for understanding language through audition and/or speechreading, while others require exposure and experience with a variety of speakers in order to achieve success. The oral interpreter should be able to understand a wide variety of dialects and accents, spoken by persons of different races and countries. Additionally, the oral interpreter needs to be able to understand the speech and language patterns of various hearing-impaired persons who use oral language communication. If the oral interpreter has difficulty discriminating words in the message, understanding the syntax or semantics of the sentence, or remembering and repeating it in meaningful speech, then the version presented by the oral interpreter will differ from the intent of the speaker. A training program can help the prospective oral interpreter to improve listening skills (McLaughlin and West, 1978), memory span, attention, speed, and flexibility in rephrasing for consumer ease in understanding the message.

THE MESSAGE

The Basic Framework

Phonetic Factors   What does the speechreader see that allows differentiation among the speech sounds of English? Sanders (1971) cited four factors that impact upon the ease of speechreading individual sounds:

1. The degree of visibility of the movement
2. The rapidity of articulatory movements
3. The similarity of the visual characteristics of the articulatory movements involved in the production of different speech sounds
4. Intersubject variations in the visible aspects of articulatory movements involved in the production of any given sound

Visibility   The professional oral interpreter has learned that the basic visible information comes from the movements of the articulators and relates to their place of articulation. Because movements involving the lips and the tongue are more easily seen, they are considered the most helpful for recognition of a vowel or consonant (Berger, 1972; Sanders, 1971).

Mobility of the jaw (height of mouth opening) allows the speechreader to see the tongue as it moves toward the front or back of the palate for sounds such as /t, d, n, l, k, g/. Clear enunciation requires mobility of the lips, an important cue for certain vowels and consonants; notice the change in lip shape from a tight circular movement, as for the vowel in "pool," to a wide smiling movement in "peel." The teeth serve as a landmark to indicate that certain sounds are in process. If the teeth are visible, the movement identifies certain sounds, such as /f, v/ and the voiced or voiceless /th/. If the teeth are not visible, the experienced speechreader would anticipate words that did not include these sounds. When the sound is made farther back inside the mouth, it will be less visible.

It is well-accepted that when individual sounds are placed in words, the sounds are influenced and altered by neighboring sounds. This is called phonetic adaptation. The position of the articulators for one sound determines the movements necessary to produce adjacent sounds. This can be demonstrated by the variation in tongue-palate contact for /k/ in front of two different vowels in the words "key" and "caught."

Speed   A change in the rate of speaking from average to fast causes the articulators to modify their movements by falling short of their target. If the modification goes far enough, the sound may actually change and take on a characteristic of the neighboring sound, e.g., "give me" becomes "gimme." These changes should not have a significant impact on the speechreader (see discussion of linguistic factors). Experienced speechreaders do not seem to have difficulty with the normal rate of speech, which is 120 words per minute (Sanders, 1971).

Homophenes   Although no two speech sounds are produced in exactly the same way, many speech sounds (/t,d/, /k,g/, /f,v/, /s,z/, etc.) have visible movements that are identical (homophenous). It is assumed that 40 to 50% of speech sounds are homophenous (Berger, 1972). Individual sounds, groups of sounds, words, phrases, or sentences that look the same on the lips are said to be homophenous.

In conversational speech, i.e., in context, *it is possible* to distinguish among homophenes by relying on the linguistic redundancy of the message, e.g., "My next coat/goat is going to be fur." The importance of contextual cues is demonstrated by the fact that at times the speechreader, the listener, and the reader all have similar problems with the accurate perception of English. Although homophenous words look alike on the lips (fine, vine), homophonous words sound alike to the listener (ate, eight), and another category of words are read differently but look alike on paper (read; read—present and past tense, respectively). A general lack of knowledge about this information has incorrectly focused the blame for inability to speechread on homophenous words rather than on the hearing-impaired consumer's skill or the oral interpreter's/speaker's competence. Homophenous words will not automatically cause confusion. Linguistic factors (see next section) such as the consumer's predictive ability must be considered as well.

Individual Differences   In production of speech sounds individual differences may be attributable to variations in the structure of the speech mechanism, regional or social variations in production of sounds, or differences in auditory perception of the sounds (Sanders, 1971).

Speechreaders often report that it is easier to understand relatives or friends than persons who are not as well-known. When the person is familiar, knowing their dialect, speech habits, and personality contributes to speechreading proficiency (Berger, 1972). Berger found that black speechreaders were able to speechread black speakers best and white speechreaders were able to speechread white speakers best; the differences were statistically significant. This information suggests that it is easier to speechread those with features one has had more experience with, thus highlighting the value of a brief conversation or warm-up period between the oral interpreter and speechreader.

Linguistic Factors   Berger (1972) suggested as much as 50% of the English language is redundant. This fact assists the speechreader confronted by homophenous words, making it easier to anticipate what will be said in general. Many words can be predicted from the meaning of other words already understood in the sentence, "I wrote a _____ to Mother." Many words can be predicted from the grammar of the language because words must be combined to form acceptable sentences in English. In addition to being grammatically correct, the sentence must make sense, as in the sentence, "He had to drag/track himself out of bed." The knowledge of grammar plus the ability to effect closure play an important role in perceiving sentences through speechreading (Lowenbraun and Affleck, 1970). Furthermore, this predictive ability is based on the knowledge that certain combinations of sounds do not occur in English words (/pg, tf/); that certain sounds occur infrequently (/t, d, n, s, r, l/); and that certain sounds are not found as initial consonants (/ng, zh/) nor as final consonants (/j, w, h, wh/, etc.) (Fairbanks, 1960). On the average pronouns and verbs seem to be the easiest to speechread; sentences using few words or syllables are easier than longer sentences with more syllables; and phrases are easier than individual words or sentences (Berger, 1972). Frequently used words tend to be speechread better than those infrequently used. One-syllable words are more difficult, while two- and three-syllable words are easier and thus recognized more frequently.

It is possible, therefore, to perceive an incomplete message as a whole by mentally filling in portions that are not clearly understood. For the speechreader and the oral interpreter, this process of *closure* involves use of all linguistic cues when either visual or auditory information is insufficient.

The prosodic features of language involve the rhythm and melody of speech (Borden and Harris, 1980). These features are superimposed on a word, phrase, or sentence. They include stress, intonation, duration, and juncture. They are important to understanding the meaning of the speaker because they reveal attitudes and feelings.

Differences in stress can change the meaning of a word or sentence. Moving the stress from one syllable to another can change some nouns into verbs, e.g., 'permit becomes per'mit. For the listener, stressed syllables or words tend to be louder. For the speechreader, stress may be seen as more accurate articulation of a word or syllable, with vowels having longer duration (Borden and Harris, 1980).

The intonation or pitch pattern used for a word, phrase, or sentence can clearly express the attitudes of the speaker, changes in meaning, or the way a person feels (Borden and Harris, 1980). Intonation also plays an important role in guiding the listener in perceiving the intended groupings of words as a phrase with specific meaning (Sanders, 1977). The listener's knowledge of the language makes it possible to correctly perceive the meaning intended by the speaker. Changes in the intonation pattern for the same words can suggest different meanings to the listener. Specific intonation patterns categorize declarative statements, questions, and incomplete sentences. Anger, happiness, or enthusiasm is usually expressed by large changes in intonation patterns, and calm, quiet feelings have smaller variations in intonation patterns. The speechreader may miss these auditory cues if they are not supplied visually by the oral interpreter, who must use facial expressions, natural gestures, and body language to convey the intonation.

Duration and juncture add to the linguistic cues of a sentence by modifying the length or the boundary of individual sounds, syllables, or phrases (Borden and Harris, 1980). For example, vowel duration is modified according to whether the following consonant is voiced, voiceless, or a continuant, e.g., "leave," "leaf," or "leap." Juncture relates to changes in duration and sound changes, as demonstrated by moving the /n/ in "a name" to "an aim". Speechreaders are able to recognize changes in duration and can use them as cues for word identification (Berger, 1972).

Nonverbal Factors   Jacobs (1982) provided a succinct review of research on nonverbal language communication. In her review, Jacobs pointed out that nonverbal language must be learned from childhood in order for the person's sensitivity to nonverbal stimuli to increase with age. Mehrabian (1971) reported that when a person simultaneously uses words, facial expressions, tone of voice, posture, and gestures, 55% of meaning comes from facial expressions, 38% from tone of voice, and only 7% from words. If the facial expression used by the talker contradicts the words used, the listener will rely on the facial expression for meaning. Obviously, the nonverbal cues are very powerful. Birdwhistell (1970) estimated "no more than 30 to 35% of the social meaning of a conversation or an interaction" (p. 158) are transmitted through words, which implies that 65 to 70% are from nonverbal language. Jacobs (1981) graphically demonstrated the many nonverbal language cues available for the speechreader who is sensitive to them.

Sanders (1971) also illustrated ways in which nonverbal cues contribute to accuracy in predicting the verbal message. For example, he described how natural gestures can substitute for a spoken word and may involve the head, face, shoulders, hands, and arms through "the nod of approval or disapproval, the protruded tongue, the shrug of the shoulders, the extended hand, or a raised hand in a classroom" (p. 119).

Experienced speechreaders are sensitive to and knowledgeable about inferring meaning from nonverbal communication. When used appropriately, facial expressions, natural gestures, and body language can clarify information transmitted by the articulators indicating a question, a command, a request, joy, anxiety, etc. Nonverbal cues that are either inappropriate for the message (i.e., lack of facial expression when it is implied) or represent personal mannerisms (i.e., head-bobbing and meaningless hand, face or body movements) decrease the understanding of the message and confuse the speechreader.

How the Oral Interpreter Deals with the Message

Whenever possible, the speechreading consumer and the oral interpreter should meet prior to the start of an interpreting assignment to determine whether the speechreader wants exact repetition of the speaker's remarks (transliteration) or modification as appropriate (interpreting). This meeting helps the oral interpreter to become familiar with the communication needs of the consumer as well as the topic and any specific terminology or names that may arise during the interpreting process. The oral interpreter may be involved in various specialized interpreting assignments (Caccamise et al., 1980), e.g., legal, religious, performing arts, television, and telephone (Castle and Rizzolo, 1984). At the end of the interpreting session, a meeting between the interpreter and consumer gives each person an opportunity to present any constructive suggestions that may improve the interpreting process in the future.

When the consumer is a hearing-impaired person, the initial meeting gives each person an opportunity to become familiar with the other person's communication style—speech, vocabulary, and sentence structure. An awareness of the general level of receptive and expressive language and speechreading abilities of the hearing-impaired person influences the choice of vocabulary and style of interpreting used by the oral interpreter. The oral interpreter should ask the hearing-impaired person how he or she would like information involving proper names and numbers presented. In some environments, the hearing-impaired person may accept limited use of fingerspelling, signs, or writing in addition to oral spelling or writing in the air because there are different degrees of oral functioning (Thompson, 1965). For example, when dealing with numbers, the fingerspelled "six" may be preferred to the gesture of six fingers.

As with any other type of interpreting, i.e., foreign language (Van Reigersberg, 1970) or sign language (Caccamise et al., 1980), fatigue affects the accuracy of the message transmitted because of the mental and physical processes involved. Optimally, for lengthy assignments, oral interpreters should try to alternate every 30 minutes. Because of the limited number of certified individuals in the 1980s, an oral interpreter may have to continue for an entire session.

When the speaker is using vocabulary and a style of speaking that is clearly difficult for the speechreader, an oral interpreter must judge how to convey that information. Repetition of words does not significantly improve their comprehension by the speechreader. Using synonyms, rephrasing the message, or adding a clarifying word or phrase may be more successful. Using words that are more familiar, multisyllabic, or include more visible elements of speech adds more cues for speechreading (Berger, 1972). The oral interpreter must be almost intuitive in modifying and presenting the message to enhance speechreading. This ability is based on a strong understanding of speech science and linguistic theory.

Appropriate phrasing breaks long sentences into visually meaningful units. When a new term or a proper name is used for the first time, the oral interpreter may choose to emphasize it by pausing briefly immediately after the word and using very clear but slower pronunciation, which indicates the number of syllables for that word, e.g., manufacturers, Smith-Kettlewell. This technique is useful also when multisyllabic words or less visible words are spoken. Maintaining eye contact with the consumer is an important way to obtain verbal or nonverbal feedback regarding the success of the message transmitted (Caccamise et al., 1980).

Often, a speaker pauses and vocalizes "er" or "uh" while thinking about the next statement. The oral interpreter repeats these vocalizations to faithfully convey the style and degree of fluency of the speaker. If there is a silence of several seconds, the oral interpreter can signal the end of a phrase or sentence by bringing the lips together lightly rather than leaving the mouth wide open. Simultaneously, the oral interpreter may look away from the speechreader. This change of eye contact is another signal that the oral interpreter is waiting for the speaker to continue. However, if the speaker has lost his or her place on the page or if there are problems with the microphone or loudspeaker system, for instance, the interpreter should let the speechreader know what is happening. In a group discussion or in a question and answer period, the oral interpreter should show who is speaking by pointing to the location of the person or verbally describing the location, e.g., "The woman in the back row."

If the speaker is using a soft voice or if the pace is too fast, the oral interpreter should not try to stop the speaker but instead can indicate the problem by saying, without voice, "I missed that" or "too fast" to the speechreader. The consumer can then decide whether or not to make a request of the speaker, either directly or via the interpreter. The interpreter remains unobtrusive to the speaker and to the general audience at all times. In the case of a speaker's sustained rapid pace, the interpreter may have to summarize the content.

Ideally, the interpreter paces himself or herself two or three words behind the speaker, particularly if the hearing-impaired person is participating in a discussion, so that the consumer's comments are timely. However, this ideal pace may vary within a presentation because lag time depends on the size of the chunk being processed, e.g., whether an entire phrase or a single homophenous word is involved. It is most important for the oral interpreter to convey the information clearly and accurately while staying as closely behind the speaker as possible.

Sometimes the speaker is poorly organized. When this occurs, the oral interpreter may not wish to proceed until the speaker comes to the point. This situation may create a problem of credibility for the oral interpreter because the hearing-impaired audience may not be aware of whether the speaker or the oral interpreter is at fault.

Often, when the speaker is difficult to understand, hearing people in the audience may watch the oral interpreter. Some speakers have distracting speech characteristics that result in a word or part of a word not being heard by the audience, e.g., varying patterns of speaking rate, with shotgun bursts of speech alternating with pauses or uneven control of vocal loudness. The speaker may be a person with a hearing impairment or another physical disability that affects speaking ability. Regardless of the speech style of the speaker, the oral interpreter should try to maintain a smooth flow of words with meaningful pauses. The oral interpreter must be aware of and in control of the sounds of lip and tongue contacts and escaping breath that occurs when repeating words without using voice. These sounds are very annoying for hearing persons in the vicinity of the oral interpreter. The oral interpreter should use clear speech, facial expression, and body language to transmit the mood and style of the speaker. Concentration on the task at hand is necessary; other thoughts should be put out of mind, and visual or auditory distractions must be ignored.

Voice Interpreting   The hearing-impaired person should indicate if he or she will be participating in any way during the interpreting assignment. Many hearing-impaired persons are unaware of whether or not their spoken language is understood by strangers. Unfavorable room acoustics, use of a microphone, or environmental noise can interfere with oral communication by a hearing-impaired person. When speaking with only one person, before a small group of people or before a large audience, it is to the advantage of the hearing-impaired person to ask the audience as well as the oral interpreter if he or she can be understood in that particular environment. Because of the familiarity of the oral interpreter with the speech of hearing-impaired persons, he or she may not be the best judge of the speaker's intelligibility. The oral interpreter may be helpful by setting up an agreed upon system of nonverbal cues, which would give the hearing-impaired person feedback about adequate loudness, rate, and clarity during the speaking process. During the presentation by the hearing-impaired person, the oral interpreter should convey information about any noises, e.g., airplanes flying overhead or construction work, that may distract the attention of the audience.

If the hearing-impaired person chooses to have the oral interpreter repeat his or her remarks, there should be some decision about whether to use the *simultaneous* or *consecutive* mode of interpreting (Witter-Merithew and Dirst, 1982). Simultaneous interpreting occurs when the oral interpreter's voice overlaps the voice of the hearing-impaired person, which can be distracting. In this case, the oral interpreter should use a microphone. Consecutive interpreting requires the hearing-impaired person to speak and then pause after a sentence or short paragraph to allow the oral interpreter to repeat the information phrase-by-phrase. This type of interpreting is more time-consuming and lends itself best to a one-to-one situation, e.g., a doctor's office. If the hearing-impaired person serves as a platform speaker, a copy of the prepared speech will help an oral interpreter to convey the message with accuracy.

When voicing for a hearing-impaired person, the oral interpreter needs to use appropriate language, intonation, and expression in order for the intent of the message to be understood. Because hearing-impaired persons have varying degrees of speech intelligibility, the oral interpreter needs to rely on speechreading, natural gestures, and facial expressions when possible, along with a knowledge of the language and previous experience with many hearing-impaired persons, to assist in understanding the speech-language patterns at hand. In a legal setting, an oral interpreter may be requested to transliterate, i.e., repeat precisely, word-for-word (including faulty grammatical phrasing) what the hearing-impaired person has said.

In some assignments, the oral interpreter may be standing in front or to the side, unable to watch the hearing-impaired person speak. If another interpreter is available, a "buddy" system may be useful. In this situation, the buddy is seated facing both the oral interpreter and the hearing-impaired speaker. The buddy watches, listens, and conveys, without voice, the message spoken by the hearing-impaired person to assist the oral interpreter. In a large hall with several oral interpreters, an FM system may be more practical than the buddy system. In this arrangement, one oral interpreter faces the hearing-impaired speaker. The interpreter speaks into a microphone, and the message is transmitted by radio frequency into the small FM receivers worn in the ear of each of the other oral interpreters.

THE ENVIRONMENT

The Basic Framework

Lighting, Distance, and Angle   Studies on the effects of lighting, distance, and angle on the speechreading process (Erber, 1974) reveal that when the light is focused on the oral cavity, the speechreading scores are affected only slightly by changing the intensity of lighting through a wide range. Speechreading comprehension dropped sharply only when the lighting was so dim that gross shapes and shadows of the mouth and head could be seen. For successful speechreading, these studies suggested that overall lighting of the room does not seem to be as important as the amount of light on the mouth and face. Light fixtures mounted on the ceiling tend to place the speaker's face in shadow and make it difficult to see the oral cavity and discrete articulatory movements within the mouth such as /t, d, n, l, s, z, k, g/.

Light coming from a window, lamp, or spotlight located behind the speaker or oral interpreter places a shadow on the face, making speechreading very difficult (Jacobs, 1981, 1982). Any change in room lighting after showing slides, videotapes, or movies requires a brief time for the eyes of the speechreader to readjust. The amount of light that permits clearest vision depends on the task. Too much light intensity will produce glare, making it more difficult to see.

Furthermore, research (Erber, 1974) suggests that as long as the oral cavity is illuminated, speechreading comprehension will not be significantly affected whether the oral interpreter: 1) sits or stands; or 2) directly faces the speechreader or has turned his or her head no more than 45° to the side. However, speechreading comprehension will deteriorate when the oral interpreter is positioned at an extreme angle, e.g., facing 90° to the side.

Decreasing the distance between the oral interpreter and the hearing-impaired consumer increases speechreading comprehension. Research suggests up to 10 feet between speechreader and speaker/oral interpreter, with 5 to 8 feet being a good conversational distance (Erber, 1974; Jacobs, 1982; O'Neill and Oyer, 1973).

Auditory and Visual Interference   Speechreading supplements the listening process by adding 20% to 30% of the message for hearing-impaired persons who can perceive auditory information through amplification (Erber, 1981). Clearly, the ability to use both sensory channels maximizes the information received.

For the hearing aid user who depends habitually on residual hearing to support speechreading in noninterpreted situations, i.e., in one-to-one conversations, it may be very difficult to combine the visual with the auditory signals in an interpreted situation. It is difficult to determine the value of the oral interpreter for this type of person (Titus, 1978); consumers need to judge each situation on an individual basis.

Inherent in the interpreting process is a brief delay between the speaker's remarks and the time it takes for the oral interpreter to repeat the message. This time lag between the auditory and visual signals may serve to confuse rather than enhance the speechreading process for the hearing-impaired person who benefits from auditory cues. Because of this time lag, some hearing aid users may prefer to turn off the amplification when interpreting begins.

The use of amplification can add numerous auditory distractions and interfere with concentration on and perception of the message. The transmission of sound to the oral interpreter and the hearing-impaired consumer may be affected by the architectural features of the room, e.g., reflection or reverberation of sound from room surfaces, the direction of sound from the speaker in relation to the listener's head, and distance from speaker to listener (Niemoeller, 1981). Acoustic conditions are frequently poor in churches and meeting halls. In these locations, the speechreader may have to rely more on visual cues. However, room noise from heating, ventilating, and air conditioning systems may be more harmful to auditory speech perception by the oral interpreter and the hearing-impaired person. Unexpected, intermittent distractions, whether auditory or visual, may be more disruptive than expected, continuous ones. However, continuous auditory distractions, i.e., white noise, speech, or music, have been found to significantly affect speechreading performance (O'Neill and Oyer,

1973). For the hearing-impaired person, such auditory distractions can cause greater dependence on speechreading.

How the Oral Interpreter Deals with the Environment

Neesam and Falberg (1965) reviewed many of the environmental factors that interfere with receptive communication by the hearing-impaired person. Although their information is directed primarily to the sign language interpreter, many of the points are applicable to the oral interpreter as well.

In consultation with the hearing-impaired person, the oral interpreter should facilitate an optimum environment, visually and acoustically. The hearing-impaired person should be aware of his or her range of visual reception and should suggest a particular location for the oral interpreter if any visual impairment exists.

Overhead room lighting often is inadequate for speechreading. The research clearly indicates speechreaders benefit when additional lighting can be used and adjusted to focus specifically on the mouth of the oral interpreter. Therefore, the oral interpreter should make every effort to have available a portable light with a 25-watt light bulb and extension cord. This portable light can highlight specific articulatory movements to facilitate speechreading cues, particularly when overhead lights are dimmed or turned off for movies or slides. The interpreter should inform the speechreader about the environmental light and indicate how it can be helpful.

The oral interpreter should not sit or stand in front of any visually distracting background, such as defective flourescent lights, low swinging lamps, windows without curtains, doors, hallways, or patterned wallpaper. Ideally, the background should be plain and of contrasting color. If both oral and sign language interpreters are used, they should be placed at least several feet apart to reduce the distraction of signs in the visual field of the speechreader.

The clothing, glasses, jewelry, or makeup worn by the oral interpreter can be an additional distraction. Clothing should contrast rather than blend with skin color but should not be vividly striped or patterned. The oral interpreter should determine if there is any light reflecting from jewelry or eyeglasses because this can be very annoying for the speechreader. For women, the absence of any makeup may be as detrimental to a speechreader as the overabundance of makeup. Use of some makeup, e.g., mascara, rouge, or lipstick, helps to define the facial structure and compensate for shadows frequently on the face. The lip movements of the oral interpreter will be more noticeable when lipstick is used; a brown tone for men and a noniridescent red color for women. The oral interpreter should try to have a neat, well-groomed appearance.

The nature of the interpreting situation (Caccamise et al., 1980; Neesam and Falberg, 1965) determines whether the oral interpreter sits or stands and should not affect speechreading proficiency significantly. However, the interpreter should be facing the speechreader with his or her head at no more than a 45° angle and not more than 10 feet away.

Sometimes it is difficult to see whether a hearing-impaired person is using amplification; this is particulary true when interpreting for a group. Thus, as a matter of routine, the oral interpreter should inform the speechreader of any obvious auditory conditions that may interfere with or support the use of amplification for reception of sound. Some facilities have induction loop, FM, or infrared sound systems that, when used by a hearing-impaired person, tend to reduce environmental noise and reverberation while increasing the loudness of the speaker's voice. The oral interpreter as well as the hearing-impaired consumer need to be aware of the presence of such systems.

CONCLUSION

To the naive observer, the task of the oral interpreter seems relatively easy. To the oral interpreter, each assignment is a challenge in processing receptive and expressive communication rapidly and accurately for speechreaders, the ultimate consumers. The effective oral interpreter is a skilled practitioner, applying a knowledge of theory from many disciplines in order to enhance the communication process. The information in this chapter is presented to enable the prospective oral interpreter to see the complex set of tasks more clearly in order to prepare to meet the communication challenge.

ACKNOWLEDGMENT

The materials herein were produced in the course of an agreement between the Rochester Institute of Technology and the U.S. Department of Education.

REFERENCES

Berger, K. W. 1972. Speechreading Principles and Methods. National Educational Press, Baltimore.

Birdwhistell, R. L. 1970. Kinesics and Context. University of Pennsylvania Press, Philadelphia.

Borden, G. J., and K. S. Harris. 1980. Speech Science Primer. Williams and Wilkins, Baltimore.

Castle, D. L., and M. Rizzolo. Telephone interpreting for oral deaf persons. In: A. Witter-Merithew and L. A. Siple (eds.), Curriculum Guide for the Instruction of Oral Interpreting. A. G. Bell Assoc., Washington, DC. In preparation.

Caccamise, F., R. Dirst, J. Stangarone and M. Mitchell-Caccamise. 1980. General factors to consider in interpreting assignments. In: F. Caccamise, R. Dirst, R. D. DeVries, et al. (eds.), Introduction to Interpreting, pp. 15–31. RID, Silver Spring, MD.

Erber, N. P. 1974. Effects of angle, distance, and illumination on visual reception of speech by profoundly deaf children. J. Speech Hear. Res. 17:99–112.

Erber, N. P. 1981. Speech perception by hearing-impaired children. In: F. Bess, B. A. Freeman, and J. S. Sinclair (eds.), Amplification in Education, pp. 69–88. A. G. Bell Assoc., Washington, DC.

Fairbanks, G. 1960. Voice and Articulation Drillbook, 2nd Ed. Harper and Row, New York.

Jacobs, M. A. 1981. Associational Cues. Rochester Institute of Technology, National Technical Institute for the Deaf, Rochester, NY.

Jacobs, M. A. 1982. Visual communication (speechreading) for the severely and profoundly hearing-impaired young adults. In: D. G. Sims, G. G. Walter, and R. L. Whitehead (eds.), Deafness and Communication, pp. 271–295. Williams and Wilkins, Baltimore.

Jeffers, J., and M. Barley. 1971. Speechreading (Lipreading). Charles C Thomas, Springfield, IL.

Lowenbraun, S., and J. Q. Affleck. 1970. The ability of deaf children to use syntactic cues in immediate recall of speechread material. Except. Child. 36:735–741.

McLaughlin, J. E., and E. A. West. 1978. The interpreter as listener: Effective listening for interpreters. In: F. Caccamise, J. Stangarone, and M. Mitchell-Caccamise (eds.), Potpourri, pp. 72–81. Proceedings of the 1978 RID Convention, Rochester, NY.

Mehrabian, A. 1971. Silent Messages. Wadsworth Publishing, Belmont, CA.

Neesam, R., and R. Falberg. 1965. Physical Factors in Interpreting. In: S. P. Quigley (ed.), Interpreting for Deaf People, pp. 11–17. U. S. Department of Health, Education, and Welfare, Washington, DC.

Niemoeller, A. F. 1981. Physical concepts of speech communication in classrooms for the deaf. In: F. Bess, B. A. Freeman, and J. S. Sinclair (eds.), Amplification in Education, pp. 164–179. A. G. Bell Assoc., Washington, DC.

O'Neill, J. J., and H. J. Oyer. 1973. Aural rehabilitation. In: J. Jerger (ed.), Modern Developments in Audiology, 2nd Ed., pp. 211–252. Academic Press, New York.

Sanders, D. A. 1971. Aural Rehabilitation. Prentice-Hall, Englewood Cliffs, NJ.

Sanders, D. A. 1977. Auditory Perception of Speech. Prentice-Hall, Englewood Cliffs, NJ.

Thompson, R. F. 1965. Interpreting for the orally oriented deaf person. In: S. P. Quigley (ed.), Interpreting for Deaf People, pp. 25–29. U.S. Department of Health, Education, and Welfare, Washington, DC.

Titus, J. R. 1978. The comparative effectiveness of presenting spoken information to postsecondary oral deaf students through a live speaker, an oral interpreter, and an interpreter using signed English. Doctoral dissertation. University of Pittsburgh, Pittsburgh, PA.

Van Reigersberg, S. 1970. Observations on foreign language interpreting. In: L. J. DiPietro (ed.), Proceedings of the First Convention of the Registry of Interpreters for the Deaf, pp. 3–8. Delavan, WI.

Witter-Merithew, A., and R. Dirst. 1982. Preparation and use of educational interpreters. In: D. G. Sims, G. G. Walter, and R. L. Whitehead (eds.), Deafness and Communication, pp. 395–406. Williams and Wilkins, Baltimore.

CHAPTER 10

THE CONTENT OF PRACTICUM OBSERVATION AND SUPERVISED INTERACTION

Kirsten Aase Gonzalez

CONTENTS

From students at almost every workshop and short course given on oral interpreting has come the plea for more practica—opportunities to practice the skills learned from previously presented theory and demonstration, with observation and constructive criticism from instructor, peers, and consumers. Such practica are necessarily limited in short refresher courses. The practicum ideas offered in this chapter are designed for a full-semester course of one 3-hour class a week. A 1-week intensive practicum course of 48 to 54 hours would amount to approximately the same in-class time. For inexperienced students, a minimal preservice training period should be a 2-semester course or the equivalent—the first semester addressing required competencies (knowledge, attitudes, and introduction to skills); the second, focusing on skill development through practicum (site visitation, observation, practice under supervision, and group analysis of student performance).

A 2-year oral interpreter training program that would culminate in an Associate of Arts Degree is foreseeable. Such a program would require both general education and specialized courses, reflect a major in oral interpreting, or be offered as an option in an established sign language interpreter training program (see Chapter 9).

Practicum activities generally follow formal lectures and demonstrations illustrating skills to be practiced; thus, a coordinator of practicum would report directly to the director of the comprehensive training program.

The use of videotapes for self-evaluation is a desirable option in almost all practica; otherwise, the critique comes solely from external observers.

It is highly desirable to obtain heterogeneity of educational, social, and vocational background; speechreading skills; speech intelligibility; and personal adaptation to hearing impairment among hearing-impaired participants and presenters in the program. Students will benefit by firsthand observation of these variations.

Students are expected, working individually or in some groups, to become familiar with the many environments (social, educational, and vocational) in which hearing-impaired speechreaders are functioning with varying degrees of personal satisfaction. Such settings can include:

Health services (medical, dental, social, and mental)

Places of work (offices, factories, staff meetings, and union meetings)

Government and community service meetings at all levels (school board, and city council; legislative hearings)

Activities and meetings of deafness-related organizations, e.g., A. G. Bell Assoc., Oral Deaf Adults Section (ODAS) NAD, RID, SHHH, at local, state, and national levels

Churches, temples, and synagogues

Schools at all levels, both special and integrated

Professional organization meetings and conventions at local, state, and national levels

Recreational activities (clubs, special and regular summer camps, and school games and dances

Activity within a group training setting can be individualized by using a variety of instructional strategies. Evans (1981) suggested a range of format options that combine active and passive learning:

Role playing (consumers, both hearing and hearing impaired and interpreter, including planned errors)

Demonstrations (include practicing opportunities)

Group experiences

Panel, utilizing guest speakers

Discussions with an appointed leader

Brainstorming (specified agenda)

Work stations (used with media)

Independent activities (summary project to be shared with group)

Media (utilized as a supplement to lecture, for demonstration or for practice)

Group project (goals and committees specified), utilizing a one-task agenda

Simulation (of an unusual condition or circumstances)

After discussing the role of the hearing-impaired speechreader in a training course and in practica, this chapter offers a few comments on speechreading and its practice (refer also to Chapter 7). The organization of skills and practicum discussion which then follows is based on the author's adaptation of the Skills Section of the 1979 *Guidelines for the Preparation of Oral Interpreters* (RID, 1979) (see Chapter Appendix A).

A paragraph or two discussing each skill precedes practicum descriptions relating to that skill. Where appropriate the practicum activities are written up in "cookbook" style: objectives, preparation and materials, procedure, and follow-up.

THE ROLE OF THE HEARING-IMPAIRED SPEECHREADER

Hearing-impaired speechreaders are essential to the quality control in any training program in oral interpreting. These prime consumers of oral interpreting services are helpful in many capacities. They may be employed as full-time or part-time professional staff members (curriculum consultants, supervisors of practicum, coursework instructors, and guest lecturers). They can encourage students to become acquainted and comfortable with them—as individuals and as potential consumers. This "getting acquainted" can be accomplished in the classroom, through panels and discussion groups, and outside at informal social gatherings. Diversity is important. Variations in age at onset of hearing loss, sex, educational background, vocational experience, speechreading capabilities, personality, and speech intelligibility should all be considered when inviting hearing-impaired persons to participate in practicum activities. Chapter Appendix B lists resources for contacting hearing-impaired speechreaders in the community. Chapter Appendix C shows a sample letter for approaching the contact.

Hearing-impaired speechreaders in the class, itself, are valuable, but they must not be regarded simply as "captive consumers" on which to practice. Not all hearing-impaired individuals are experienced in the use of oral interpreters or educated in what should be expected of them; those who are experienced will be especially valuable in critique and evaluation. Carefully devised feedback or evaluation forms can help guide responses, making this resource useful to student interpreters. Busy persons cannot be expected to travel long distances and repeatedly volunteer their time for the benefit of oral interpreting students.

Some suggestions for "getting acquainted" activities follow. Practicum activities for various skills are discussed later in the chapter; the participation opportunities for hearing-impaired speechreaders will be delineated.

Activity 1 (In Class): Getting Acquainted—A Panel Presentation

Objective   To introduce students to a variety of hearing-impaired speechreaders (prelingually deaf and adventitiously hearing-impaired in later childhood or adulthood) for the purpose of breaking down preconceived stereotypes and learning more about the commonalities and individualities within each classification. Listening and speechreading practice for students to take place as they communicate with hearing-impaired persons who have voices and speech patterns of varying intelligibility.

Preparation and Materials   If the choice is available, consider presenting more than one panel (four to six people each in a 90-minute session at different times). Choose a wide representation for one panel; a specific group for another (e.g., young people attending different types of secondary education programs). Seating should allow panelists to see each other as well as the class (a semi-circle is common). Class and room size may require microphones; a smaller room with natural voices is preferable. Individual students and hearing-impaired guests should be given time to interact informally. Ideas for class questions should be developed at an earlier time. A sample list of questions is given in Chapter Appendix D.

Procedure   Invite panelists to introduce themselves in a brief personal sketch. Direct the discussion only as needed to elicit additional information and prevent monopoly of time by any individual. If there is doubt that a given panelist is intelligible to the students, ask. If needed and if acceptable to the panelist, proceed to provide an oral interpreter who specializes in, for example, Visible-to-Spoken (V/S) interpreting services for the class.

Follow-Up   After the panel has left, class discussion can begin with the following lead questions: "Were the students' questions answered?" "Were attitudes and preconceptions changed or confirmed?" "Did there seem to be different styles of processing information by the panelists?" A short paper may be assigned for students to analyze their observations.

Activity 2 (Out of Class): Attending a Meeting

Objective   Same as for Activity 1.

Preparation and Materials   If an ODAS group of the A. G. Bell Assoc. is active in the area, the instructor should call or write the contact person to arrange for a group of students to visit a meeting or social gathering. The instructor should provide class members with complete information, including a map. Before the event, the instructor should lecture on the purpose and history of the National ODAS and the outreach activities of the local chapter.

Procedure   Go. Enjoy. Learn. Students should be encouraged to approach individuals, introduce themselves, and ask questions at opportune times.

Follow-Up   Discussion at the following class meeting can be led by the instructor's questions: "Any surprises?" "Difficulties in understanding speech?" "Comfort level?" "General impressions?" "Difficulty in making oneself understood?"

Activity 3 (Out of Class): Social Interaction

Objective   Same as for Activities 1 and 2.

Preparation and Materials   If the class or instructor hosts the gathering, a theme, refreshments, and other party preparations are in order. Invitations to hearing-impaired persons should be sent and RSVPs received well in advance.

Procedure   Planned games or activities that require interaction between normally hearing and hearing-impaired guests are encouraged. One imaginative instructor invited a graphologist to her home and had normally hearing and hearing-impaired persons pair off to have their handwriting analyzed.

Follow-Up   Discussion should revolve around ease of communication, use of body language, eye contact, consumer comfort, and individual differences.

SPEECHREADING

Speechreading is the set of skills that makes oral interpreting possible and the limitations of which makes oral interpreting necessary. Students need to be made aware of both the possibilities and the limitations early in the training course. Oral interpreting, Spoken-to-Visible (S/V) assumes speechreading skills on the part of the consumer, while oral interpreting, Visible-to-Spoken (V/S), assumes speechreading skills on the part of the interpreter.

Speechreading, of course, involves not only watching the mouth but also making use of all visual input that accompanies speech. The work of the oral interpreter is to offer clear articulation, natural expression and gestures, and supplementary support techniques when necessary so that the speechreader neither strains to understand nor is in any doubt about the meaning of the message.

If possible, the practicum activities in speechreading described in this chapter should have hearing-impaired speechreaders present in order to illustrate the reality of proficient speechreading and to give valuable feedback to students about the techniques that facilitate or hinder the process.

SKILLS REQUIRED OF ORAL
INTERPRETERS: SPOKEN-TO-VISIBLE (S/V)

Chapter Appendix A identifies the skills required of oral interpreters, Spoken-to-Visible. The following analysis of the elements of the oral interpreter's performance applies to Spoken-to-Visible (S/V) as well as Visible-to-Spoken (V/S) interpreting and transliterating. At least one suggestion for practicum activity is described for each of the skill factors listed.

Short-Term Auditory Memory Skills

Listening and memory skills shall be adequate for accurate reception and retention of the spoken message and its faithful reproduction.

Through careful listening, the oral interpreter should be able to deal appropriately with familiar but unexpected content, unfamiliar terminology, and uncommon accents.

Practicum 1: Transliteration of Familiar Vocabulary

Objective   To hone accurate listening skills; specifically, to listen precisely and repeat accurately and clearly, the familiar but unexpected.

Preparation and Materials   Audiotapes and scripts or read-aloud materials that contain nonsensical information but use only familiar words and proper sentence structure can be prepared. Examples of two such short passages can be found in Chapter Appendix E.

Procedure   Allow each student to orally transliterate a passage for the class. Hearing-impaired students can choose to practice their own speechreading skills by watching carefully or to observe critically with script on hand.

Follow-Up   Brief constructive observations can be offered by peers, instructors, and the student. (Did the interpreter maintain a smooth flow in accurate repetition, illustrating the tone of voice and mood of the speaker? Facial expressions? Eye contact? Did the interpreter show his or her *own* surprise or reaction?) Discuss what would be appropriate.

Practicum 2: Transliteration of the Unfamiliar

Objective   To develop the ability to listen to and accurately repeat spoken messages that contain words unfamiliar to the interpreter, especially in the fields of science and social science.

Preparation and Materials   It may be possible to obtain audiotapes (and transcriptions) from convention proceedings of professional organizations such as the American Medical Association, the American Psychological Association, or the American Association for the Advancement of Science. Centers for disabled students at colleges and universities may be willing to loan textbooks recorded for the blind. Chapters from college textbooks can be read aloud or taped. Audiotapes of college lectures may be useful for practice both in presenting technical terminology and in coping with the problems of speakers who mumble, speak in fragmented sentences, or digress from an announced topic. Each tape requires an accurate script, in which technical terms and other possibly unfamiliar words will be underlined (cued) for observation by the instructor and hearing-impaired students.

Procedure   Students will orally transliterate the taped material, paying special attention to rendering technical terminology precisely, while being observed by classmates and instructor. Hearing-impaired students may attempt to speechread or may follow with a script.

Follow-Up   Discussion will include constructive criticism from peers and instructor, noting whether unfamiliar words were pronounced accurately and whether the interpreter continued smoothly or became flustered. What can the interpreter do to prepare in anticipation of such problems? Tapes could be made available for students to practice privately.

Experienced interpreters have the ability to remember what has just been said long enough to repeat it accurately while at the same time hearing and remembering new information long enough to express it, while at the same time . . . etc.! The S/V oral interpreter is screening the incoming message for words or phrases that may cause difficulty to speechreaders and making almost instantaneous decisions about using one or more support techniques that will facilitate more accurate reception by the speechreading consumers. All this involves complex mental processes, with simultaneous but discrete receptive and expressive activities.

The oral interpreter is expected to remember what is heard only long enough to express it. Where there is a long time lag (two to three sentences) between the spoken word and the interpreter's expression of it, short-term auditory memory is sorely taxed.

Practicum 3: Transliteration of Numbers

Objective   To develop good short-term auditory memory skills.

Preparation and Materials   Lists can be prepared, for example, of increasingly complex sentences containing a series of items or numbers increasing from three digits to seven. Audiotapes can be made from these lists. Sentences for memory practice can be found in Chapter Appendix F.

Procedure   The instructor reads each sentence or number series to the class once, after which the class repeats it aloud. Students can also use taped materials for individual practice. The materials can be used again, this time with students starting to repeat the sentence after the first few words have been heard. Hearing-impaired students can participate by speechreading the instructor but probably will not be able to use the tapes.

Follow-Up   Testing can be done by using similar materials and having students write down what they can remember of each sentence or number sequence. Discussion can center on speed/time lag, rhythm, and fluency.

Lipreadability

The oral interpreter's voiced or voiceless speech shall be easily understood by hearing-impaired speechreaders.

Without exception, hearing-impaired speechreaders who were asked what characteristics should be required for oral interpreters began by saying, "Easy to lipread." All other skills were regarded as secondary. Although this statement is subjective, an objective equivalent might be "the ability to make speech sounds as visible as possible without distortion."

Practicum 1: Clear Articulation

Objective   To record performance and direction for improvement in developing clear articulation (pretest and post-test).

Preparation and Materials   Videotaping equipment (optional) and audiotaped passages or written passages to read aloud; form or paper with carbon for notes by instructor.

Procedure   Each student interprets or orally transliterates a one- to two-minute passage presented by a classmate. The instructor makes notes suggesting specific improvement needed in the student's articulation; a copy of the notes is given to the student. Hearing-impaired students may participate by speechreading a reader and silently articulating his words. If videotaping is done of each student, he or she can also analyze his or her own articulation.

Follow-Up   Later in the course (after studying articulation and speech production), the same material and procedure can be followed, with reference to the original notes to evaluate improvement. If available, new and old videotapes can be compared. Discussion should be on clear articulation, omissions, and the comfort factor.

Practicum 2: Position of Speech Production Organs

Objective   To develop flexibility of speech production organs and muscles and a kinesthetic awareness of their position when making specific speech sounds.

Preparation and Materials   A list of phonemes in the English language and *Fox in Sox* by Dr. Seuss (Seuss, 1965) or other "tongue twister" books can be used.

Procedure   Exercise tongue, lips, cheeks, and neck by placing them in various exaggerated positions, e.g., stretching. Produce isolated phonemes, both voiced and unvoiced, so that the sound is appropriate but the movements are highly exaggerated. Slowly and distinctly, read aloud from *Fox in Sox* or other tongue twister sources while exaggerating all movements.

Follow-Up   Students may recite poetry or sing at home, continuing to use precise but exaggerated speech production movements. Discussion should be on awareness of muscle and organ placement and relationships, and silent and voiced clarity.

Practicum 3: Awareness of Distortions

Objective   To be aware of distortions produced by overarticulation and underarticulation in a person's own and in others' speech and the problems these create for the speechreader.

Preparation and Materials   Videotaping equipment and passages to read aloud are both optional.

Procedure   Each student will read aloud, talk, or recite, first in his "normal" manner, then using articulation he or she feels would be easiest for speechreaders to understand, and finally in a highly exaggerated manner, spending about 1 minute on each mode.

Follow-Up   Speechreaders in the class, or guests, should indicate which mode was preferable to them and why. If videotaped, the student can critically review his or her own style of speech production. Discussion should be on impact on message comprehension, the comfort factor, and voice quality.

Practicum 4: Natural Enunciation

Objective   To develop clear, natural articulation without using voice.

Preparation and Materials   Videotaping equipment with microphone is optional. Passages can be read or recited—1 or 2 minutes each.

Procedure   Each student reads or recites a passage aloud and then repeats the same passage without voice. The class and instructor watch for changes or distortion in articulation when "silent" speech is used as well as listen for distractions, such as lip smacks, clicks of teeth, or hisses of breath, that may inadvertently be made during the "silent" reading. Critiques will be offered for student self-improvement.

Follow-Up   If this practicum is videotaped, the student can verify the feedback and use the tape for review. Discussion should be on natural movements (even when not using voice), clarity, and comfort level.

Verbal Support Techniques

Verbal support techniques (addition, substitution, or rearrangement of words or phrases) shall be used in an appropriate manner when interpreting to clarify and facilitate a speechreader's comprehension.

Interpreters will have learned when studying speechreading what some of the "problems" are for the speechreader (e.g., homophenous words in ambiguous contexts, low visibility words or phrases, and poor pacing). Practica for verbal support techniques involve learning to identify an existing problem and justifying the selection of a particular verbal technique to remedy it.

Practicum 1: Interpretation Using Synonyms and Antonyms

Objective   To demonstrate the ability to use appropriate synonyms and antonyms when substituting or adding words for clarity, i.e. vocabulary-building.

Preparation and Materials   Distribution of lists of words should be grouped according to part of speech—i.e., noun, verb, adverb, adjective; Transparencies and an overhead projector or chalkboard may be used to supplement.

Procedure   Students are asked to write two or three synonyms beside each word on a given list, which is then projected on a screen or written on the chalkboard. The class also contributes to the list. Class discussion, under the instructor's guidance, permits an analysis of each suggested synonym (e.g., Are both nouns?), appropriateness (Is the synonym too "rare" or too colloquial?), meaning (Was the original concept retained?), and finally, whether it has improved visibility over the original (input from speechreaders solicited). The same procedure may be used with antonyms.

Follow-Up   At the end of the unit or course, similar lists can be included in a written test, in which synonyms and antonyms meeting all the requirements cited above are requested for each word.

Practicum 2: Interpretation of Homophenes

Objective   To demonstrate the ability to recognize homophenous words and utilize an appropriate verbal support technique, when required, or repeat the original wording.

Preparation and Materials   Several 2-minute audiotapes should be developed on nontechnical subjects, with scripts carefully cued ("problems" underlined, with notes on some possible solutions).

Procedure   The instructor (with cued script) and other students watch closely while one student interprets orally from the audiotape. The instructor observes whether the student: a) recognizes a homophenous word and deals with it appropriately; b) fails to deal with a problem; or c) modifies a nonproblem word or phrase (i.e., uses clarification techniques when none are needed).

Follow-Up   Feedback from instructor, students, and especially from hearing-impaired persons, should follow each student's efforts. These materials and procedures are appropriate for pre- and posttesting. Discussion should be on the decision making process, use of clarifying words, and excessive deletions.

Practicum 3: Interpretation Involving Phrasing

Objective   To recognize the importance of rhythmic phrasing in the process of speechreading and oral interpreting and to phrase appropriately when oral interpreting, changing the phrasing of the spoken message when necessary.

Preparation and Materials   A passage is selected by the instructor to be videotaped or read aloud.

Procedure   The instructor reads the passage aloud four times: 1) rapidly and evenly, with no change of pace (newscaster-style); 2) jerkily and unevenly, alternating rapid and slow pace, with awkward pauses; 3) slowly and carefully, with self-conscious articulation, a stolid pace, with no variations whatsoever in phrasing; and 4) with natural, appropriate phrasing. Students observe and listen.

Follow-Up   The students discuss the pros and cons of each version (input from hearing-impaired speechreaders is valuable here). If a videotape is made, it can be used later—with the sound turned off for speechreading practice and with the sound on for oral interpreting practice, concentrating on problems of phrasing.

Nonspoken Support Techniques

Nonspoken support techniques (facial expression, gesture, body movement, manual alphabet, number configurations, and mirror-writing, pad and pencil) shall be employed as necessary for clarification of difficult to speechread words and to convey more precisely the tone or mood of the speaker.

Speechreaders rely heavily upon facial expressions, gestures, and body movements as natural components of communication that normally accompany the spoken word. These components should thus occur naturally in the process of oral interpreting and, as adaptive techniques, should be consciously added when appropriate. In most oral interpreting, facial expressions are subtle and very dependent on the immediate context, while gestures are subdued.

Practicum 1: Muscle Warm-Up

Objective   To loosen and "warm up" the muscles of the face, shoulders, neck, and arms; to promote unself-conscious, natural facial expressions, and gestures.

Preparation and Materials   A professional mime or actor can be brought in to lead exercises, or the instructor may look to an exercise book for suggestions.

Procedure   Instructions are followed from the leader or book to methodically stretch and contract muscles of the face, shoulders, neck, and arms.

Follow-Up   Repeat these exercises periodically to reduce tension (e.g., during a class break) and as readiness for oral interpreting or other practicum activities.

Practicum 2: Facial Expressions

Objective   To accurately recognize and produce facial expressions that convey certain common states of being.

Preparation and Materials   For a class of 20, prepare 10 sets of index cards. On one side, print or type a word conveying an emotion (e.g., anger) or state of being (e.g., fatigue) and one or more synonyms (see the examples given in Chapter Appendix G).

Procedure   Divide the class into pairs that sit facing each other, each person with one half of a set of shuffled cards, placed face down. Alternately, each partner turns up one card and attempts to convey through facial expression alone its contents to the other partner. If the partner identifies the word or offers an acceptable synonym, he or she is given the card; otherwise, the card is shown to the partner and set aside. This continues until all the cards have been attempted.

Follow-Up   The instructor leads a class discussion of reasons for difficulties with this exercise, e.g., "wrong," ambiguous, or insufficient facial expression; limited perception or vocabulary on the part of the guesser; or subjectivity of word interpretation, lack of clear context.

Gestures should reinforce, rather than replace, the spoken word and should be used only when truly communicative; a habitual, vague gesture is not helpful. Gestures must never obscure a speechreader's full view of the face and, with few exceptions, should not be formal signs.

Practicum 3: Transliteration and Interpretation Using Nonspoken Cues

Objective   To use natural, expressive gestures in oral interpreting to clarify and communicate meaning.

Preparation and Materials   A carefully cued script may be audiotaped in advance or read aloud to the class (see Chapter Appendix H).

Procedure   The student orally interprets a narrative read aloud or presented on videotape, using appropriate gestures and facial expressions. Students and instructor observe (the latter using a cued script) and critique. Input from hearing-impaired speechreaders is especially valuable.

Follow-Up   The student should be given the opportunity to repeat this procedure some time later, specifically applying earlier suggestions. Discussion questions should center on use of space, whether facial expressions are synonymous with the speaker's intent, and the use of posture and natural gestures.

For proper names and homophenous numbers, the oral interpreter may use the manual alphabet and/or signed number configurations *if* the client has requested this modification and if the oral interpreter can do so fluently and accurately. Printing words or numbers in the air (at chest level) or using a pad and pencil are also acceptable options.

Practicum 4: Transliteration of Proper Names and Numbers

Objective   To convey smoothly and accurately proper names, homophenous numbers, and key "problem" words or phrases by selective use of one or more options, including the manual alphabet and number configurations, mirror-writing, and pad and pencil, as appropriate.

Preparation and Materials   Written material containing many numbers and proper names (e.g., history or algebra "lecture"), to be read aloud in class or audiotaped in advance.

Procedure   Students interpret orally for the class for 5 minutes each, first using mirror-writing when appropriate (2 minutes); then, if competent, using fingerspelling (the manual alphabet) and number configurations (2 minutes); and finally using pencil and pad (1 minute).

Follow-Up   Feedback is provided by the instructor and class (hearing and hearing-impaired) on fluency, clarity, and appropriateness of the support techniques used. Discussion questions should include clarity, placement, and accuracy of fingerspelling and of mirror-writing, and smooth use of pad and pencil?

Finally, the time comes to put it all together.

Practicum: Evaluation of Interpretation

Objective   To demonstrate the ability to receive and transmit accurately the content and tone of the message of a speaker through clearly articulated and smoothly phrased speech (without voice) and the use of appropriate verbal and nonverbal support techniques.

Preparation and Materials   Prepare a number of 3-minute audiotapes or printed material, to be read aloud. Invite to class a group of hearing-impaired speechreaders who have had experience using oral interpreters. Arrange seating and lighting so that the student oral interpreter is clearly visible to all speechreaders. Prepare evaluation sheets (see Chapter Appendix I) for later completion by the visiting evaluators.

Procedure   Introduce speechreaders and indicate proper seating. Have one student adjust the distance and lighting in consultation with the invited guests. Distribute evaluation sheets, with carbon inserts, for assessment of each interpreting performance—one copy for the practicing student, one for the instructor. Have each student interpret orally a full 3-minute videotape.

Follow-Up   After the guest consumers have completed the evaluation sheets for each student interpreter, invite them to analyze the style and adaptive techniques of that interpreter, offering suggestions. Write thank you notes to the "evaluation team." Provide an opportunity for further instructor-student discussion of evaluation sheets.

SKILLS REQUIRED OF ORAL INTERPRETERS: VISIBLE-TO-SPOKEN (V/S)

The practicum activities described above can frequently be used, with adaptations, for Receptive Oral Interpreting: the Visible-to-Spoken (V/S) mode.

Auditory Attention and Auditory Memory

Listening, speechreading, and auditory memory skills shall be adequate for accurate reception, retention, and repetition of the message of hearing-impaired persons whose speech and language have varying degrees of intelligibility and grammatical accuracy.

Practicum 1

Objective   To develop skills in listening to and comprehending the speech of hearing-impaired persons in order to accurately convey their message to other hearing-impaired and hearing persons.

Preparation and Materials   Invite one or more hearing-impaired individuals to visit class and lecture, tell a personal experience, or read from instructor-prepared material. The instructor should have a written copy of the material to be used. If possible and acceptable to the speaker, have videotaping equipment (including sound) available.

Procedure   Introduce each speaker and allow him or her to speak for 5 to 15 minutes. Students should listen carefully and make notes. They should not ask questions or ask for repetitions during the lecture. (Videotapes of these lectures, with sound, will provide invaluable material for later practicum activities.)

Follow-Up   After guest speakers have left, administer a written test (to be corrected in class) on the content of the lecture. Discussion questions should center on reasons for misunderstandings, deciphering techniques, and the comfort factor. Students should use videotapes individually for listening and speechreading practice.

Consumer Comprehension

The oral interpreter's voiced speech or written communication of a hearing-impaired person's spoken message shall be easily understood by hearing persons through two modes: 1) simultaneous, and 2) consecutive.

Practicum 2

Objective   To project a clear voice that will carry over that of the hearing-impaired speaker, in the process of simultaneous oral interpreting (Visible-to-Spoken); to pace comfortably in the consecutive mode.

Preparation and Materials   Five-minute videotapes of hearing-impaired persons may be used or hearing-impaired individuals may be invited to speak, following orientation to the purpose of the practicum. Audiotaping equipment should be available.

Procedure   While being audiotaped, each student orally interprets what the hearing-impaired speaker says, concentrating on the quality of voice projection and accuracy, demonstrating first the simultaneous mode, then the consecutive mode.

Follow-Up   Class and visitor discussion regarding the problems encountered by the hearing-impaired speaker and the interpreters should ensue. Discussion questions should revolve around faithfulness to the speaker's message, nonspoken behaviors, clarity and projection of voice, rhythm and time lag, English structure, and the comfort factor? Later, students may listen to audiotapes of their performances. Hearing-impaired students need to rely on feedback from class and their instructor regarding their voice projection and clarity of speech.

Verbal Support Techniques

Verbal support techniques (addition, substitution, or rearrangement of words or phrases) shall be used in an appropriate manner when necessary for clarification of a hearing-impaired person's spoken message.

Practicum 3

Objective   To develop the ability to use verbal support techniques, including the use of grammatical English, as necessary, when interpreting orally, Visible-to-Spoken.

Preparation and Materials   Videotapes or a scheduled visit by hearing-impaired speakers who use nonstandard English (e.g., ungrammatical sentences, omission of phrases, or mispronounciation of words) will be required. Alternatively, a literal transcription of such speech could be provided. Audiotaping equipment is desirable.

Procedure   Where a videotape or speaker is provided, the students practice Visible-to-Spoken oral interpreting in pairs, first *transliterating* the original message and then interpreting, with special attention paid to using appropriate standard English. Where a transcription is used, students are asked to rewrite it in standard English.

Follow-Up   After the speaker has left, the class may discuss accuracy of message, smoothness of phrasing, appropriateness of changes, and fluency and time lag.

Nonverbal Support Techniques

Nonverbal support techniques (facial expression, gesture, body movement) shall be used in an appropriate manner when necessary for clarification and/or to convey accurately the tone or mood of the speaker.

Various practicum activities relating to facial expression and use of gesture (described earlier) apply equally to this section. However, such support techniques as manual alphabet and mirror-writing are normally not necessary when interpreting in the Visible-to-Spoken mode.

ADAPTATION SKILLS

The Skills Section of the *Guidelines for the Preparation of Oral Interpreters* (1979) also relates to adaptation skills of the oral interpreter and modification of the environmental factors that influence the quality of oral interpreting services:

The oral interpreter shall demonstrate the ability to adapt his or her oral interpreting skills to various situations for which they are requested (one-to-one, group, platform, telephone, etc.).

The primary techniques for practice in dealing with different situations involve setting up mock situations and arranging for role playing. A few suggested techniques are:

1. *One-to-One*   This technique really involves a trio when the interpreter is included. Trios may include doctor, patient, and interpreter; job applicant, employer, and interpreter; or lawyer, client, and interpreter. It should be noted that the hearing-impaired person may be the doctor *or* the patient, the employer *or* the job applicant. Scripts can be written by an appointed trio for a class "performance," or students can be assigned a role "on the spot" and required to improvise. Hearing-impaired speechreaders are invaluable in playing both consumers and interpreters.

2. *Groups*   Groups can involve such situations as a board of directors meeting, therapy session, college seminar, staff meeting, informal get-together. More than one hearing-impaired person may be active in the group. A short time lag between the speaker's and interpreter's words is essential in this situation in order to ensure that

the hearing-impaired members of the group have an opportunity to participate actively.

3. *Platform*   This more formal type of oral interpreting requires a certain amount of stage presence and poise because the interpreter is usually positioned in front of a large group of people. The location may be a classroom, conference, or convention; auditorium event (travelogue, convocation, faculty meeting, or entertainment); or large business meeting. An appropriate appearance (clothing, accessories, and hairstyle) is an important factor and is a topic included in practicum discussions. Adaptation to the differing needs of several consumers is also an item for discussion during platform interpreting role playing.

4. *"Odd" Situations*   Professional oral interpreters may be invited to lecture on specific skill adaptations in unusual situations, such as guided tours, animal obedience training courses, or dance classes—situations in which the leader or primary speaker may be constantly moving while speaking.

5. *Telephone*   Oral interpreting for a telephone user who is hearing-impaired involves adapting skills to the instruments at hand and to the individual needs of the client, i.e., does he or she prefer to speak for himself or herself or does he or she require Visible-to-Spoken oral interpreting as well? The interpreter may encounter: 1) the regular phone with one handset; 2) two extensions so that the client and the interpreter may use separate handsets; 3) a "watch case" listening device connected to the phone for the interpreter; or 4) a conference phone. These instruments should be obtained for use in student role playing.

The second group of adapting skills the oral interpreter must develop involves changing the environment itself:

> The oral interpreter shall demonstrate the ability to adapt environmental factors to produce optimum speechreading and listening conditions for the consumers of oral interpreting services.

Lectures on environmental factors (lighting, seating, distance from speaker, and acoustic conditions) influence both the interpreter's ability to maintain a professional performance and the speechreader's ability to benefit optimally from it. Practicum activities that follow may take the form of field trips to a courtroom, lecture hall, auditorium, classroom, church, office or meeting room. Each will enable students to pay special attention to critical environmental factors that affect the interpreter and speechreading consumer.

CONCLUSION

Classroom activities are an integral part of the practicum experience. In this familiar and comfortable environment, students can apply principles from formal coursework, observation, demonstration, and team practice under expert instructor supervision.

The natural supplement is to carefully plan site visitations and field trips to settings where hearing-impaired speechreaders function in an integrated social, educational, or vocational environment. Each of these opportunities adds to a student's perceptions of the roles of consumer and interpreter and the suitableness of the physical environment in which they interact.

The formal preservice preparation of oral interpreters is relatively new. As experience is gained by instructors, interpreters, and consumers, greater understanding of the complex skills involved in proficient oral interpreting will add to available materials, professional literature, research, and the cultivation of training courses.

The specialized field of oral interpreting is growing; understanding of the full spectrum of practicum experience is essential to its refinement. The ultimate goal of professional interpreter training is professional interpreter performance—the speechreader's entitlement.

REFERENCES

Evans, J. 1981. Inservice training for the 1980's. Early Child. 2:67–74.
Guidelines for the preparation of oral interpreters: Support specialists for hearing-impaired individuals. 1979. Volta Rev. 81:135–145.
Seuss, D. 1965. Fox in Sox. Random House, New York.

APPENDIX A

Adaptation of Skills Section: *Guidelines for the Preparation of Oral Interpreters* (1979)[1]

I. The oral interpreter shall demonstrate the ability to receive and transmit accurately the content and tone of the message of a speaker (hearing or hearing impaired) through clearly articulated and smoothly phrased speech, with or without voice, using appropriate verbal and nonverbal support techniques (*1, 3, 4, 5, 6, 8, 9, 10, 11, 12*).

   A. Oral interpreting: Spoken to Visible (S/V)
      1. Listening and memory skills shall be adequate for accurate reception and retention of the spoken message and its faithful reproduction (*1, 3, 6*).
      2. The oral interpreter's voiced or voiceless speech shall be easily understood by hearing-impaired speechreaders (*6, 10, 11*).
      3. Verbal support techniques (addition, substitution, or rearrangement of words or phrases) shall be used in an appropriate manner to clarify and facilitate a speech reader's comprehension (*1, 5, 6*).
      4. Nonverbal support techniques (facial expression, natural gesture, body movement, manual alphabet, number configurations, mirror-writing, and pad and pencil) shall be employed as necessary to clarify difficult to speechread words and to convey more precisely the tone or mood of the speaker (*1, 5, 8, 11, 12*).

   B. Oral interpreting: Visible to Spoken (V/S)
      1. Listening, speechreading, and auditory memory skills shall be adequate for accurate reception, retention, and repetition of the message of hearing-impaired persons whose speech and language have varying degrees of intelligibility and grammatical accuracy (*1, 3, 9*).
      2. The oral interpreter's voiced speech or written communication of a hearing-impaired person's spoken message shall be easily understood by hearing persons (*9, 10*).
      3. Verbal support techniques (addition, substitution, or rearrangement of words or phrases) shall be used in an

---

[1] Numbers correspond to skills as listed in the Guidelines.

appropriate manner when necessary for clarification of a hearing-impaired person's spoken message (*1, 6, 9, 10, 11*).

   4. Nonverbal support techniques (facial expression, natural gesture, and body movement) shall be used in an appropriate manner when necessary to clarify and/or to convey accurately the tone or mood of the speaker (*1, 5, 9*).

II. The oral interpreter shall demonstrate the ability to adapt his or her oral interpreting skills to various situations for which they are requested (one-to-one, group, platform, telephone, etc.) (*2, 4, 7*).

III. The oral interpreter shall demonstrate the ability to adapt environmental factors to produce optimum speechreading and listening conditions for consumers of oral interpreting services (*2*).

APPENDIX B

Suggestions for Finding Hearing-Impaired Speechreaders in the Community

1. To reach local Oral Deaf Adults Section (ODAS) chapter members and provisional members (age 18 to 21), contact the chairperson of ODAS, Alexander Graham Bell Association for the Deaf, 3417 Volta Place, NW, Washington, D.C. 20007. ODAS is usually comprised of people who have been deaf or severely hard of hearing since childhood and have relied on speechreading for many years. A high percentage of its members are college-educated and/or professional.

2. To reach local parents with school-age, hearing-impaired children and youth, contact the chairperson of the International Parents Organization (IPO) of the A.G. Bell Assoc. (address above).

3. To reach hearing-impaired students in secondary schools, contact the special education office of the local school district. The names and addresses of such students will not be made available, but the district might be willing to forward an informational letter to them or inform the oral interpreting instructor of parent meetings that might be visited.

4. For private schools for aural/oral education for hearing-impaired children in the vicinity that offer various kinds of cooperation and support, contact A.G. Bell Assoc. (address above).

5. To identify adventitiously deafened adults, contact local retirement homes or a senior citizen organization. The instructor can send information to be posted, as well as a specific day and time when he or she can visit with hearing-impaired individuals who may have difficulty using the telephone or finding transportation.

6. To contact various hearing-impaired speechreaders, phone the State Registry of Interpreters for the Deaf (RID) chapter (see yellow pages of the telephone book).

7. To reach hearing-impaired students and/or staff, contact centers for the disabled or handicapped in nearby colleges or junior colleges.

8. To find out about services for the hearing impaired, contact the state department of rehabilitation.

9. Hearing aid dealers are listed in the yellow pages of the telephone book.

10. Otological, ENT, or speech and hearing clinics (listed in the yellow pages) are usually willing to post information about the class and instructor's need for guest lecturers and demonstrations, and evaluation participation.

APPENDIX C

Sample Letter or Flyer for Making Contact with Hearing-Impaired Speechreaders in the Area

WE ARE LOOKING FOR HARD-OF-HEARING AND DEAF PERSONS WHO USE SPEECH AND SPEECHREADING (LIPREADING) AS THEIR PRIMARY MODE OF COMMUNICATION

_____(Institution)_____ is conducting a program of instruction for oral interpreters.

Oral interpreting is a support service for those hearing-impaired (hard-of-hearing and deaf) persons who rely primarily on speechreading (lipreading) and speech, rather than on sign language, for communication. Oral interpreters provide an opportunity for hearing-impaired speechreaders to derive full benefit from social, religious, educational, and work environments where the use of their speechreading skills may be limited or prevented due to unavoidable circumstances.

The students in our program aspiring to become certified oral interpreters need to have greater contact with the people they will serve. If you are a hearing-impaired speechreader and would like to volunteer an hour or two of your time, please contact:

(Name)

(Phone number, voice and TDD)

(Mailing address)

(Phone number, voice and TDD)

(Mailing address)

APPENDIX D

Suggested Questions to Ask a Panel of Hearing-Impaired Persons

1. At what age did you lose your hearing? What was the cause of your hearing loss? How severe is your hearing loss?
2. What kind of educational background do you have? Do you feel it was appropriate, given your present situation?
3. What is your occupation now? How did you prepare for and/or get this job? Do you feel it is right for you? Are there communication problems at work because of your hearing loss? If so, how do you handle them?
4. What communication mode(s) do you use now? If more than one, which do you prefer? Why?
5. How did (does) your hearing loss affect your social life?
6. Have you ever used an oral interpreter? If yes, under what circumstances? What was positive and what was not useful about the experience? When do you think you would use an oral interpreter now?

APPENDIX E

"Familiar But Unexpected": Listening Practice (Spoken-to-Visible, Practicum 1)

Yesterday I took my daughter to the movies. I didn't want to take Jenny too, but my daughter insisted. Jenny's mother and I are not close friends, although Jenny and my daughter usually get along quite well. Of course, we walked to the movies. I had my doubts about the whole arrangement, though, and they were confirmed. The theater people would not let Jenny in. They probably didn't have any seats big enough for an elephant, even a small one like Jenny.

Last week I decided to make meatloaf. It is one of my favorite meals because I can use so many leftovers. This time I started with a pound of good, fresh, ground horsemeat. To this I added one egg, bread crumbs, chopped onion, and a cup of fresh garden snails left over from the night before. A half-teaspoon salt, a dash of pepper and some crumbled paper for flavor finished that recipe. My family loved it.

APPENDIX F

Sentences for Memory Practice (Spoken-to-Visible, Practicum 2)

1. Yesterday I went shopping at the grocery store.
2. I had not been shopping since Friday, August 15, and was out of just about everything.
3. First I got basic nonfood products: paper towels, paper napkins, plastic bags, and soap.
4. Then I went to the produce department and got apples, bananas, grapes, cherries, and oranges.
5. I needed vegetables for a salad so I picked up fresh mushrooms, onions, green peppers, tomatoes, celery, and two kinds of lettuce.
6. Then I went to the dairy section and got eggs, whole milk, sour cream, cottage cheese, half-and-half, nonfat milk, and ice cream.
7. I was about to leave when I remembered I needed hotdogs, mustard, relish, hotdog buns, potato chips, soda pop, beer, and film for my camera.
8. When all this was added up at the checkout stand, it came to $37.59 but I only had $26.35 so I gave that to the checkout girl and wrote a check for $11.24.
9. Whew!

APPENDIX G

Facial Expressions: Practice
(Spoken-to-Visible, Practicum 3)

1. HAPPINESS (joy, delight, gladness, pleasure, contentment)
2. SADNESS (grief, sorrow, despondency)
3. FEAR (horror, terror, anxiety, apprehension)
4. DISGUST (repugnance)
5. ANGER (rage, fury, irritation, annoyance)
6. SURPRISE (shock, astonishment)
7. DOUBT (disbelief, suspicion)
8. ARROGANCE (pride, haughtiness)
9. FATIGUE (exhaustion, tiredness, weariness)
10. CONTEMPT (disdain, scorn)
11. SHYNESS (coyness, bashfulness)
12. ENTHUSIASM (eagerness, anticipation)
13. INDIFFERENCE (apathy, nonchalance)
14. PAIN

APPENDIX H

Cued Script: Natural Nonverbal Cues (Spoken-to-Visible, Practicum 4)

Two or 3 years ago, I decided to fly home for Christmas. I had just gotten a brand-new *kitten* and *I didn't have anyone to take care of her*, so I decided to take her with me. I went to the vet to get some medication to help her sleep because it was going to be a long trip. *I didn't have enough money* to rent one of those cages you can get from the airport, so I decided I would *put her in a blanket and pretend she was a baby.* On the plane, all the stewardesses were very helpful and interested in my "baby." They would ask, "Is it a boy or a girl? *May we see it? Can I help you with anything?* How old is it?" All this made me very nervous. I found myself *telling lies right and left* and *assuring* them that the "baby" was asleep. After 4 hours of this, *I was a nervous wreck!*

Finally we arrived home. By then *my clothes were wet with sweat* because I was so nervous, and I wanted to get off the plane as quickly as I could before the kitten woke up. Just as I was about to leave the plane, the friendly stewardess at the door asked, *"May I see your baby?"* I was so tired of telling lies that I finally *lifted up the blanket.* My kitten *opened up her little eyes* and gave a soft "meow." The stewardess *was so shocked*, she screamed! I hurried off the plane, *holding tightly to my now active little "baby."* I'll *never* try to get away with that again!

APPENDIX I

Spoken to Visible: Speechreader's Evaluation[2]

Student _____ Date _____

Topic _____

Evaluator _____

I. Listening and Memory Skills
   A. Time Lag
      ___1. Excellent (keeps up with speaker)
      ___2. Good (occasionally behind, but able to keep up)
      ___3. Average (frequently behind, misses some information)
      ___4. Poor (unable to keep up, loses the message)
   B. Deletions
      ___1. Excellent (almost no deletions, all information included)
      ___2. Good (minimal deletions, message conveyed clearly)
      ___3. Average (many deletions, message garbled)
      ___4. Poor (many deletions, message lost)

II. Lipreadability
   A. Articulation (mouth movements)
      ___1. Excellent   ___Overexaggerated
      ___2. Good   ___Stiff
      ___3. Average   ___Mumbled
      ___4. Poor   ___Other (Explain: _____
      _____)

   B. Pronunciation
      ___1. Excellent   ___Interpreter's accent evident
      ___2. Good   ___Overexaggeration of speaker's
      ___3. Average   accent
      ___4. Poor   ___Other (Explain: _____
      _____)

   C. Rhythm and Pacing
      ___1. Excellent   ___Halting
      ___2. Good   ___Runs words together
      ___3. Average   ___Too steady (monotonous)
      ___4. Poor   ___Unfaithful to speaker's pacing
      ___Other (Explain: _____
      _____)

---

[2] This Speechreader's Evaluation Form is adapted from the form used in the Interpreter Training Program at the Community College of Denver, North, 3645 West 112th, Westminster, Colorado 80030 (Kenneth Bosch, Director; Lindsey Antle, Coordinator).

III. Verbal Support Techniques
    A. Use of Synonyms
        ___1. Excellent   ___Uses when unnecessary
        ___2. Good   ___Uses inappropriate synonyms
        ___3. Average   ___Uses insufficiently
        ___4. Poor   ___Other (Explain: _____
                                  _____)

    B. Use of Paraphrasing
        ___1. Excellent   ___Paraphrases when unnecessary
        ___2. Good   ___Paraphrases inaccurately
        ___3. Average   ___Loses other message while
        ___4. Poor   paraphrasing
                                  ___Other (Explain: _____
                                  _____)

IV. Nonverbal Support Techniques
    A. Facial Expression
        ___1. Excellent   ___Expressionless
        ___2. Good   ___Exaggerated expression
        ___3. Average   ___Expression does not match
        ___4. Poor   message
                                  ___Other (Explain: _____
                                  _____)

    B. Eye Contact
        ___1. Excellent   ___Watches speaker, not con-
        ___2. Good   sumer
        ___3. Average   ___Minimal or no eye contact
        ___4. Poor   ___Unrelieved, staring eye contact
                                  ___Other (Explain: _____
                                  _____)

    C. Gestures
        ___1. Excellent   ___Uses signs (except fingerspell-
        ___2. Good   ing or numbers)
        ___3. Average   ___Habitual and unhelpful ges-
        ___4. Poor   tures
                                  ___Excessive and/or exaggerated
                                  ___Minimal to none
                                  ___Other (Explain: _____
                                  _____)

D. Body Shifting
    ___1. Excellent   ___Too much
    ___2. Good   ___Too little
    ___3. Average   ___Inappropriate and/or distract-
    ___4. Poor   ing
    ___Other (Explain: _____
    _____)

V. Appearance
  A. Posture
    ___1. Excellent   ___Too tense
    ___2. Good   ___Too relaxed
    ___3. Average   ___Slouched
    ___4. Poor   ___Unnatural
    ___Other (Explain: _____
    _____)

  B. Facial Hair (if any)
    ___1. None
    ___2. Neat, not distracting
    ___3. Moustache covers upper lip
    ___4. Beard not neatly trimmed
    ___5. Other (Explain: _____)

  C. Hairstyle
    ___1. Neat, not distracting
    ___2. Needs trimming (Explain: _____
    _____)

  D. Dress
    ___1. Excellent   ___Too highly patterned
    ___2. Good   ___Too highly colored
    ___3. Average   ___Inappropriate for setting
    ___4. Poor   ___Other (Explain: _____
    _____)

ROLE MODELS AND RESOURCE NETWORKS

CHAPTER 11

THE CODE OF ETHICS: SOME INTERPRETATIONS

Rebecca H. Carlson

CONTENTS

Professionally trained and certified interpreters/transliterators (sign language and oral) conform to a set of standards for acceptable behavior and performance that is formally identified as the Code of Ethics. It has been developed, adopted and upheld by the Registry of Interpreters for the Deaf, Inc. (RID) to protect the rights of hearing and hearing-impaired (deaf and hard-of-hearing) consumers of interpreting services as well as the interpreter, who acts as a communication facilitator. Why, then, is the Code of Ethics far too often misrepresented, misunderstood, and misused? A partial answer lies within this chapter.

HISTORY

Interpreting is a relatively young profession. Less than 20 years ago a "Workshop on Interpreting for the Deaf" was held at Ball State Teachers' College in Muncie, Indiana. The outcome was the formation of a new organization, called the National Registry of Professional Interpreters and Translators for the Deaf. This was later shortened and renamed the RID.

The original statement in founding an interpreter organization in 1964, read: "The purpose of the organization is to promote recruiting and training of more interpreters for the deaf, both manual and oral, and to maintain a list of qualified persons" (Quigley, 1965). From its inception, the RID was to be an organization to support all hearing-impaired individuals (including both sign language users and speechreaders). "I am led to wonder how the oral deaf person . . . will fare in a large meeting where the speaker is some distance away. I hope this workshop will provide some answers, and that the oral deaf who are with us will help us develop them" (Smith, 1964, p. 33).

Although no formal Code of Ethics was developed at Ball State in 1964, a committee was established to address the question of ethical behavior and these guidelines were advanced:

> An interpreter should possess:
> 1. A proficiency in manual and/or oral communication
> 2. A high moral character
> 3. A professional attitude which will inspire ethical conduct
> 4. An understanding of deaf people
> 5. An education sufficient to embrace the problems of life and a sophistication to cope with its varieties. (Smith, 1964)

These original guidelines form the foundation from which the current Code of Ethics evolved.

The following year (1965) at the Governor Baxter State School for the Deaf in Portland, Maine, a second workshop on interpreting was held. The proceedings from this workshop were printed and entitled *Interpreting for Deaf People* (Quigley, 1965). Quite unintentionally, that publication, which included the Code of Ethics, became the textbook for many sign language interpreter training programs. Thus, the first formal code of ethics was widely circulated.

This code emphasized behavior indicating high moral character and impartiality regarding interpreter attitude and behavior as well as faithfulness to the content and spirit of a speaker's remarks and confidentiality regarding all aspects of an assignment. It also covered a variety of situations, such as legal settings, volunteer services offered without charge, and a general dress code. However, the paternalistic overtones were eliminated when the style changed from a command format to one that stresses guidelines and permits interpretation of what is "reasonable" in carrying out the major tenets of the code.

There is a critical need for more written information regarding implementation of the Code of Ethics for use by consumers and interpreters alike. A case book of situations demonstrating appropriate behavior in professional and personal dimensions of interpreting could well be used by instructors of preservice preparation programs. The Code is an often requested topic for professional growth workshops, indicating recognition of the fact that oral or sign language interpreting requires more than application of professional and technical skills. In order to be effective, the code's formal principles must be applied in humane and logical ways.

PURPOSE

In all dimensions of human interaction in the 1980s, individuals are either governed by formal rules of behavior or traditional, informal patterns of response. By general agreement, a person would greet the President of the United States quite differently from his or her best friend, for example. Some "rules" for interaction are written as laws, regulations, or contracts; others are unwritten but equally binding and automatic in application, such as the standard greeting, "Hello (or Hi!), how are you?" "Fine!"

Child development specialists say that children enjoy and even want limits set for them. There is a sense of security and self-confidence that develops when a person knows what is generally expected in the way of performance in a given situation. The conduct of an interpreter, the hearing and the hearing-impaired consumer is conditioned by the principal tenets of the Code of Ethics, which relate to both personal and professional deportment; all three classifications of individuals are protected. Thus, a stable framework exists to ensure a trusting relationship between the interpreter and consumer. It is ironic that from this foundation, built on trust, springs such an active potential for harm and misuse of power on the part of active members of the triad.

THREE MAJOR TENETS

Three fundamental tenets of the Code of Ethics carry mandated compliance by the interpreter as well as by the normally hearing or the hearing-impaired consumer.

1. *Confidentiality*   Keep all assignment-related information strictly confidential.
2. *Impartiality*   Maintain impartiality in behavior and attitude. Render the message faithfully, always conveying the content and spirit of the speaker and refraining from censorship or embellishment.
3. *Integrity*   Accept assignments using discretion with regard to demeanor and information, in full consideration of the skill, setting, and consumers involved.

Through the setting of behavioral limits, the Code offers protection to an interpreter and consumer alike. The normally hearing speaker or consumer is secure in the knowledge that all he or she says will be conveyed fully and clearly to the hearing-impaired individual. In turn, the hearing-impaired speaker or consumer knows his or her information will be conveyed without editing or censorship. Protection of the interpreter stems from a clear definition of roles, which require each person to accept responsibility for his or her own actions.

The Code guarantees full communication to the hearing-impaired consumer under the mandate of *impartiality*. The same interpersonal communication that many people take for granted as a natural part of daily life can become a conscious struggle for a hearing-impaired person. In the broader sense, the basic human rights as set forth in the Declaration of Independence have involved a battle of accessibility for hearing-impaired individuals who only recently have gained access to a formally trained and professionally certified interpreter of their choice: an oral interpreter or a sign language interpreter.

APPLICATION

The Code of Ethics can be read, understood, debated, applauded, and memorized, but the Code is not necessarily followed until it has been internalized. The integrity of the set of ethics is not argued; it is the application that requires constant attention.

Clearly Defined Positions

In some situations, application of the code is clearly presented in the *Guidelines*, undergirding each specific principle. If an interpreter is asked, "What happened when Johnny went to the nurse's office?" the correct response is one which protects his or her right to confidentiality. The response might be, "You might want to ask Johnny when you see him."

What would your response be in the following situation? You are an oral interpreter for a speechreader who is making a presentation to a panel of judges. After the session, another speechreader wants to know how his friend did; were the judges fair?

If the friend did well, it seems harmless, on the surface, to say "Fine!" However, if the friend made a poor showing, what would you say? Would your immediate reaction be different? The guidelines of the Code remind a reader that "even seemingly unimportant information could be damaging in the wrong hands. Therefore, to avoid this possibility, interpreter/translators must not say anything about any assignment." Clearly, the interpreter cannot divulge information learned while interpreting. As one speechreader chided, "It is not your news. It is mine!"

Culton (1974) focused on the imperative of confidentiality, as the hearing-impaired individual views it, from the point of view of the professional relationship that must be preserved between interpreter and client. "In most cases where there is a choice, a deaf person will choose an interpreter with inferior skills, or even resort to pad and pencil, in order to preserve their right to privacy" (p. 179).

"Function in a manner appropriate to the situation" is a dimension of the concept of integrity described in the Code guidelines. Let's look at another situation. You are an oral interpreter during a group discussion. The content of the discussion has deteriorated and the group has become disorganized. You can see very clearly how to redirect the group so that they can complete the task at hand.

To step out of your role as interpreter is to betray the trust between you and the consumers, who depend on you to provide a communication bridge. You are not present to be a participant, a group facilitator, or consultant. As an interpreter, you are conveying the spoken thoughts of one individual to another. Even though your actions may be motivated by very good intentions ("I'm only trying to help"), *don't!* Don't voluntarily extend your role to "chairperson"; keep out, or you may be asked to stay out.

In these illustrations, as in numerous daily situations, the answer to "What should I do?" is fairly clear, with directions clearly stemming from the Code of Ethics. When an interpreter knows what *should* be done, what is right and proper, he or she must then muster the courage to do it. Often, it is not easy, but there is not much to debate.

To the extent that the interpreter and normally hearing and hearing-impaired consumers understand the subtle dimensions of the Code, the interaction will unfold naturally and fairly. In both preservice and in-service orientation, experienced interpreters can demonstrate in practical ways how the Code of Ethics of interpreting influences them. Reaching out to other disciplines to hear lectures by specialists in law, medicine, and advertising on the subject of ethics in general is valuable.

The task of consumer education is being assumed by the Registry of Interpreters for the Deaf, the Oral Deaf Adults Section (ODAS) of the Alexander Graham Bell Association for the Deaf, and the National Association of the Deaf, as well as specialists in this dimension of professional preparation of oral and sign language interpreters.

Ambiguous Situations

For every interpreting situation in which the appropriate behavior is self-evident and clear-cut, interpreters must wrestle with a multitude of dilemmas.

Consider the following example: You are interpreting for a speechreader enrolled in a highly technical course at a university. It is late in the afternoon and you can see the student (Jack) is not understanding the material being presented. What is your role as an interpreter? Do you begin to explain the content more fully? Do you stop the speaker? Do you continue interpreting as usual?

If the answer is not clear, ask this rhetorical question of yourself, "If Jack were a hearing person and no interpreter was present, what might happen?" Jack might continue to sit and listen, hoping to get the information from the textbook. He could ask the instructor to expand his remarks. He might be absorbing the lecture completely and actually working out another problem in his head! The critical point here is: Jack would reach an independent decision on what course of action to take. The presence of an interpreter should not alter this logical process.

Consider this type of situation. You are an oral interpreter for a speechreader who is part of a professional team of four. During the discussion, it is decided to set up a meeting with a fifth individual. You happen to know this person has a conflict on the appointed date. Do you volunteer the information in the interest of efficiency or remain silent?

If the answer is unclear, ask yourself this question? "If I don't speak up, what is the worst consequence of my silence? Can I live with it?" In this instance, a rescheduling of the meeting and some inconvenience seem tolerable.

In a situation where you are unsure of the "right" behavior, ask yourself this question: "As a self-reliant individual who enjoys independence, how would *I* want the interpreter to act if *I* were the hearing-impaired client?" You would probably want to retain your autonomy and would resent behavior that prevented you from doing so.

CANONS OF BEHAVIOR

1. *Focus on your function, not your feelings* Interpreters are involved in human interactions. They witness emotions that range from confrontations, arguments, and temper flare-ups to scenes of extreme sorrow. When an interpreter becomes distracted or preoccupied with emotions that are evoked, the precision of professional interpreting is affected. The challenge, instead, is to direct your energy toward careful, eloquent expression of another's emotions.

2. *Avoid "owning" other people's emotions and decisions* Events may not turn out as you would wish; people make independent decisions, and in turn, each must accept the consequences. If an instructor becomes angry with a student, do not internalize that anger as your own. If a hearing-impaired court witness is hostile, the sole responsibility of an interpreter is to accurately convey the message to include mood, emotional tone, and content.

3. *Your primary responsibility is self-control and self-discipline* These follow the Code of Ethics and should prevent you from step-

ping in to control a three-party situation: the hearing consumer, the hearing-impaired consumer, and you, the interpreter, as communication facilitator. Interference with the independent judgment and actions of others can result in resentment and resistance. Learn to control the one person you are responsible to—yourself.

4. *Identify your "should" list*   Everyone has a primary set of values that governs their lives and reflects their personal upbringing and previous experiences. From these values stems a "should" list of how to control personal behavior in daily living. For instance, one "should" might be to respect individuals in authority, i.e., teachers, police officers, and community leaders. In this example, if a hearing person in the audience shows disrespect for the hearing-impaired leader through comments or tone of voice, how will this affect interpreting? The interpreter's instinct might be to soften the comments and smooth over the condescending tone; his or her "should" prompts this reaction. While interpreting, the "shoulds" of the Code of Ethics are paramount. Although personal values are concepts to be cherished, interpreters are asked to identify them and for the duration of an interpreting assignment, to lay them aside.

SUMMARY

The Code of Ethics of the RID provides a structural frame of reference to facilitate full communication between normally hearing and hearing-impaired persons, with the interpreter as communication facilitator. It is a sound nucleus, governing conscientious and "correct" behavior by all parties concerned. It should be presented to preserve students in interpreter preparation programs early in the sequence of coursework so that it becomes, not an instrument of rigidity, but a functional set of guidelines to encourage rather than limit creative problem solving and rapid decision making.

Rapid decision making is the heart of creative interpreting—whether to paraphrase a speaker's particular statement to facilitate a speechreader's comprehension or to repeat it verbatim; and how to precisely mirror the mood and tone of a speaker's remarks for the consumer. These professional and technical skills demand intense concentration on the part of an oral interpreter. Self-control is expected of normally hearing and hearing-impaired clients as well as the "bridge" builder—the interpreter.

Interpreting is an occupation that offers challenge, usefulness, and adventure. Interpreters play a critical role in many situations involving dynamic human interactions. For those who choose to absorb the skills, knowledge, and attitudes required to supplement extensive firsthand contact with and appreciation of those whose chosen mode of communication is speech and speechreading, oral interpreting can be a fulfilling part or full-time career.

REFERENCES

Code of Ethics. 1980. In: R. D. Dirst (ed.), Oral Interpreter Evaluation Manual for Evaluators, Appendix. RID, Inc., National Evaluation System, Silver Spring, MD.

Culton, P. 1974. The professional approach. In: J. Palmer (ed.), The Interpreting Scene, pp. 175–180. Proceedings. Second National Workshop/Convention of RID, August 14–17, 1972, Long Beach, CA.

The interpreter. 1979. In: C. Yoken (ed.), Interpreter Training: The State of the Art, pp. 4–9. The National Academy of Gallaudet College, Washington, DC.

Morgan, S. M., and R. H. Carlson. 1980. Creative problem solving for interpreters. In: Proceedings, 6th National Workshop/Convention of the R.I.D. Decade of Interpreter Awareness in a Century of Interpreter Awareness, pp. 11–19. RID, Inc., Silver Spring, MD.

Quigley, S. (ed.). 1965. Interpreting for Deaf People. U.S. Department of Health, Education and Welfare, Washington, DC.

Smith, J. (ed.). 1964. Workshop on Interpreting for the Deaf. Vocational Rehabilitation Administration, Washington, DC.

CHAPTER 12

TESTIMONY FROM SPEECHREADERS

CONTENTS

SATISFIED YANKEE FAN

Ken H. Levinson

Since the age of 21 months, I have had to contend with a radio-like box that would reach beyond my 95–100 dB loss and amplify every conceivable sound on earth so that I could enjoy the fruits of speech, music, and all the creatures of sound. Then 2 years ago, a threshold shift caused my hearing to drop about 5 to 10 dB across the speech range. This pushed me to the point where the doctors feared that further direct amplification would destroy whatever residual hearing I had left. That meant no more hearing aids. Well, actually, I was only allowed to wear the aid 1 or 2 hours a day. In reality, however, this amounted to getting off the phone and relying totally on speechreading whenever carrying on daily conversation.

WHY THE INTERPRETER?

The bottom line in getting an interpreter in the "Fortune Five Hundred" company where I am employed is the extra cost to the employer for such services. There were other factors involved that made my case somewhat different from a normal situation. First of all, there was no question as to the need for an oral interpreter. My ability to perform adequately as a manager depends on communication with many different people. The cast of characters includes my boss, co-workers, staff, and company executives. The last category became the most important in terms of getting the interpreter because interface with executives is the most critical in terms of selling the services of the audit department, where I hold an executive position. Having the oral interpreter on board would enhance my ability to function and communicate in a more normal fashion. Since getting the interpreter, I have been absolutely amazed as to how much communication is really required. It seems as though I'm constantly having conversations and/or meetings with one person or another. I no longer need to rely on others to communicate to the executives for me; that makes my visibility within the company much greater and, I hope, more positive.

The second major factor is that the department shares two sec-retaries, and I cannot train one of them to be an oral interpreter because it would take time away from her responsibilities to other members of the department. Since the communications requirement is so great, the need was there to add another employee solely for the purpose of interpreting.

Now we can label this member of the cast of characters. The interpreter's name is Leah. She is certified by the National Registry of Interpreters for the Deaf (RID) and was an instructor in an interpreter training program until affected by cutbacks in federal funds. Not only is she very highly qualified, but we have become fast friends, although sometimes I wonder if her husband and I are actually closer. After all, we're both baseball freaks and die-hard Yankee fans!

USE OF THE INTERPRETER

Leah is what I call an exceptionally good interpreter. When she interprets, she is only three or four words behind the speaker. This makes telephone conversations seem as though there is no third party involved. In terms of managerial effectiveness, I feel I get close to 90 to 95% of the message she repeats without voice. The staff no longer have qualms about calling me from the field. Previously, lengthy discussions would be saved for face-to-face meetings, or the staff person might feel compelled to drive back to the corporate office to tell me. Of course, this easier access over the phone gives them the opportunity to bother me as well.

Telephone Usage

When we first started using the phone with the staff, it was a bit strange for them. Most of them would say, "Leah, tell Ken this and that." Now they have all gotten so used to it that most of them now talk directly to me about company matters and then, before hanging up, will say, "Hi Leah, how are you doing today?" They care how Leah is doing. Me? I'm just the boss. Leah has a very outgoing and friendly personality, and this plays a crucial role in her effectiveness as a genuine part of Corporate Audit rather than just some kind of support service specialist.

Friends that I talk to all want to know how in God's name I can hear what they are saying on the phone. Feedback I get from talking to them in person is one of amazement. They all say that talking to me on the phone is the same as carrying on a normal conversation. The three- or four-word delay that exists goes unnoticed by virtually everyone until it is explained to them. There are times, though, when I want the listener to know I am hearing impaired (for example, when ordering theater tickets), and I will have Leah talk on the phone because I doubt they'd ever believe me if we did it our normal way.

Meetings

The other participants do the talking, and I "listen" through Leah. The reasons for this are twofold. First, the three- or four-word delay in Leah's interpretations is added to the natural delay any hearing-impaired person has in translating visual cues to auditory ones. As a result, the opportunities to interject my opinion or added information into group conversations are diminished because hearing people develop a natural capability of taking advantage of conversational pauses. The second reason for low participation is that speechreading everything continuously is an extremely strenuous task, and often times, I have to take a mental break. This doesn't happen over the phone because the back and forth exchange provides that respite. My ability and motivation to respond also depend on the group size and who the participants are. Many people just naturally like to control conversations, and others would rather follow.

Distractions

Signing, for example. Leah is basically a sign language interpreter and still does some moonlighting as one. On the job, however, signing is kept to a minimum. I would guess that maybe 5% or less of the words are actually signed. Phone conversations generally are strictly oral. The only time Leah signs is if she feels that I may not be getting a particular word and, even then, she usually just fingerspells the first letter of the word. Sometimes, it's still difficult for her to know what I understand and what I don't. A lot of that is easing off because she's becoming familiar with the vocabulary used in our department. At times, she will also sign a bit more at conferences or large meetings where there may be some misunderstanding as to what an "oral" interpreter is. If she only interprets orally, it can be perceived as a side conversation between Leah and myself. In addition, Leah sometimes needs to sign to give herself some kind of break from a strict oral mode as she has no one available to "sit in" for her when she tires.

PRACTICAL ADAPTATIONS

This brings me to another point. Interpreting can be a very strenuous and exhausting job. Breaks are essential but often unavailable. Leah and I try to work things out so that her breaks are maximized with no loss of information to me. All-day conferences, for example, pose real hardships on Leah. Hence, if a speaker is talking about something I already know or don't want to hear, I let Leah stop. Funny thing is that when this happens, we start chatting about personal matters, such as joining her and her husband for dinner and Hill Street Blues.

What about other distractions? Remember, Leah is a human being (so she told me during the interview) and that means yawning, sneezing, scratching, moving, and brushing her hair back. And this one sneezes! It's just my luck to have an interpreter who is allergic to offices. In any event, if the interpreter were doing 20- to 30-minute shifts, these distractions would be minimal, but Leah doesn't have that luxury. In all fairness then, I have to let her indulge in her foibles. It's rough, but she makes up for it when she interprets things like yawning at the other end of the phone. The shock expressed by some of my friends when I ask them if I'm keeping them awake is worth it.

CONCLUSION

So now you have the story. How it came to be. Why I needed her. And how she does her thing. Having an oral interpreter has helped me so much I can't begin to say. I mentioned earlier that I was surprised how much I needed to use her. When we were asking the company for such services, we estimated that I would need the interpreter for about 30% of the time. Now, it's more like 80%. Just goes to prove the old adage—give them an inch and they'll take a mile. Or is it because Leah feels more comfortable being with a Yankee fan? After all, she married one!!

I ORGANIZE FOR WHAT I NEED

Mark L. Stern

INFORMAL ORAL INTERPRETERS

A Family Affair

My mother had served as an informal oral interpreter off and on for most of my life, but she rarely interpreted more than a few sentences or a sentence fragment at any one time. Usually, she could summarize the situation for me in two or three words. She was actually an interpreter/editor—skilled in reducing public statement to a minimal comment. In fact, our system was practical. If the President of the United States gave a 30-minute speech on television and I asked my mother what it was about, she usually said, "Wait a minute . . . I have to listen a little more" and then she would sum it up in a succinct phrase such as, "The economy is in bad shape." I was content to have these summaries because I did not always want to take time to watch the whole speech. Also, I knew I could read the text in detail in the morning paper if I wished. However, I gradually became more interested in public events and wanted to follow certain public meetings on the spot.

My father, brother, and sisters also acted as sporadic oral interpreters at home. My sisters were especially helpful with telephone calls. My older sister, Ami, interpreted on the phone until she was about 14 and became too busy with her own phone calls; then my younger sister, Rachel, inherited the post. At age 4, Rachel was still too young to dial accurately; I dialed the number, and Rachel did the oral interpreting. When I was 14, I received a TDD (telecommunication device for the deaf) and my telephone communication opportunities were expanded. However, Rachel still interpreted when I called a hearing friend to get the homework assignment or to find out about a social event.

The School Environment

In school, classmates were often volunteer oral interpreters, giving me a running summary of what was happening in a class presentation or assembly. My friend, Jimmy Baldinger, was particularly supportive in this way. He offered me selective interpreting; we knew each other well, and he had the ability to sift out unimportant information quickly and get to the core. At an assembly, he would choose some statements and skip others. It worked very well for me, but only such a good friend can serve as a selective interpreter. From my point of view, he knew what was important and unimportant, and I had confidence in his selection.

At our school, which is a Quaker school, we had Meeting for Worship weekly. These Meetings were mostly silent, where everyone in the room would sit in reflection until someone from anywhere in the room would speak out on a subject of spiritual, personal, political, or social importance. When someone spoke out at the silent meeting, my friend, Jimmy, who was often sitting next to me, oral interpreted (in his usual selective way) what was being said. One time during the meeting, another student stood up and said that he had been observing

Jimmy's interpreting to me and felt that Jimmy and I had a special kind of friendship—one that allowed one person to interpret the Meeting for another.

PROFESSIONAL ORAL INTERPRETERS

Although I had observed professional oral interpreters at an Alexander Graham Bell Association Family Outing in Emmittsburg, Maryland, I had followed them rather unconsciously. I did not consider how they could really help me until, in 1978, I was invited by Anne Adams to speak on a panel of oral deaf adults at the Bell Convention in St. Louis, Missouri. There were at least 10 people on the panel, sitting on a platform at a long table with microphones between each two persons. It was hard to crane my neck to follow the remarks of the sixth or eighth person down the line, especially when the speaker's face was partially obscured by the microphones and profiles of other panel members. The oral interpreter was in plain view, right in front of me. I had some reservations about looking at the interpreter because I was worried whether the audience would wonder why I was not lipreading the other speakers. One of the reasons we had been invited to speak on the panel was to serve as role models for other young hearing-impaired people. Sitting up there, looking out at the hot room packed with 200 people, I wondered if they thought I was a poor role model because I could not speechread all the other speakers on the panel—and sideways at that!

I did not use interpreters for classes in junior high and high school because Sidwell Friends School had small classes. The teachers almost always had time to spend with me, and everybody was very supportive and understanding. But I have used interpreters on several special occasions through my high school years.

First Experiences

The first time I used an oral interpreter at school was an evening lecture on Human Growth and Development, given by Dr. Estelle Ramsey of Georgetown University. Dr. Ramsey was known to be a provocative speaker; the school dining room was crowded with many of my fellow students, teachers, and parents. Barbara Williams, my interpreter, had worked as an interpreter in the school system in nearby Montgomery County. She had also interpreted for me once at the Smithsonian Institution at a photography lecture given by Ansel Adams. I knew she was excellent for lecture interpreting. However, at that time I still had some anxiety about using an interpreter in such a big setting at school. I tried to make the arrangements as inconspicuous as possible by having the interpreter sit next to me (not in front of me) so that she looked like a member of the audience. It was not that I lacked self-confidence but rather that I did not want to have to explain about the interpreter and I did not want my friends to look at me differently—as someone isolated from the group. I wanted all the information, but I wanted just as much to be part of the crowd.

The next time I used an interpreter at school was at another evening meeting. This one was about alcohol and drugs and included a panel of students, faculty, and parents. This was such a pivotal topic at school that I did not want to miss the event and read about it in the school paper 3 weeks later. I knew everyone would be talking about it, and I could not afford to wait to be up to date. My interpreter was Sarina Roffé, who was a parent of a hearing-impaired child and had been trained and certified as an oral interpreter. At that meeting, I started to realize that sometimes I wanted the *whole story* instead of an edited or selective summary. Also, at a meeting where everyone has an opinion, the interpreter is particularly useful in allowing the speechreader to follow the questions and answers back and forth between the speaker and the audience, which may be as interesting as the formal presentation because it allows the person to keep up on "real time" and fully participate. The problem in school is that the person needs to know *beforehand* if a word-for-word interpretation is important or if he or she can rely on good friends to give an abbreviated version.

Communication of Needs

As I became more used to interpreters, I had to analyze myself so that I could gain maximum benefit from them. For example, I find that I need to be well-rested or I am defeating the purpose. Still, I sometimes have to stop watching for a while and look around the room because my eyes can become atrophied from looking at the same lips for so many hours in a row!

I have developed nonverbal ways of telling the interpreter that I understand or do not understand. At the same time, the interpreter gives me clues that transmit the *feeling* of the speaker through expression, gesture, and eye movement. This helps to give me a sense of the mood, which is as important as the words. Therefore, the interpreting relationship is not only a matter of the skill of the interpreter but also of the skill of the hearing-impaired person. I do not sit there passively but put in as much effort as the interpreter.

In January of 1982, some school friends and I worked as volunteers at the Annual Meeting of the American Association for the Advancement of Science (AAAS) in Washington. AAAS makes all its meetings barrier-free to disabled individuals. As part of that policy, it provides oral and manual interpreters upon request at all of its symposia. My friends were enthusiastic about attending the lecture at which the well-known scientist, Carl Sagan, would be the speaker. Even though I could read Sagan's books and watch him on television, it was exciting to see him in person in a room with 1,000 other spectators and follow his speech through an oral interpreter.

In my senior year, I had quite a bit of trouble speechreading my United States history teacher. I missed a lot of class discussion, but I was able to do fairly well because I was allowed to borrow his lecture notes and make copies for my review. He prepared his lecture notes word-for-word and with extreme care, albeit written in a long, scrawly hand. The stack of notes rivaled the thickness and weight of the Random House Dictionary of the English Language. But I did get the identical facts and background comments that were presented to all the students. At the end of the semester, my teacher scheduled a review session on the Saturday before exams. For a change, I decided (with my teacher's approval) to have an oral interpreter at that session. Sharon Coale, a speech pathologist who had helped me throughout 4 years of high school, was my interpreter. She had not had professional interpreting experience, but we knew each other well, so speechreading was not a problem. The session was quite a challenge for her, considering that this teacher often stops in mid-sentence and never picks it up again! He was very well-liked by the students and the classroom atmosphere was spirited. Various members of the class kept shouting questions and remarks, some of which were absolutely irrelevant. It gave me insight on what the class discussions must have been like all semester—a three-ring circus! I realized that I did not want to know every remark that every student made; it was simply too much to absorb and take seriously. I learned that I had to judge how much I wanted to know and then instruct the interpreter.

Characteristics of an Effective Interpreter

My experience with Sharon made me realize what it takes to be a skilled oral interpreter. It requires a sustained pace and rhythm and analysis of the spoken material for accommodation to "unlipreadable" words or phrases while repeating in a clear, distinct, but nonexaggerated way what is being said. Facial geometry, choice of nondistracting clothes, and appearance are also important. In planning, the logistics of a setting must also be considered. I care about lighting, proper viewing angle, and the distance between me, the interpreter, and the speaker. I want a sense of the entire room and the atmosphere—I cannot sit too close, or my eyes will cross; I cannot sit too far away, or I will have to squint to see. At some angles, I have to strain my neck to see the speaker. Continued practice has taught me how to assess these variables quickly and position myself to best advantage.

Graduation Day

My high school counselor and advisor for 4 years, Ele Carpenter, and I analyzed the tricky seating and processional pattern planned for the out-of-doors graduation. My place in the procession allowed no room for error. Dr. Joseph Rosenstein, my oral interpreter, sat in front of me, diagonally across the narrow grass aisle as a member of the audience. I could see him clearly, yet there was enough space for me to walk down the aisle to receive my diploma. I enjoyed Roger Rosenblatt's commencement address about grown-ups immensely, with his insightful observations drawn as a senior staff writer for Time Magazine. Since this was probably one of the most important events in my life so far, I was grateful for the support help I received as well.

Thus far, I have been lucky to have access to some of the best oral interpreters available—naturally talented, well-trained, and experienced. I have rarely been frustrated by their inability to convey the full message to me, yet I realize that I may not always be so fortunate. I am no longer self-conscious about using oral interpreters because I recognize there are times when I want all the information being presented and I must organize for what I need.

MY EXPERIENCES WITH ORAL INTERPRETING

Barbara G. Biddle

As a college student, I applaud the advent of oral interpreters on the educational scene. As a college senior, I hope tomorrow's oral interpreters are better prepared than those who pioneered in our lecture classes.

In high school, I wondered why teachers moved around so much and turned their backs to the class as they talked. I've now decided it's because they are concentrating on *what* they are teaching rather than *how* they are delivering the material. This sometimes works a hardship on the entire class, and especially the hearing-impaired student whose only recourse is to depend on an interpreter.

THE EARLY YEARS

A Unisensory Program

My profound hearing loss was identified at 11 months of age, and I was fitted with binaural hearing aids at once. For 2 years, I had intensive auditory training in a special unisensory program at the University of Denver Speech and Hearing Center. This experience introduced me to the world of sound, and I began to understand that sounds have meaning. Today, I still use my residual hearing to good advantage and now benefit from combining listening and speechreading skills.

A Regular Preschool, Kindergarten, and First Grade

After much listening therapy I attended a "hearing" preschool, kindergarten, and first grade. Then I went into a public school with classes for the hearing impaired and at fourth grade, my parents decided I needed the challenge of a good residential school. They chose one in St. Louis, which I attended through the eighth grade. My self-confidence and independence grew as a result of this change, and when I came home to enter high school, we chose a good private school with small classes.

At first I felt shy and uncomfortable. This was quite a change from the environment I'd been in throughout my lower- and middle-school years. Here, I was—one of four hearing-impaired students in a high school of 300, fresh from a school of 200 deaf students (resident and day), where I had known everyone. Involvement in the sports program saved the day for me. It helped me make friends and prove that I could be a competitor *and* a team player. I was on the diving team and lettered in basketball, volleyball, and field hockey. (To this day my favorite sports are team sports because of the friendships they build.) I was glad that my communication skills let me participate in the social activities of the school.

I did very well academically, with the help of notetakers in lecture classes and an outside tutor for literature and math. There were times I felt "lost" in class, but by studying hard outside, I managed to keep up.

AND ON TO COLLEGE

After looking at several options, I chose Utah State University in Logan because of the structured support services for the hearing impaired. Yes, I'd completed high school with a minimum of help, but I felt ready to have someone smooth the way by handling these kinds of supplemental assistance for me. It looked as though Utah State was doing this well.

Training My Own Oral Interpreters

Colleges were just beginning to provide *oral* interpreters in my freshman year, so as I learned my way around in another environment, I helped "train" several of these to adapt to needs and preferences of an oral person. How helpful it would have been to have had well-trained, certified oral interpreters in that first year. Some interpreters were "dead pan," which made a lecture boring, and I would sometimes feel hypnotized in my efforts to watch. Sometimes they were so far behind the professor that they found it hard to catch up and so lost the train of thought—then had to pick it up again wherever they could. Sometimes the interpreter would see a puzzled look on my face and stop to explain (without voice) something he or she thought I didn't understand. Well! By the time he or she started listening to the professor again, we might have missed a full minute or more of the lecture and were far behind on the information being covered. We finally got that straightened out by making sure the interpreter continued to channel the professor's remarks and let a tutor deal with vocabulary and concepts I found puzzling.

Although our campus had certified sign language interpreters, we had only one certified oral interpreter for a short time. Funding problems prevented the university from developing a corps of certified oral interpreters, and it seemed that as soon as student interpreters developed good skills, they were graduating or transferring. We were training new interpreters constantly. Eventually, the Coordinator of Support Services decided to train some community-based people who were interested and had previous experience with speechreaders. This is finally building a good base of experienced oral interpreters.

A Range of University Activities

In addition to my accidental role of "training" new interpreters, I pledged Alpha Chi Omega and became active in HISA (the Hearing-Impaired Student Association). As a recreation education major, I volunteered with multiple sclerosis patients in a swimming program and also worked at the Exceptional Child Center. During two summers and one spring break, I was fortunate enough to have jobs with camping programs for handicapped children. All this sparked an interest in my pursuing a Master's Degree in Therapeutic Recreation. It also helped me earn the Achievement of the Year trophy at the 1981 Robins Awards at Utah State (the annual Robins Awards honor the top student in nine different categories). I treasure that award and appreciate all of the support which made my achievement possible!

I wonder how different things would be if every oral deaf college student could have a certified oral interpreter for lecture classes. Certification means well-trained individuals who: 1) use clear articulation; 2) know how to use pacing and phrasing techniques to make speechreading easier; 3) add natural gestures to help a student make use of associational cues; and 4) make appropriate word substitutions for higher visibility on the lips.

In my junior year, I decided to try a certified sign language interpreter. These were available at Utah State, I suppose, because the Registry of Interpreters for the Deaf (RID) has been certifying this specialist longer than the oral interpreter. By this time, I had taken a college course in sign language and wanted to compare the interpreting mode. The signing interpreter repeated each sentence of lectures without voice, too, but could not use the natural gestures with which I am so familiar and which I find so helpful. I experimented back and forth and began to request signing interpreters for my social psychology and kinesiology classes because the unfamiliar terminology seemed difficult for me to speechread and could be fingerspelled. Using an interpreter, in *either* mode, is a mixed blessing. I wish we could find an FM loop amplification system for the classroom that works for me because I'd much rather look *and* listen when conditions permit.

In the meantime, I hope better training can be offered to oral interpreters *and* to the students who need them. Keeping speech skills up to par at the same time that a person is working hard academically is not always easy. But it *is* necessary if his or her goal is to function in the broader world. Systems need to work together to help students meet this challenge.

SOME "WHAT IFS"

I wonder how different my life might have been if my parents had not
  believed I could develop spoken language. My parents and my
  sister have always "been there" to offer encouragement.
I wonder how different my life might be if the professional people my
  parents consulted (teachers, doctors, audiologists) had discour-
  aged us from the life goals we set. Almost without exception, they
  have been supportive.
I wonder how different my life might be if our *friends* had not cheered
  me on as I mumbled, fumbled, stumbled, and got up to try again.
  Friends of all ages—my peers, my sister's friends, and my parents'
  friends.
I wonder how different my life would be if I had not been born with
  a recessive genetic deafness. But then, I would not be the person
  I am and my Dad says, "I wouldn't want her to be different than
  she is."

That's quite a lot of love to live up to!

TESTIMONY FROM A HEARING-IMPAIRED JUROR

Barbara Chertok[1]

A CALL TO JURY DUTY

An unexpected letter arrived, informing me that I was being considered for jury duty. I dashed off a short reply to the jury commissioner immediately, telling of my eagerness to serve and including a paragraph that explained that because I was profoundly hearing impaired, I would request the court to provide an oral interpreter to assist me during the trial, should I be selected.

A second letter came informing me that my request for a manual interpreter would be honored. To clarify the matter, I sent another letter explaining the difference between an oral interpreter and a manual interpreter.

In a few weeks time, a summons arrived in the mail requesting that I appear at the Montgomery County Circuit Courthouse in Rockville, Maryland on June 21, 1982, at which time I would be part of a jury pool under consideration for selection as a juror.

Holding the actual summons in my hand, something clicked in my brain. Having been previously advised by the jury commissioner that over the past several years 30 other persons with a hearing impairment had failed to be selected for jury duty, I was all the more determined not to become number 31. I also wanted to give full visibility to the new and largely unknown medium of oral interpreting for speechreaders.

The specialist known as an *oral interpreter* was officially recognized at the first National Oral Interpreter Evaluation/Certification Workshop, sponsored by the Alexander Graham Bell Association for the Deaf in St. Paul, Minnesota, October, 1979. It was there that the first 51 oral interpreters in the United States were formally evaluated[2] and certified by the National Registry of Interpreters for the Deaf (RID). I was privileged to be a part of this pioneering effort and to become certified as an Oral Interpreter: V/S (visible to spoken). This means I can be called upon to read the lips of another hearing-impaired

---

[1] The author lost her hearing suddenly at the age of 21 due to a virus. She is currently employed part-time as the staff coordinator of the Oral Deaf Adults Section (ODAS) of the Alexander Graham Bell Association for the Deaf, Inc. in Washington, D.C. She serves as a consultant on one board and several committees of other organizations of and for the hearing impaired (deaf and hard of hearing). She resides in Bethesda, Maryland with her two teen-age children.

[2] A portion of the evaluation addresses knowledge of the Code of Ethics for certified interpreters (RID) and application of its three basic concepts—*confidentiality, impartiality*, and *integrity*.

person, whose speech is not sufficiently intelligible, for the benefit of a third person or group.

Request for an Oral Interpreter

Now to the task of assuring that I would be selected as a juror. My first call went out to the jury commissioner, requesting again that the court provide me with an oral interpreter. Knowing very well that he would have difficulty in securing one because there are not yet many oral interpreters who are formally certified by RID, I offered to furnish an exceptionally qualified one. It was agreed upon, and at the same time, the commissioner confirmed that the interpreting costs would be paid for by the court.

Rounding up the Specialists

My second call was to Richard Dirst, a free-lance interpreter and former Executive Director of RID who holds certification as an Oral Interpreter: Comprehensive (OI:C). He agreed to act as my oral interpreter and arranged to meet me at the courthouse on the specified day.

Next, I contacted Judith Toth, a member of the Maryland House of Delegates, who is hearing impaired and who sponsored a bill allowing for manual (sign language) interpreters in the courtroom. Upon being made aware of the oversight, she kindly reworded the bill to include oral interpreters. The bill is still under consideration. We arranged to meet at the courthouse.

My final action was to alert the local newspapers, television stations, and various organizations of and for the deaf and hard of hearing in the area. Everyone was genuinely delighted with the prospect of my being chosen to serve on the jury.

The big day arrived. Armed with my personal oral interpreter, my own hearing-impaired delegate from Annapolis, and my very best smile, I entered the jury lounge along with more than 100 other prospective jurors. Here I met the jury commissioner for the first time and introduced myself. He greeted me cordially, offering to bring up a chair so that my interpreter could sit directly in front of me while the jury process was being explained to all.

Answering Preliminary Questions

Shortly thereafter, I was assigned to the courtroom of Judge Rosalyn Bell. Once inside, Dick and I, along with 55 other persons, were seated. The judge sat on a dais and seated to her right were the defendant and his two attorneys and the two plaintiffs and their attorney. The elimination process began with the judge asking if any of us knew the defendant, the plaintiffs, or their attorneys. As people raised their hands,

I looked around hoping to find a reason to approach the bench and talk with the judge face to face in order for her to know that we could communicate easily. Just then, Dick noticed that the defendant was wearing a hearing aid attached to his eyeglasses. I immediately raised my hand and was asked to approach the bench. Dick accompanied me. I then explained to Judge Bell that I wanted her to know that I, too, wore a hearing aid, as did the defendant. She thanked me for bringing this to her attention.

At this point, all three attorneys came forward and asked the judge for permission to question me. They wanted to know: Would I be impartial toward the defendant, who was also hearing impaired? Would this influence my decision? How did I lose my hearing? When did I lose my hearing? How much hearing did I have?

With the help of my interpreter, I answered their questions to their satisfaction. However, before they retreated, I made it a point to tell them how important I felt it was for a hearing-impaired person to be selected to serve on the jury in view of the fact that in recent years, 30 others before me had failed.

IN ACTION AS A JUROR

The judge announced that a jury had been selected and that the list of 12 names would be read. A hush fell over the room as the numbers and names began to be called off. Suddenly, I felt what it must be like to be a finalist in the Miss America Beauty Pageant. Just at that moment, Dick was repeating to me, without voice, "Number nine, Barbara Chertok." I squealed with delight. It took a long while before the wide grin on my face began to fade. Thus, I began jury duty as the first hearing-impaired person in Maryland and the first hearing-impaired juror in the United States to use an oral interpreter.

SEATING ARRANGEMENTS

At the suggestion of Judge Bell, I seated myself at the far left end of the second row of the jury box, with Dick in the seat next to mine. The seats were really too close together to accommodate us comfortably, our knees bumping together as we swiveled in order to face one another. However, it was the best possible arrangement because the witness stand was in my direct line of vision, enabling me to glance at the witness whenever I had a free moment to look away from my interpreter. Because there were only 12 seats in the jury box and Dick was occupying one of them, the judge allowed one of the jurors to sit outside the jury box and next to the alternate who is always seated there. No one objected to this arrangement. I was delighted that throughout my jury duty experience, everyone connected with the trial was especially cooperative with Dick and me.

The Oral Interpreter's Role

The trial lasted for 4 days. The last half of the fourth day we moved to the deliberation room. My interpreter was allowed to accompany me. Here we sat around a long, oval-shaped table discussing the case and trying to arrive at a verdict. In order to give Dick a much deserved rest, I read the lips of those jurors who were easy to read.

Four days of speechreading was exhausting for me as well as for my interpreter who, in addition to mouthing the words being spoken, had to let me know who was doing the talking by pointing to that person. But it was exhilarating as well. It renewed my energy and spurred me on to know that someone as profoundly hearing impaired as I am was sitting on a jury and participating in the highest form of civic duty, helping to pave the way for others with a hearing impairment. When asked by several people at the close of the trial as to how much I missed, I could honestly answer, "Not much more than the hearing jurors probably did." One of the defendant's attorneys was quoted by a newspaper reporter as saying, "She probably knew more about this case than anybody else in this courtroom, except for the judge."

Interest of the Media

The publicity surrounding my jury duty was evident. On the second day of the trial, there were a few reporters present. On the third day of the trial, there was an artist from a major newspaper present making sketches of Dick and me and some courtroom scenes. That same day, the judge was asked if she would allow a television cameraman and newspaper photographer to enter the courtroom. After obtaining permission from everyone in the courtroom connected with the trial, for the first time in history, the judge then allowed them to enter the courtroom and film and photograph my oral interpreter and me. Interviews on television, radio, and by publications followed to add to the excitement.

Now as I begin to wind down after this momentous experience and word filters through to me that another hearing-impaired person has already been selected for jury duty, I sigh and say, "Amen."

FROM AN ORTHODONTIST'S EXPERIENCE

James C. Marsters

"Dr. Marsters?" asked a young audiologist. "Tell me something about yourself and why you feel so strongly about oral interpreting."

I responded, "I am congenitally deaf as a result of maternal rubella and unable to use a hearing aid for practical speech discrimination. As an orthodontist with a successful 30-year, solo practice in Pasadena, California, I feel it is critical to the success of my practice and to my personal happiness to sometimes have access to oral interpreters."

"But," she persisted, "you have graduated from colleges and graduate and dental schools and seem to function very well without an oral interpreter. Why do you feel you need one? How is that kind of a specialist used?"

I am frequently asked questions like this and my response follows a general pattern along these lines:

Patients who have difficult speech patterns and certain facial characteristics or who are deeply frightened are difficult, if not impossible, to speechread. It is important to me to have competent chairside assistants and a receptionist who are relatively easy to speechread and who can, when necessary, convey to me in an unobtrusive manner the statements and questions of patients, parents, and others so as to enhance my effectiveness. I may also need oral interpreting during telephone conversations, meetings, and seminars.

Few of my patients are hearing impaired. A successful dental-orthodontic practice outside of institutions cannot be limited to hearing-impaired individuals; considering a random two hundred of my patients at any one time, only one is deaf. Yes, hearing-impaired people may come many miles to my office feeling confident of communicating with me because I, too, am hearing-impaired. However, I have had hearing patients who commuted thousands of miles as well as others coming from within Pasadena for orthodontic treatment. I feel it is important to be a good, sensitive, caring, and communicative specialist in a highly competitive professional field. Oral interpreting helps to make this possible.

MEETINGS AND CONFERENCES

As an expert examiner for the California State Board of Dental Examiners, which licenses dentists to practice in California, I sometimes take an oral interpreter to all-day meetings where there is much discussion and lecturing taking place. I also try to take (or hire) oral interpreters when going to conventions, meetings, or conferences so that I may gain more information from the occasion. I have had some interesting experiences: Some hearing participants do not believe that interpreters are needed, preferring to feel that the hearing-impaired professional is whole and receiving everything said. I need to take care of myself and profit from a meeting and the time and expense of having an oral interpreter rather than fostering someone else's delusions; I find it necessary to educate people as to the value of an oral interpreter and overcome objections. Some audience members have expressed indignation that someone should be so rude to a speaker as to be talking to me all through a meeting! I sometimes need to explain beforehand to a speaker or the audience what I am doing. This increases the appreciation and awareness of the audience as to the value of oral interpreting.

STAFF SELECTION

I evaluate potential staff members (a receptionist, business manager, dental hygienist, and chairside assistant) for distinctive open speech and personality first—and then for their professional skills.

Oral interpreting training prepares the staff member to help with telephone calls, conferences, meetings, patients (adults and children), and other professionals.

Note-taking training techniques using pen and pad, a video terminal, and/or a silent printer are also very helpful, especially during long meetings or conferences.

Spouses, family members, and other relatives, in my judgment, seldom make good professional oral interpreters because of their psychological need to dominate, intimidate, or control the hearing-impaired family member. They do, however, make excellent on-the-spot oral interpreters; the professional should not abuse this family convenience. It is better to have someone outside of the family as an oral interpreter.

Professional Vocabulary

Professionals need to provide oral interpreters with specific vocabularies commonly used in the course of professional duties, for example, in orthodontics and dentistry:

Banding	Scaling
Protrusive	Maxilliary
Mesial	Direct bonding
Occlusal	Bicuspids
Mandibular	Incisal
Retrusive	Periodontics
Posterior	Interproximal
Distal	

Special vocabulary lists should be made available to oral inter-

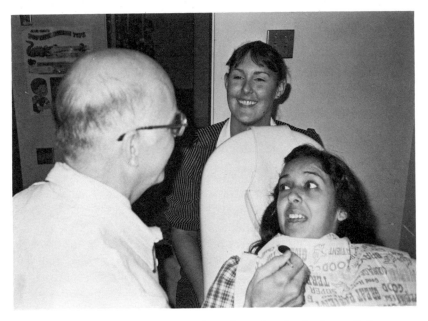

Figure 12.1.   Team effort: preliminary discussion and professional consultation.

preters during their course of preservice training. They will have much more confidence in communicating with the professional who is a speechreader when the terminology is familiar (see Figure 12.1).

Prior to my personal consultation, it helps to have the appropriate staff member ask a patient specific questions about his or her needs. Very often, the patient is unable to overcome the psychological block of relating to any professional, but can relate more easily to a female staff member who then relays the information by telling me privately or by writing it down. This is especially helpful on an initial visit as well as during subsequent appointments.

I then ask the patient what I can do for him or her or what the problem is and I let him or her talk. In the event I have difficulty in speechreading the patient, the staff member stands behind the patient and relays the information silently and unobtrusively.

Should the patient need to talk while I am doing adjustments or preparatory work outside of the mouth, it is helpful to have the chair-side assistant engage him or her in conversation so that I can proceed without interruption. I am very sensitive to the patient's needs while working with him or her.

Angles

In the dental chair, a patient is usually tilted back so that speechreading as well as working is easier; it is further enhanced if the dentist works while sitting in a mobile chair to the side or front of the patient. Sitting at the patient's eye-level tends to lessen his or her anxiety, which is heightened when the dentist is hovering over him or her.

Some people can be speechread better facing front; some more easily from a three-quarter front view; and others from the side or profile, where the tongue can be seen more easily. Seeing the entire face, not just the lips and oral cavity, is important for facial cues. Seeing the throat, chest, and entire body is also very useful because of the revealing cues that rate of breathing and body language may offer.

Alexander Graham Bell had an hearing-impaired wife. Dr. Bell and male members of the Grosvenor family (of National Geographic fame) usually brushed whiskers and mustaches clear of the lips and inclined their head back to enhance speechreading for Mrs. Bell and other hearing-impaired people. Several times, I had the pleasure of being a recipient of this thoughtfulness on the part of the Grosvenors. Tipping the head back a bit when talking to a speechreader allows the light to play on the lips and oral cavity; this angle also forces the lips to be parted further so that the tongue and oral cavity are more visible.

Lighting

Good lighting is conducive to good speechreading. In the dental chair a patient is usually positioned favorably, facing a window, dental light, and ceiling lighting.

Offices usually have overhead ceiling lighting, which is frequently fluorescent; when abetted by mustaches, noses, and protrusive upper teeth or lips, it casts unfavorable shadows on the mouth. Better lighting often is needed to improve speechreading conditions.

Convention and conference rooms or halls frequently have poor lighting. It may be wise for a hearing-impaired professional to bring his or her own supplementary lighting, pitched from a low angle, to enhance the faces of the oral interpreter and/or speaker. It is also good show business to have good lighting as surely anything worth hearing should also be well worth seeing!

Dim lighting and back lighting are to be avoided because they cause darkness of the lips and oral cavity; the whole blends into one, flat dimension rather than a vibrant three-dimension. The speechreader needs to position himself or herself carefully with his or her back to a light source for ease in conversation. If the lighting is poor, then the person can be taken to brighter light and told, "Now we both can see better!"

Figure 12.2.   Telephone interpreting.

TELEPHONE INTERPRETING

Most hearing-impaired professionals need access to the telephone. Patients, parents, colleagues, and business people expect to be spoken to personally. If the hearing-impaired person's speech is intelligible, he can do his or her own talking, while the oral interpreter listening in on a separate telephone extension silently repeats to the speechreader what is being said while it is being said (see Figure 12.2). The professional then is able to speak for himself or herself. When all this is done well and simultaneously, the person at the other end is seldom aware that the oral interpreting is taking place. This builds a hearing-impaired person's self-esteem, encourages improvement in his or her speech and voice, and also increases the confidence of the other party. In the instance of an individual whose speech is not so intelligible, the oral interpreter can repeat the message verbally to the listener.

Adaptive telephone equipment includes:

1. *An extension telephone*   There is a drawback to this—some oral interpreters have a tendency to do the intelligible speechreader's talking for him or her, which is an undesirable occurrence.

2. *A simple receiver with a handle on it* (single receiver headset or handset) This is available without a microphone from the telephone company's Department of Special Services for the Handicapped. It is simply wired into the base of the single telephone being used. If properly connected, a dial tone is heard when the telephone's handset is off the cradle.

3. *A wireless telephone extension* The oral interpreter using a wireless telephone simply presses the "mute" button so that his or her breathing or clearing of the throat cannot be heard. The hearing-impaired professional uses the regular telephone. This allows excellent freedom of movement.

4. *Tactile set (vibratory)* Sometimes I use this so that I can feel when the other person is talking by placing my fingers on the vibrating pad. This keeps me from interrupting and gives me a sense of the other person's personality and mood. This often works on dial-type telephones, but sometimes there is a problem when used with touch tone telephones.

5. *Voice into computer printout devices* Currently available, these voice-activated computers are extremely limited in vocabulary and may have to be imprinted with the user's speech/voice patterns. Computer designers say that computer printout devices for hearing-impaired people are at least a decade or two away from general availability.

6. *Telecommunication devices for the deaf (TDD)* Devices such as teletypewriters and evanescent, liquid crystal, or television displays are principally used in communication between hearing-impaired persons when normal telephone facilities are involved. The first devices were originally financed, developed, and promoted by three speechreading deaf men; these various devices now number over 100,000 stations worldwide!

7. *Telephone answering services* These services involve TDDs and inward WATS lines, which receive calls by TDDs or voice and briefly relay messages between parties. I use TDDs when oral interpreters are not available to receive and send emergency information.

8. *Amplified telephones* These telephones can be used, with or without a hearing aid, by persons who have functional residual hearing. In the event that the hearing-impaired person has poor speech discrimination over the telephone, the familiar "20 questions" can be used: leading questions are answered by "yes," "no," "maybe," or "please repeat." The tactile set or other vibratory, needle-gauge, or light-indicating sets can also be used.

CONCLUSION

An oral interpreter is a necessary adjunct in my life, enhancing my effectiveness in the office, at meetings, and on the telephone. Oral interpreters should be qualified staff members, not family members. The limited number of certified oral interpreters in the 1980s serves to highlight the need for their continued training and evaluation/certification by the RID. Visual media, such as movies, videotapes, slides, printed material, and actual demonstrations, will enhance the development and use of oral interpreters and improve the effectiveness of hearing-impaired persons in verbal communication.

When I experience poor speechreading reception attributable to poor speech patterns, I usually tell the speaker I am hearing impaired but that I speechread well. I then ask if he or she could speak more carefully *but not louder*. This often improves communication for both of us.

ORAL INTERPRETATION AND THE SCIENCE PROFESSIONAL

Nansie S. Sharpless

Not long ago, I presided at a symposium during an annual meeting of the American Association for the Advancement of Science (AAAS). I also attended several other scientific symposia, participated in the audience discussion, and moderated a press conference. None of these activities would be considered especially remarkable for a woman with my professional background and position. But I happen to be completely deaf, and I was "listening" to the speakers through the ears of an oral interpreter. For the first time in 35 years, I was actually able to fully enjoy the words of a lecturer.

A TEEN-AGER. . . . AND DEAFENED

When I was suddenly deafened at the age of 14, I was halfway through the ninth grade. Because I had learned to speak naturally, by listening, my language and reading abilities were normal. I was well-equipped to meet the challenge of a return to regular school and to continue to live among hearing people; this my parents decided I should do. Of course, in 1946, there was no specially trained support team for hearing-impaired students and there were no interpreters in the classrooms. Even if interpreters had been available, however, I seriously doubt that I could have used them. Although I started immediately to take instruction in speechreading, it was many years before I could carry on a relaxed conversation by this method. Although I finished high school and college right on schedule and earned a Master's degree in medical technology, I did so by relying primarily on the textbooks and on notes from my fellow students. I paid scant attention to the teachers.

EXTERNAL BARRIERS TO FULL COMPREHENSION

As my speechreading skills improved, my circle of friends gradually widened and my social life expanded, but I never developed the ability to follow rapidly moving group discussions or lecturers in the classroom. Furthermore, the facial characteristics of some individuals make their speech difficult or impossible to speechread. In direct, one-to-one conversation, people with illegible countenances can usually be persuaded to write instead of speak, but this is impractical in group situations. There were, of course, many activities in which I could engage without impediment. Reading, sewing, visiting museums, traveling, and gardening, to name a few, don't require the ability to hear. But the intellectual stimulation afforded by group discussions, lectures, travelogues, or sermons was missing and not easily acquired from books.

THE ORAL INTERPRETER: A NEW DIMENSION

Almost 30 years elapsed between the time I lost my hearing and my first encounter with an oral interpreter. During this interval, two important events shaped my future. First, after much soul-searching, I decided to leave my job as a medical technologist and in 1967, at the age of 35, returned to school to obtain a doctoral degree in chemistry. As a student, I began to attend and to present the results of my research at professional meetings. Although my speech is sufficiently clear to be understood by most members of an audience, someone always had to relay the questions from the audience to me. My research advisor usually volunteered to do this, but a great deal of mental dexterity was required. She was seldom able to relay more than a brief summary of the question. Interaction with colleagues is a very important part of a scientist's professional life; almost all exchange of ideas occurs during seminars, group discussions, or at professional meetings. These areas of communication are definitely the most difficult for a speechreader. After I had acquired my doctorate, my need for a more efficient and independent means of communicating with other researchers became acute.

IMPACT OF FEDERAL LEGISLATION

The second, and decisive, event was the passage of the "nondiscrimination" Section 504 regulations of the 1973 Rehabilitation Act, which stimulated increased awareness of the civil rights of disabled people. This new climate led John Gavin, a deaf biologist, to approach AAAS with the concerns of disabled scientists. Dr. Gavin was invited to organize the first AAAS symposium to address the problems and potentials of handicapped scientists. As a panelist, I pointed out that one of the major barriers to full participation of hearing-impaired individuals in scientific professions is the inaccessibility of professional meetings. AAAS annual meetings are now accessible to all disabled scientists. Both oral and sign language interpreters are provided routinely. I have been one of their most enthusiastic consumers.

OBSERVATIONS ABOUT INTERPRETERS:
SIGN LANGUAGE AND ORAL

At the first interpreted AAAS meetings, all of the interpreters were sign language specialists. Because some of my hearing-impaired colleagues[3] and I have never learned sign language, we had to experiment. We found that it is necessary to have separate oral and manual interpreters because the exaggerated arm movements associated with the simultaneous method are distracting to "pure" speechreaders. Although many of the sign language interpreters turned out to be very good oral interpreters because they had already learned to listen and transmit simultaneously, others were impossible to speechread. I was delighted, therefore, when the National Registry of Interpreters for the Deaf started formal evaluation and certification programs for oral interpreters in 1979. Now that oral interpreting has become recognized as a special form of support service for the hearing impaired, the quality of oral interpreting at the AAAS annual meetings has improved markedly. Nevertheless, not all of my encounters with interpreters have been entirely successful.

FACTORS INFLUENCING THE BONDING PROCESS:
INTERPRETER AND SPEECHREADER

I've found that there are a number of factors, other than the interpreter's formal training, which can contribute to the success or failure of the oral interpretation. Some of these are:

---

[3] Approximately 20% of the more than 500 handicapped scientists, engineers, and medical practitioners listed in the 1978 edition of the AAAS *Resource Directory of Handicapped Scientists* (edited by J. A. Owens, M. R. Redden, and J. W. Brown) are hearing impaired.

1. *My own speechreading ability* I believe that I am a fairly proficient speechreader. I am completely integrated to the extent that all of my close friends have normal hearing and none are familiar with sign language. I once attempted to learn sign language but was unsuccessful. I have a good command of language and a broad experiential background.

2. *The speech characteristics of the interpreter* In the interpreting situation, the effects of small speech impediments are magnified. Only people with especially clear speech make good professional oral interpreters. All prospective oral interpreters ought to have themselves checked objectively. Obviously, people with braces, full beards, or foreign accents make poor oral interpreters.

3. *The speech characteristics of the person being interpreted* This is an occupational hazard that cannot be readily controlled. Interpreters, both oral and sign language, differ in their ability to follow speakers with foreign or regional accents or speech impediments. Disorganized, rapid presentations are, of course, poorly understood by everyone.

4. *Auxiliary aids supplied by the interpreter* It is helpful if the interpreter uses slightly exaggerated gestures occasionally if they are related directly to the material being interpreted. Animated facial expressions and direction of gaze give added clues. Proper names and exact locations are especially hard for a speechreader; it helps if the interpreter has a small pad of paper handy to write out these words. In group discussions, the interpreter should indicate who is speaking. During slide presentations, the interpreter should stop briefly so that the hearing-impaired person can read the material on the slide. During this time, the interpreter might also glance at the slide because some of the technical vocabulary will be presented there.

5. *Auxiliary aids obtainable by the hearing impaired user* If there is a printed program, I check the name of the speaker and the title of the talks I will attend. If abstracts are available, I read them in advance or between speakers. The press room at AAAS meetings often has complete summaries of the speeches that can sometimes be obtained to read in advance.

6. *Auxiliary aids supplied by the speaker* Scientific presentations are almost always illustrated. Tables, graphs, or pictures are customarily shown on projected slides. Printed handouts are sometimes distributed.

7. *The physical characteristics of the room* In scientific meetings, the room is often darkened for slide presentations. In these situations, it helps if the oral interpreter has access to an auxiliary

lighting system. The interpreter should be spotlighted and seated directly in front of the speechreader who then has a clear view of the interpreter's face as well as that of the speaker and the blackboard or screen. Major traffic areas should be avoided so that latecomers do not have to walk between the interpreter and the speechreader. Absence of vibrations or visual noise (a flapping window shade or tapping foot, for example) also contributes to a good interpreting environment.

8. *The content of the material being interpreted* My own familiarity with and interest in the material being interpreted strongly influence my ability to follow the interpreter. Lectures on broad, abstract issues are usually read from a prepared text without illustration. These are very difficult to follow. On the other hand, I have greatly enjoyed symposia on such diverse topics as laetrile (I am well-read on the subject), cocaine (an area in which we are currently doing research), the boomerang, computer animation, and underwater archaeology, to name a few. Oral interpreters have been of invaluable help in the numerous business and committee meetings I attend. I am currently president of the Foundation for Science and the Handicapped, a member of the Board of Directors of the Alexander Graham Bell Association for the Deaf and of the AAAS Committee of the Office of Opportunities in Science. None of these activities would be possible without the assistance of the professional oral interpreters I have used at their meetings, supplied by each organization without charge.

The interpreter's familiarity with the language being used is a critical factor. I have found that most interpreters have difficulty with highly technical scientific presentations. Because AAAS symposia are intended for a broad audience made up of people from many disciplines, complex technical jargon is seldom used. This may explain why the interpretation at the AAAS meetings has been so successful. In contrast, at scientific meetings intended for specialists in a narrow discipline, it is customary to schedule 12 or more speakers in one 3-hour session. Each speaks for 10 minutes while showing about a dozen slides. A 5-minute discussion period follows, and then the next speaker is introduced. Even an interpreter with a doctoral degree in the subject would have trouble with sessions of this kind, not to mention the problems the speechreader has trying to follow multiple visual clues in a darkened room. It is not surprising, therefore, that the few times I have taken an interpreter to a scientific meeting of this type, there have been disasters. Fortunately, many scientific organizations have started to use poster sessions as well as slide presentations at their annual meetings. The poster session is an ideal format for a hearing-impaired person.

CONCLUSION

During the past 7 years, I have made increasing use of oral interpreters to at least partially overcome the barrier to professional advancement caused by inaccessible scientific meetings. Oral interpretation has some distinct advantages over sign language interpretation at scientific sessions. It is faster, especially in the numerous situations where there are no signs for technical terms, which must then be fingerspelled. There is a greater vocabulary range and the person receives the words in complete sentences with normal English syntax. This is very important, I believe, because it facilitates the hearing-impaired person's effective interaction with other scientists. Since I have started to use oral interpretation, I have, for the first time, been able to participate fully in group discussions, serve on committees, direct business meetings, and attend lectures. Oral interpreters have opened new professional doors for me and enabled me to expand my world considerably.

APPENDICES

APPENDIX I

Guidelines for the Preparation of Oral Interpreters: Support Specialists for Hearing-Impaired Individuals

INTRODUCTION

Winifred H. Northcott, president (1978–80),
Alexander Graham Bell Association for the Deaf

The current educational and social environment is one of respect for individual differences among deaf and hard-of-hearing people regarding their expressed mode of communication preference in daily living. Recently, there has been a groundswell of interest and action directed toward the formal preparation and eventual certification by the Registry of Interpreters for the Deaf, Inc. (RID) of a new, additional support specialist—the Oral Interpreter (as distinct from the Manual Interpreter). The Oral Interpreter is to be available on request for those deaf and hard-of-hearing individuals who rely upon speechreading, with or without auditory input, as their preferred means of interpersonal communication.

In 1977, strong regulations were written to implement Section 504 of the Rehabilitation Act of 1973 which provides that:

> No otherwise qualified handicapped individual in the United States shall, solely by the reason of his handicap, be excluded from the participation in, be denied the benefit of, or be subjected to discrimination under any program or activity receiving federal financial assistance.

This small section of the law is administered by the Office of Civil Rights. Violation of the rights of a handicapped person (deaf or hard of hearing, in this instance) carries the threat of sanctions, including the withholding of federal funds for demonstrated discrimination. The missing link has been the Oral Interpreter.

Definition of Terms

An Oral Interpreter is usually a hearing person. He or she will proceed at a normal rate of speed and enunciation and will generally be a few words behind the speaker in the smooth repetition of statements. A skilled Oral Interpreter will sometimes rephrase or add a word or phrase to give higher visibility on the lips for added comprehension. Natural body language and gestures give added flavor.

Oral Interpreting   the incidental or substantial rewording of the speaker's remarks, presented with or without voice and always with natural lip movements.

Oral Translating   verbatim presentation of the speaker's remarks by means of natural lip movements, with or without voice.

Reverse Oral Interpreting   verbal rephrasing of the message of a hearing-impaired (deaf or hand-of-hearing) person who may or may not use voiced speech, standard inflectional patterns, and grammatical construction.

Reverse Oral Translating   vocal expression of the exact words of a hearing-impaired (deaf or hard-of-hearing) speaker who may or may not use voiced speech, standard inflectional patterns, and grammatical construction.

Earlier Activity

At the biennial National Convention of the Alexander Graham Bell Association for the Deaf, held in Boston, June 1976, one section presentation was titled: "Oral Interpreters: A Missing Link Among Support Specialists for the Hearing Impaired." In response to deaf and hard-of-hearing panelists at the convention who presented "The Case for Oral Interpreters," Carl Kirchner, then president of the Registry of Interpreters for the Deaf, concluded his formal paper with the statement:

> The RID, Inc. expresses its willingness to work with the Alexander Graham Bell Association and its hearing-impaired members to establish a certificate for oral interpreting. Hopefully, with your help and guidance, such a certificate could be established. The RID stand ready and willing to serve.

The next move was up to the A.G. Bell Association. It took the form of a published article in *The Volta Review* (Northcott, 1977) identifying the various dimensions of professional training and specialization that must be considered in exploratory discussions prior to implementation of training programs and eventual certification of graduates as Oral Interpreters by the Registry of Interpreters for the Deaf.

Subsequently, RID invited the A.G. Bell Association and the National Technical Institute for the Deaf (NTID) to share the responsibility of defining certification requirements for Oral Interpreters.

In parallel action in 1978, the Council of Directors of Federally Funded Post-Secondary Programs for the Deaf convened to develop "Policies, Procedures, and Guidelines for the Implementation of the National Interpreters for the Deaf Training Act of 1978," which were submitted to the U.S. Office for Handicapped Individuals. Named in the guidelines are four deaf parent/consumer groups: International Parents' Organization (AGB), International Association of Parents of the Deaf, National Association of the Deaf, and Oral Deaf Adults Section (AGB).

Dr. William Castle, chairperson, convened a meeting of representatives of the four groups listed above in St. Louis on June 23, 1978 during the biennial National Convention of the A.G. Bell Association. The purpose was to include reference to Oral Interpreters at different points throughout the document relating to implementation of the National Interpreters for the Deaf Training Act of 1978. However, a separate section on Oral Interpreters was neither developed nor appeared in the final document.

Thus, on October 27–28, 1978, in Washington, D.C., the A.G. Bell Association held a workshop. "Focus on the Oral Interpreter," to revise a first draft of these guidelines, originally written by Winifred H. Northcott. Following formal presentations, 25 deaf and hearing participants worked in small groups through discussion and consensus votes to modify, expand, and shape the list of competencies (knowledge, skills, and attitudes) required for efficient performance as an Oral Interpreter. Deaf and hearing individuals from inside and outside the A.G. Bell Association, oral and manual interpreters, public school administrators of programs for hearing-impaired persons, and representatives from NTID and the National Association of the Deaf (NAD) comprised the group. ODAS member Beth Powell took the leadership role of workshop coordinator and deaf individuals were the formal discussion chairpersons. These guidelines are the product of this endeavor.

The A.G. Bell Association enthusiastically endorses the assurance of separate but equal specialists—the Oral Interpreter and the Manual or Simultaneous Interpreter—in order that the rights of every deaf and hard-of-hearing individual to full participation in society be preserved. Each person is entitled to receive support when needed, both during school years and as adults, in the mode of communication of his or her choice (*Oral* or *Simultaneous* method). This may be by means of speechreading alone (with amplification as appropriate), supplied by an Oral Interpreter on request, or a combination of speechreading and sign language as presented by a Manual Interpreter, on request.

On June 23, 1978 the Council on Education of the Deaf (CED)* formally resolved upon action on the Board of Directors of each of its constituent organizations that:

---

* The constituent members of the Council on Education of the Deaf are the Alexander Graham Bell Association for the Deaf, the Conference of Executives of American Schools for the Deaf, and the Convention of American Instructors of the Deaf.

CED views the role of Oral Interpreter as a necessary adjunct to equal opportunity for all hearing-impaired individuals (deaf and hard of hearing) and recommends that agencies involved with the provision of or training or certification of Simultaneous or Manual Interpreters for the Deaf consider the establishment of guidelines, competencies and criteria for certification of Oral Interpreters as soon as practicable.

Thus, we leave the era of rigidity related to methods of communication, with its defenses and accusations reflected in value judgments, and take advantage of the current process by which alternatives to individualized services required by a single deaf or hard-of-hearing person are assured under Section 504 of the Rehabilitation Act of 1973. In this hospitable environment, the fledgling Oral Interpreter is recognized as a valuable member of the support team.

REFERENCE

Northcott, W. H. The Oral interpreter: A Necessary support specialist for the hearing impaired. *The Volta Review,* 1977, *79,* 136–144.

THE ROLE OF INTERPRETERS FOR THE DEAF

James Stangarone, President, Registry of Interpreters for the Deaf

Since the Registry of Interpreters for the Deaf, Inc. pioneered the certification of over 2000 sign language interpreters, it is again most appropriate for this organization to certify Oral Interpreters for the deaf. At present, RID has over 3500 members of whom 2100 are certified. These members are located within 60 chapters in 42 states. This vast network of interpreters has been providing services to deaf individuals in medical, educational, legal, cultural, religious, and mental health settings.

We are now working with the National Technical Institute for the Deaf to develop a prescreening program and actual certification procedures. When this project is completed, a workshop will be convened to bring together members of various organizations who provide direct or indirect services to deaf individuals. The certification procedures will be presented at this workshop and, if approved, will be given to the RID for implementation.

The Registry of Interpreters for the Deaf has also developed its own "Principles, Guidelines and Standards for RID, Inc. Accreditation of Interpreter Training Programs." The training and certifying of oral interpreters has been included within this process.

We would like to take this opportunity to thank the National Technical Institute for the Deaf and the Alexander Graham Bell Association for the Deaf for the outstanding contribution they have made in preparing the guidelines for this project.

THE ORAL INTERPRETER OR TRANSLATOR

The services of an Oral Interpreter may be required in a variety of situations depending upon the modality preference of individuals with varying degrees of hearing loss. Among the more common instances are: group discussions in a classroom or lecture hall, public speeches and programs, conversation (interviews, person to person), professional settings (courtrooms, consultations, conferences), and media (television, radio, telephone).

> *An interpreter shall not espouse any particular mode of communication (oral, simultaneous, or manual) as superior to another, but shall be guided by the expressed wishes of the consumer(s) as to the mode of communication to be employed.*

A. *Personal Characteristics*   The following characteristics are conducive to speechreading without strain:
    1. Facial characteristics conducive to speechreading:
        a. mobile lips,
        b. no deformation of teeth, lips, jaws,
        c. precise enunciation and diction,
        d. expressive face and eyes,
        e. well-trimmed beard and mustache, if any;
    2. Experience in communication with a variety of deaf and hard-of-hearing individuals;
    3. Clear speech;
    4. Appropriate regional or ethnic accent;
    5. Clothing suitable for occasion including lack of distracting jewelry and/or sunglasses.
B. *Knowledge*   The Oral Interpreter should have working knowledge of the following:
    1. The role and function of an Oral Interpreter and translator;
    2. Homophenes (low visibility words) and how to rephrase them for increased comprehension;
    3. Public speaking techniques;
    4. Principles of communicative and interpersonal dynamics;
    5. Variability of the responsive behavior of hearing-impaired (deaf and hard of hearing) individuals;
    6. Procedures and protocol for special situations (i.e., telephone);
    7. Current trends in education of the hearing impaired (deaf and hard of hearing);

8. Hearing aids—their uses and limitations;
9. Theories and practices of mainstreaming hearing-impaired children in the regular classroom—integration and assimilation as processes;
10. Telecommunication systems and other devices and their use;
11. Formal systems of speechreading/speechreading instruction;
12. Psycho-social aspects of deafness;
13. Professional organizational activities, certificates, publications, and educational/work environments related to hearing-impaired individuals of school and post-school age;
14. Facial/body language—client/interpreter feedback;
15. Various etiologies of deafness.

C. *Skills*   The oral interpreter shall demonstrate the ability to:
1. Transmit effectively the style, mood, and intent of the speaker(s);
2. Adapt the environment to meet the needs of clients in one-to-one or group situations;
3. Apply appropriate auditory and visual memory techniques in the process of interpreting and translating;
4. Identify a client's primary channels for receptive and expressive communication;
5. Identify in an unobtrusive manner a change in speakers as well as a change in subject;
6. Rephrase sentences for maximum visibility when necessary while retaining their original meaning;
7. Demonstrate ability to use the variety of telecommunication systems and devices;
8. Demonstrate appropriate public speaking techniques as they apply to oral interpreting and translating;
9. Be able to interpret verbally the statement of hearing-impaired individuals having varying degrees of speech intelligibility (reverse interpretation or translation);
10. Exhibit precise speech production;
11. Give evidence of smooth, not choppy, interpreting style;
12. (Optional) Use conversational sign language and fingerspelling for the purposes of reverse interpreting and translating.

D. *Attitudes*   The Oral Interpreter is one who:
1. Is sensitive to the dignity of each hearing-impaired individual;
2. Recognizes the purposes of the various organizations of and for hearing-impaired individuals and communicates them without bias;

3. Supports professional organizations related to the promotion of speech, speechreading, and use of residual hearing;

4. Is willing to continue to develop and upgrade professional competence;

5. Performs in accordance with national, state, and local guidelines and regulations, and the code of ethics;

6. Relates positively to all hearing-impaired consumers of interpreting services;

7. Demonstrates willingness and patience to work with hearing-impaired individuals with varying degrees of speechreading proficiency;

8. Recognizes personal performance strengths, weaknesses, and limitations and invites constructive suggestions for improvement as an Oral Interpreter;

9. Demonstrates a sensitivity to clients' preferences in the interpreting situation.

E. *Environment* It is the responsibility of the Oral Interpreter to consult with the client and facilitate the following:

1. Lighting and seating arrangements for maximum efficiency in speechreading (individual or group);

2. Optimum auditory environment when the client uses hearing, with or without an aid.

F. *Curriculum* Any program designed for the training of Oral Interpreters shall meet the requisites below.

1. The curriculum shall contain:

   a. Formal study of speechreading systems,

   b. Social interaction with hearing-impaired (deaf and hard-of-hearing) individuals outside the training site,

   c. Educational management systems,

   d. Psycho-social aspects of deafness,

   e. Dramatic/theatrical techniques,

   f. Articulation/distinction, and

   g. Practicum (group discussions, role playing, mock evaluations, supervised practice of oral interpreting and translating, and reverse oral interpreting and translating);

2. The program shall demonstrate that its Oral Interpreter graduates meet the requirements outlined in these guidelines;

3. The program shall include a job placement component and maintain, along with AGBAD and RID, a referral list of certified Oral Interpreters;

4. The curriculum shall demonstrate that it is designed to prepare the trainees to meet the knowledge, skills, and attitude

requirements of the oral specialist certification that will be awarded by RID in compliance with Oral Interpreter guidelines and subsequent standards to be developed;

5. The admissions policy shall be consistent with that of the host institution, yet flexible enough to accommodate various levels of competence at or above the minimal requirements for entry;

6. Availability of oral deaf individuals within the host institutions for use as subjects in practicum is essential.

G. *Training Sites*   The A.G. Bell Association for the Deaf will assume a leadership role in the identification and establishment of programs for training Oral Interpreters leading to certification by RID. Training sites will be selected in accordance with need and resources available and have as a minimum the following characteristics:

1. Accreditation by its respective regional accrediting body;

2. Compliance with Sections 503–504 of the Rehabilitation Act of 1973 in providing education and employment opportunities to handicapped persons who have the capability of carrying out their employment responsibilities;

3. Program content consistent with the goals and objectives of the program for training Oral Interpreters;

4. Climate of openness, acceptance, and flexibility for the challenges presented by the program for training Oral Interpreters;

5. Demonstration of financial commitment to continuation of an Oral Interpreter training program;

6. Resources to support the program including support courses in related fields and library capability for providing professional books, periodicals, journals, and materials on topics such as deafness, use of residual hearing, and the range of achievement among deaf and hard-of-hearing individuals;

7. Demonstration of a history of sustained effort in recruitment of individuals who can benefit from the services of an Oral Interpreter.

APPENDIX II

Code of Ethics
Registry of Interpreters for the Deaf, Inc.
Silver Spring, Maryland

**INTERPRETER/TRANSLITERATORS SHALL KEEP ALL
ASSIGNMENT-RELATED INFORMATION STRICTLY CONFIDENTIAL**

Guidelines

Interpreter/transliterators shall not reveal information about any assignment, including the fact that the service is being performed.

Even seemingly unimportant information could be damaging in the wrong hands. Therefore, to avoid this possibility, interpreter/translators must not say anything about any assignment. In cases where meetings or information become a matter of public record, the interpreter/transliterator shall use discretion in discussing such meetings or information.

If a problem arises between the interpreter/transliterator and either person involved in an assignment, the interpreter/transliterator should first discuss it with the person involved. If no solution can be reached, then both should agree on a third person who could advise them.

When training new trainees by the method of sharing actual experiences, the trainers shall not reveal any of the following information:

Name, sex, age, etc. of the consumer

Day of the week, time of the day, time of the year the situation took place

Location, including city, state or agency

Other people involved

Unnecessary specifics about the situation

It only takes a minimum amount of information to identify the parties involved.

**INTERPRETER/TRANSLITERATORS SHALL RENDER THE
MESSAGE FAITHFULLY, ALWAYS CONVEYING THE CONTENT
AND SPIRIT OF THE SPEAKER, USING LANGUAGE MOST
READILY UNDERSTOOD BY THE PERSON(S) WHOM THEY SERVE**

Guidelines

Interpreter/transliterators are not editors and must transmit everything that is said in exactly the same way it was intended. This is especially difficult when the interpreter disagrees with what is being said or feels uncomfortable when profanity is being used. Interpreter/transliterators must remember that they are not at all responsible for what is said, only for conveying it accurately. If the interpreter/transliterator's own feelings interfere with rendering the message accurately, he/she shall withdraw from the situation.

While working from Spoken English to Sign or Non-audible Spoken English, the interpreter/transliterator should communicate in the manner most easily understood or preferred by the deaf and hard of hearing person(s), be it American Sign Language, Manually Coded English, fingerspelling, paraphrasing in Non-audible Spoken English, gesturing, drawing, or writing, etc. It is important for the interpreter/transliterator and deaf or hard of hearing person(s) to spend some time adjusting to each other's way of communicating prior to the actual assignment. When working from Sign or Non-audible Spoken English, the interpreter/transliterator shall speak the language used by the hearing person in the spoken form, be it English, Spanish, French, etc.

INTERPRETER/TRANSLITERATORS SHALL NOT COUNSEL, ADVISE, OR INTERJECT PERSONAL OPINIONS

Guidelines

Just as interpreter/transliterators may not omit anything which is said, they may not add anything to the situation, even when they are asked to do so by other parties involved.

An interpreter/transliterator is only present in a given situation because two or more people have difficulty communicating, and thus the interpreter/transliterator's only function is to facilitate communication. He/she shall not become personally involved because in so doing he/she accepts some responsibility for the outcome, which does not rightly belong to the interpreter/transliterator.

INTERPRETER/TRANSLITERATORS SHALL ACCEPT ASSIGNMENTS USING DISCRETION WITH REGARD TO SKILL, SETTING, AND THE CONSUMERS INVOLVED

Guidelines

Interpreter/transliterators shall only accept assignments for which they are qualified. However, when an interpreter/transliterator shortage exists and the only available interpreter/transliterator does not possess the necessary skill for a particular assignment, this situation should be explained to the consumer. If the consumers agree that services are needed regardless of skill level, then the available interpreter/transliterator will have to use his/her best judgment about accepting or rejecting the assignment.

Certain situations may prove uncomfortable for some interpreters/ transliterators and clients. Religious, political, racial, or sexual differences, etc., can adversely affect the facilitating task. Therefore, an interpreter/transliterator shall not accept assignments which he/she knows will involve such situations.

Interpreter/transliterators shall generally refrain from providing services in situations where family members or close personal or professional relationships may affect impartiality since it is difficult to mask inner feelings. Under these circumstances, especially in legal settings, the ability to prove oneself unbiased when challenged is lessened. In emergency situations, it is realized that the interpreter/transliterator may have to provide services for family members, friends, or close business associates. However, all parties should be informed that the interpreter/transliterator may not become personally involved in the proceedings.

INTERPRETER/TRANSLITERATORS
SHALL REQUEST COMPENSATION FOR SERVICES
IN A PROFESSIONAL AND JUDICIOUS MANNER

Guidelines

Interpreter/transliterators shall be knowledgeable about fees which are appropriate to the profession, and be informed about the current suggested fee schedule of the national organization. A sliding scale of hourly and daily rates has been established for interpreter/ transliterators in many areas. To determine the appropriate fee, interpreter/transliterators should know their own level of skill, level of certification, length of experience, nature of the assignment, and the local cost of living index.

There are circumstances when it is appropriate for interpreter/transliterators to provide services without charge. This should be done with discretion, taking care to preserve the self-respect of the consumers. Consumers should not feel that they are recipients of charity. When providing gratis services, care should be taken so that the livelihood of other interpreter/transliterators will be protected. A free-lance interpreter/transliterator may depend on this work for a living and therefore must charge for services rendered, while persons with other full-time work may perform the service as a favor without feeling a loss of income.

INTERPRETER/TRANSLITERATORS SHALL FUNCTION IN A MANNER APPROPRIATE TO THE SITUATION

Guidelines

Interpreter/transliterators shall conduct themselves in such a manner that brings respect to themselves, the consumers, and the national organization. The term "appropriate manner" refers to:
- (a) Dressing in a manner that is appropriate for skin tone and is not distracting
- (b) Conducting oneself in all phases of an assignment in a manner befitting a professional

INTERPRETER/TRANSLITERATORS SHALL STRIVE TO FURTHER KNOWLEDGE AND SKILLS THROUGH PARTICIPATION IN WORKSHOPS, PROFESSIONAL MEETINGS, INTERACTION WITH PROFESSIONAL COLLEAGUES, AND READING OF CURRENT LITERATURE IN THE FIELD

INTERPRETER/TRANSLITERATORS, BY VIRTUE OF MEMBERSHIP IN OR CERTIFICATION BY THE RID, INC. SHALL STRIVE TO MAINTAIN HIGH PROFESSIONAL STANDARDS IN COMPLIANCE WITH THE CODE OF ETHICS

October, 1979

APPENDIX III

National Information and Service Organizations Related to the Hearing Impaired (Deaf and Hard of Hearing)

Alexander Graham Bell Association for the Deaf, Inc.
3417 Volta Place, NW
Washington, D.C. 20007
International Organization for the Education of the Hearing Impaired
(IOEHI)
International Parents' Organization (IPO)
Oral Deaf Adults Section (ODAS)

American Speech-Language-Hearing Association (ASHA)
10801 Rockville Pike
Rockville, Maryland 20852

Council for Exceptional Children (CEC)
1920 Association Drive
Reston, Virginia 22091

The National Center, Educational Media and Materials for the Handicapped (NCEMMH)
Ohio State University
Columbus, Ohio 43210

National Hearing Aid Society
20361 Middlebelt Road
Livonia, Michigan 48152

National Hearing Association
1010 Jorie Boulevard Suite 308
Oak Brook, Illinois 60521

National Information Center for the Handicapped
Box 1492
Washington, D.C. 20013

Registry of Interpreters for the Deaf, Inc. (RID)
814 Thayer Avenue
Silver Spring, Maryland 20910

Self-Help for Hard of Hearing People, Inc. (SHHH)
4848 Battery Lane, Suite 100
Bethesda, Maryland 20814

Suzanne Pathy Speak-up Institute, Inc.
525 Park Avenue
New York, New York 10021

AUTHOR INDEX

SUBJECT INDEX